A PROCESS
CHRISTOLOGY

A PROCESS CHRISTOLOGY

by
DAVID R. GRIFFIN

THE WESTMINSTER PRESS
Philadelphia

Copyright © 1973 The Westminster Press

Book Design by Dorothy Alden Smith

Published by The Westminster Press ®
Philadelphia, Pennsylvania

PRINTED IN THE UNITED STATES OF AMERICA

Grateful acknowledgment is given for permission
to use material from the following copyrighted
works:

Paul Tillich, *Systematic Theology,* Vols. I and
II. Vol. I copyright 1951 by The University of
Chicago; Vol. II © 1957 by The University of
Chicago. Used by permission of The University
of Chicago Press and Robert C. Kimball, execu-
tor of the literary estate of Paul Tillich.

Friedrich Schleiermacher, *The Christian Faith,*
tr. from the second German edition by H. R.
Mackintosh and J. S. Stewart. Published by
T. & T. Clark, Edinburgh, 1928. Published, in
two volumes, by Harper & Row, Publishers,
Inc., 1963.

Library of Congress Cataloging in Publication Data

Griffin, David, 1939–
    A process christology.

    Includes bibliographical references.
    1. Jesus Christ. 2. Process theology. I. Title.
BT205.G67   232   73–10252
ISBN 0–664–20978–5

CONTENTS

Part III
JESUS CHRIST
AS GOD'S DECISIVE REVELATION

KEY TO REFERENCES

The following abbreviations are used both in the text and in the notes. Numbers after the abbreviations refer to pages.

Paul Tillich

ST   *Systematic Theology.* The University of Chicago Press, Vol. I, 1951; Vol. II, 1957.

DF   *Dynamics of Faith.* Harper & Brothers, 1957.

MSA   *My Search for Absolutes.* Credo Perspectives. Simon & Schuster, Inc., 1967.

H. Richard Niebuhr

MR   *The Meaning of Revelation.* The Macmillan Company, 1941.

Rudolf Bultmann

TNT   *Theology of the New Testament,* tr. by Kendrick Grobel. Charles Scribner's Sons, Vol. I, 1951; Vol. II, 1955.

EF   *Existence and Faith. Shorter Writings,* tr. and introduced by Schubert M. Ogden. The World Publishing Company, 1960.

JCM   *Jesus Christ and Mythology.* Charles Scribner's Sons, 1958.

JW   *Jesus and the Word,* tr. by Louise Pettibone Smith and Erminie Huntress Lantero. Charles Scribner's Sons, 1958.

K   *The Theology of Rudolf Bultmann,* ed. by Charles W. Kegley. Harper & Row, Publishers, Inc., 1966.

KM   *Kerygma and Myth: A Theological Debate,* ed. by Hans Werner Bartsch; tr. by Reginald H. Fuller. Harper & Row, Publishers, Inc., 1961.

S   "What Sense Is There to Speak of God?" in Ronald E. Santoni (ed.), *Religious Language and the Problem of Religious Knowledge.* Indiana University Press, 1968.

Friedrich Schleiermacher

CF   *The Christian Faith,* tr. from the 2d German edition by H. R. Mackintosh and J. S. Stewart. Edinburgh: T. & T. Clark, 1928.

Alfred North Whitehead

AI   *Adventures of Ideas.* The Macmillan Company, 1933.

MT   *Modes of Thought.* The Macmillan Company, 1938.

PR   *Process and Reality.* The Macmillan Company, 1929.

RM   *Religion in the Making.* The World Publishing Company, 1960.

SMW   *Science and the Modern World.* The Macmillan Company, 1926.

PREFACE

THIS BOOK represents an attempt to bring together three dimensions of recent theology: (1) the new quest for the historical Jesus, (2) the neo-orthodox emphasis on God's self-revealing activity in history, and (3) the theology based primarily on the process philosophy of Alfred North Whitehead and Charles Hartshorne.

The first of these has stressed that, insofar as we do have historically probable knowledge of Jesus of Nazareth, this should have a normative role in deciding what is essentially Christian, since the basic Christian confession is that *Jesus* is the Christ. The second has stressed how absolutely fundamental to Christian faith is the notion that God acts in history, and in such a way as to reveal himself. Process theology has reaffirmed the liberal thesis that Christian faith can finally verify itself only by its ability to generate an adequate, consistent interpretation of reality that will illuminate our experience.

It is not self-evident that these three notions can be brought together into a consistent position. For example, many of those in the previous generation who affirmed the centrality of God's "mighty acts" and his self-revelation evidently found it necessary to belittle the importance of the "historical Jesus" in favor of the "Christ of faith." And they often used the doctrine of divine revelation as a bludgeon against the practice of evaluating Christian faith in terms of humanly developed criteria of rationality.

However, I find that the conceptuality provided by process philosophy allows one to maintain both his formal commitment to rationality and his substantive conviction as to the truth of the essentials of Christian faith, at the center of which I place the notion of the self-revealing activity of a personal God. This can be considered the major thesis of this essay. Also I find that it is possible to join both of these elements together with the idea that Jesus of Nazareth is appropriately received as the Christ.

The confession "Jesus is the Christ" is taken here first of all as the claim that Jesus is God's decisive revelation. The Introduction discusses the basis for making this notion central to a contemporary Christology and also mentions five problems encountered in defending the intelligibility of this claim. Part I presents an examination of the theologies of Paul Tillich, H. Richard Niebuhr, Rudolf Bultmann, and Friedrich Schleiermacher, in order to illustrate that these issues have indeed caused problems for modern theologians. Parts II and III offer a constructive position that attempts to provide a satisfactory solution to these problems.

Questions will naturally be raised about the selection of theologians for study in Part I. First, it was necessary to be very selective because of limitations of space. And the necessity for selectivity was increased because of the length of the secondary studies required by the method of criticism employed. That is, the criticisms are primarily internal, and therefore rather lengthy expositions are needed in order that the authors' lack of self-consistency can be demonstrated, not merely asserted.

Secondly, Part I is by no means intended to be a survey of modern discussions of revelation in particular, or modern Christology in general. Rather, the critiques have a limited twofold purpose: (1) to emphasize by illustration the problems that have been encountered in modern theology in the attempt to make intelligible the idea of Jesus as God's decisive revelation, and (2) to point the way to a constructive solution, both by bringing out ideas that can be used positively and by suggesting the general context needed to resolve the problems.

These criteria account for the most obvious omission, that of Karl Barth. For Barth rejected the aim of trying to make the Christian doctrine of revelation intelligible in the sense intended here, i.e., showing that it and all our other beliefs can be brought into harmony. His formal position, which has aptly been termed "revelational positivism," is one which I, along with the majority of the present generation, simply cannot accept.

The impossibility of Barthianism, and the difficulties in the positions of those more liberal theologians who did try to reconcile "God's self-revelation" with "human rationality," have led in our time to various forms of nontheistic Christologies, such as those of Thomas Altizer, Paul van Buren, Gerhard Ebeling, William Hamilton, Peter Hodgson, Wolfhart Pannenberg, and Dorothee Sölle. I have not discussed these positions directly. But by presenting an alternative way of responding to the difficulties of the earlier theological positions, I have argued indirectly that these nontheistic forms of radicalism are not necessitated.

For example, the difficulty of speaking of God and his action is largely due, at the theoretical level, to the problem of evil, on the one hand, and the conviction as to the world's closedness to all outside intervention, on the other. Whitehead provides a conceptuality for overcoming both of these theoretical difficulties simultaneously. Also I do not find convincing the argument that, since God is dead experientially, all theoretical attempts to reconceive the nature of God and his action are irrelevant. For Whitehead's description of human experience suggests that whether God is *consciously* experienced is largely a matter of man's ideas and anticipations. Hence a reformation at the theoretical level can lead to a reevaluation of what the "immediate deliverances of experience" really are.

Besides the question of authors, there are many other issues which could well have been discussed in the present essay but which, because of limitations in size and scope, are not discussed. Chief among these issues is probably that of the resurrection of Jesus. It is omitted not because of skepticism regarding the ontological possibility of such an event but for the following reasons: First, the focus of this essay is on God's relation to Jesus, and I conceive of the resurrection appearances as having, not constitutive importance for Jesus' person (as they have for Pannenberg,[1] for whom not only the meaning but also the being of earlier events is determined by later ones), but only noetic significance. Second, even this noetic value is increasingly absent in our day. The resurrection of Jesus, far from being the basis for belief in his special revelatory significance, can itself be accepted, if at all, only if Jesus' special relation to God is accepted on other grounds. Third, because Christian faith (as I understand it) is possible apart from belief in Jesus' resurrection in particular and life beyond bodily death in general, and because of the widespread skepticism regarding these traditional beliefs, they should be presented as optional, whereas the present essay focuses on what I consider essential elements of Christian faith.

This essay represents a substantial revision of my doctoral dissertation. Although the reader may suspect that this explains the style of the first four chapters, these are actually new chapters. Only earlier versions of Chapters 6–10 formed part of the dissertation. As for Chapters 1–4, the heavy documentation in these secondary studies is provided because they employ the method of internal criticism and contain interpretations which I assume many readers will regard as controversial. Most of the references in these chapters are put in the text, both for economical considerations and for the benefit of those readers who wish to check them out. I hope the general reader will not find this too distracting.

My indebtedness to John B. Cobb, Jr., personally as well as philosophically and theologically, is beyond expression. When these ideas were first formulated for the dissertation, he was an ideal major professor, providing the needed combination of encouragement and criticism. He also offered further helpful advice regarding the present text. Those who know Cobb's thought will recognize his influence on virtually every page. Even many of the ideas I consider original were probably derived from him.

I am also heavily indebted to Wolfhart Pannenberg and James M. Robinson—to the former for the stimulus he provided for systematic thought when I studied in Germany in 1965–1966, and to the latter for help in regard to my understanding of the problem of the historical Jesus and of the thought of Rudolf Bultmann. I am especially grateful to Delwin Brown, who kindly read the entire manuscript and made many valuable suggestions. I am also appreciative of help received from Lewis Ford, and my student assistant, Martin Kastelic. I wish further to thank the chairman of the Department of Theological Studies at the University of Dayton, Fr. Matthew F. Kohmescher, and the University's Research Council, for needed support.

Finally, I wish publicly to thank my parents and my wife, who have provided me with the luxury of time to engage in this type of study and reflection.

D.R.G.

INTRODUCTION
Revelation and Christology

"REVELATION" was the key concept used by the so-called neo-orthodox theologians to oppose what they considered the diluted understanding of Christian faith presented by the liberals and modernists of the previous generation. Now that neo-orthodoxy is itself a matter of the previous generation, it is natural that the idea of revelation should come in for heavy criticism as well as neglect as part of the general reaction against neo-orthodoxy. Indeed, a book by a Christian theologian has even appeared with the thesis that Christianity does not have a revelation.[1]

However, although I join in the rejection of many of the theses generally identified as distinctively neo-orthodox, I believe that these theologians were essentially right in making the idea of revelation central to their theologies in general, and to their Christologies in particular. I believe that Jesus has saving significance for us first of all through his significance for our outlook on reality. His saving significance for the affective and volitional dimensions of our experience is primarily indirect, being mediated through his significance for the cognitive dimension.

Holding such a position does not necessarily imply an intellectualistic understanding of man. Indeed, Alfred North Whitehead's philosophy, upon which the present essay is heavily based, stresses the priority of the affective to the cognitive, the unconscious to the conscious, the vague to the clear and distinct. For example, it directly attacks the view of much modern philosophy that all of man's purposive and affective experiences are derivative from conscious perceptions. And it supports Freud's comparison of man's conscious rationality with the tip of an iceberg.

However, while man's consciously held beliefs are not fundamental to his being, they do, insofar as they are present, greatly influence all aspects of his life. They are not noneficacious epiphenomena floating on the surface of man's psyche, simply being tossed up by nonrational (e.g., economic or libidinal) factors and not influencing them in return. Rather, man's cognitive dimension has a degree of independence from, or transcendence over, the nonrational dimensions, and reacts on them. Man is not simply a two-level being, with a first level of natural impulse and emotion that he shares with the other animals and a second story of rationality simply added above. As Reinhold Niebuhr has stressed, man's freedom for general concepts and self-consciousness influences all dimensions of his existence, changing their character for good or for ill. And Whitehead himself, despite the heavy romantic element in his thought, has said:

A religion, on its doctrinal side, can thus be defined as a system of general truths which have the effect of transforming character when they are sincerely held and vividly apprehended. In the long run, your character and your conduct of life depend on your intimate convictions. (*RM* 15.)

The assumption behind Whitehead's statement, and basic to the present essay, is that man is a religious being in the sense that he wants to be in harmony with the ultimately real, self-existent, eternal, sacred—that which is divine. As Carl Becker has phrased it, "The desire to correspond with the general harmony springs perennial in the human breast." [2] It is because of this feature of man's nature that his emotions, attitudes, intentions, and actions will, in the long run, be brought into line with his deepest beliefs about deity.

This is why Jesus' significance for the volitional and affective sides of our being finally depends upon his significance for the cognitive side. Certainly we need images and concepts that show Jesus' relevance directly for our feeling and acting. But these notions logically presuppose his significance for our thinking about reality. If we could no longer see Jesus as of decisive importance in this regard, then sooner or later he would no longer be experienced emotionally, or as ethically relevant. This is the problem with all genuinely atheistic Christologies which express Jesus' significance for us only in terms of his direct relevance for our ethical and/or affective dimensions. If our general beliefs about the ultimate nature of reality are not seen as derived from Jesus, our character and conduct will soon cease to be informed by him, being informed instead by whatever new "revelation" of reality we come to accept. If Jesus' decisive significance for our mode of existence is to continue, it must continue to be primarily an indirect significance, via his revelatory significance for our vision of reality.[3]

There has been a tendency in modern theology to portray Jesus' benefits in terms of a personal influence on our mode of existence, either mediated indirectly through the culture (Schleiermacher) or directly through an encounter with the kerygmatic Christ (Bultmann). The impression often received by the reader is that this personal influence is more or less independent of any ideas. One of the purposes of the critiques in Part I is to show that doctrinal ideas are more central to the soteriologies of these theologians than they explicitly state.

This way of understanding Jesus' saving significance is one reason that I reject treating "soteriology" as one doctrine among others. All the doctrines in a theological position should be seen as significant for the wholeness of human existence (although the significance of some ideas will be more indirect, in that they primarily give support to other ideas which are more directly relevant to the human spirit). Insofar as there is a separate soteriological discussion, as in Chapter 10 of the present essay, it should simply make explicit the inherent salvific significance of the various doctrines constituting the theological position as a whole.

There is a second reason for not formulating *a* doctrine of salvation. Doing so would presuppose a doctrine of man's fundamental spiritual problem. But this I find impossible, due to the differences between cultures, eras, and individuals. Certainly much of the greatest writing done by Christian theologians, such as Augustine, Kierkegaard, and Reinhold Niebuhr, has been motivated by the desire to analyze man's "original" sin, and to show how all his other spiritual problems arise out of this "originating" sin. But what of the alienation of man's conscious life from the unconscious symbolizations that his civilization has fostered? What of the lack of wholeness fostered by the specialization of civilization, embodied supremely in the assembly line? What of modern man's difficulty in honestly believing there is a divine reality, and, hence, any ultimate meaning to life? These problems *can*, of course, be interpreted as flowing from some underlying perversity common to man, defined as self-centeredness or pride. But such interpretations seem more ingenious than illuminating.

This cannot be argued here, but it seems to me more helpful to think in terms of a complex of spiritual problems that are partially independent of each other. This dictates rejecting the type of soteriology that presupposes that there is one underlying spiritual problem, a solution to which will automatically solve the derivative problems. Rather than developing *a* doctrine of salvation, the theologian needs to show how the various aspects of his theological position are relevant to certain problems that are widespread in the era and tradition for which he is primarily writing, leaving it to writers in other times and places to explicate the significance of the Christian vision of reality for their contexts.

This approach, while being in one sense more relativistic than the traditional approach, is in another sense more universalistic. It is more relativistic in holding that human beings in different times and places really are different, rather than implying that they merely perceive differently their common spiritual life. It is more universalistic in holding that Jesus of Nazareth can provide the basis for the resolution of the multitude of spiritual ills that infect mankind, so that he can be the Christ for all persons, not simply those of certain eras, traditions, and temperaments. It is the traditional soteriologies which have in fact been limited in scope, with their implication that Jesus' benefits are relevant only to a few of the many spiritual ailments actually experienced by human beings.

One argument that has been used against making the notion of revelation central in Christian theology is that it was not central in the New Testament. But the presence or absence of a heavy use of a concept in the New Testament cannot settle the question of its appropriateness in contemporary theology. Revelation was not a central category for explicating Jesus' significance in the New Testament, and for good reason. Most of the major aspects of Jesus' vision of reality were largely held in common by him and the Judaism from which he emerged. Compared with the great difference, e.g., between Christian and Buddhist visions of reality, the differences between Jesus and contemporary Judaism were matters of nuance (albeit important ones) within a common framework. Hence, in describing Jesus' significance the cognitive dimension could be largely overlooked. But as Christianity came into greater contact with other outlooks that were considered real alternatives, the idea of Jesus as God's decisive revelation came to the fore, e.g., in the Logos Christology. And in *our* context, in which people are increasingly aware of a variety of ways to understand reality, and therefore their own existence, the general Biblical vision of reality cannot simply be presupposed. The validity of this vision is what is fundamentally at issue. And apart from an acceptance of its validity, none of the New Testament's ways of conceiving Jesus' significance make any sense to us. Hence in our context Jesus can only be understood as "savior" if he is seen as the decisive clue to the nature of reality.

The concept of revelation is central to the contemporary Christological task not only because it expresses a necessary aspect of Christian faith, especially in our day, but also because of the many problems involved in speaking about it intelligibly in the modern world. Of course there have always been difficulties surrounding the notion of God's saving activity in Jesus, as is shown by the attempts in the early centuries to assert the special presence of God in Jesus while holding both to his complete humanity and to his unity with God. But in the modern world the difficulties are even greater, due especially to assumptions about the autonomy of the world and human reason. I will focus on five central problems.

1. One major criticism against a theology that is based on the acceptance of "revelation" is that such a theology is necessarily irrational. Speaking of revelation, it is said, connotes a suspension of the normal philosophical criteria of rationality, i.e., consistency, adequacy to the facts of experience, and illuminating power. If theology wishes to claim to be obedient to the logos, the call to rationality, it must forsake speaking of revelation.

Certainly this attitude is widespread. Theology comes off poorly in comparison with philosophy. The theologian is said to be committed to a particular tradition's revelation, and thereby limited in his search for truth. He must make his conclusions agree with his tradition's starting point. The philosopher, on the other hand, is free to look for truth wherever it may be. He is bound by no commitments. In the bluntest language, he, unlike the theologian, is not prejudiced. Hence it seems reasonable to suppose that he is more likely to come closer to the truth about reality.

The problem of justifying the acceptance of revelation has been a major concern of much modern theology. One approach has been to equate special and natural revelation. That is, nothing is revealed in Jesus that could not already be known through creation. The Christian revelation was merely a republication of what could already be known. This position would answer the charge of irrationality, if only it were true. But, as Hume argues in his *Dialogues Concerning Natural Religion,* the Christian concept of God may be *compatible* with a thorough appraisal of nature, but it could never have been originally *inferred* from a neutral appeal to all the evidence. Only a philosopher who sees nature through Christian glasses will develop a philosophy in substantial agreement with Christian theology. Then one is back to the question as to whether seeing things from the Christian perspective is irrational.

Another approach has been that reason itself can show that certain things are in principle unknowable to, and unverifiable by, reason, so that it is reasonable to accept the authority of revelation in these matters. The problem with this type of argument is that it can be used equally in support of contradictory positions. It may show the necessity of a leap of faith, but it does not provide any basis for showing, even in retrospect, that leaping in one particular direction is better than leaping in any other. If the revelation is not susceptible to verification by rational criteria, the choice of any one putative revelation cannot be made rational.

2. A second major difficulty in speaking of revelation has been that of expressing its content. Modern theologians agree that revelation is of God himself (and not, e.g., of a number of facts about the world). But *what* of God is revealed? Giving an answer to this has been especially difficult for those modern theologians heavily influenced by Immanuel Kant, for it has seemed impossible to speak about God in himself. God could be spoken of only as experienced by man. Accordingly, there has been a tendency to say that revelation does not mediate any noetic content about God, but mediates God himself. The problem with this view, which is based on the analogy with personal communion between men, can be seen by examining instances of such communion. In any such "knowledge of ac-

quaintance," there is always some knowledge about the other person. Hence, if the analogy is to hold, the problem of formulating the knowledge about God that revelation brings cannot be avoided.

3. A third major difficulty in speaking of revelation, and probably the most serious one, involves modern presuppositions about nature and history. On the one hand, speaking of the Biblical God's self-revelation implies that he has acted in the world. On the other hand, since the scientific revolution in the seventeenth century the conviction has grown that all events have natural causes, and that the natural sequence of cause and effect is never interrupted. But is not an act of God synonymous with a miracle, an interruption of the natural causation? Also, speaking of Jesus as God's decisive self-revelation seems to imply a "special" act of God. This, even more clearly, seems to connote a miraculous interruption. Accordingly, it would seem as if speaking of God's action in the world, and particularly speaking of his special acts, is impossible for today's informed person. Hence, the idea of divine self-revelation seems no longer credible.

Some have chosen to affirm God's special activity in Jesus, while remaining agnostic as to how this affirmation is consistent with that of Jesus' full humanity and freedom.[4] This is sometimes justified on the grounds that, since the Christian knows Jesus' divinity and humanity to have been a fact, he knows it had to be a possibility.[5] But this position presupposes an authoritarian situation that no longer obtains. In our day Christian faith must base its case on its ability to generate descriptions of reality that prove themselves to be consistent, adequate, and illuminating. If the central event from which Christians derive concepts for making the rest of reality intelligible cannot itself be made intelligible in terms of these concepts, defeat is admitted at the outset. More specifically, since Christians take Jesus to be the chief exemplification of the coexistence of divine activity and creaturely freedom, failure to show the possibility of this coexistence in Jesus suggests that the notion of God's activity in the world in general cannot be made intelligible. And since the Christian God cannot be separated from the notion of his action in the world, there is truth in the observation that the "death of God" was preceded by the failure of Christology.[6]

Some have thought that the idea of divine activity could be preserved by holding that the Biblical events were fully natural, but that with the "eyes of faith" they could be designated "acts of God," since faith had found them to be revelatory of God. But the events would then be "acts of God" only in a Pickwickian sense, and theology ought to avoid such misleading language. Of course, it might be claimed that the language implying divine activity is legitimate, since faith attributes the believing perception of those events to the Holy Spirit. But the present experience of the believer is considered just as susceptible to causal explanation as are human events in the past. Hence, the problem of relating the divine causality to natural causation is merely moved from the Biblical events to the believer's psyche. And if divine causality can be intelligibly spoken of here, then there is no reason why it could not be spoken of in relation to the Biblical events themselves.

4. A fourth difficulty involves bringing "Jesus" and "truth" together. For if Jesus is to be appropriately received as the decisive revelation of God, then he must somehow be understandable as having expressed the basic truth about God. But we have become increasingly aware of the tremendous gulf separating us from the first century, and of the fact that Jesus himself shared first-century conceptions that we must consider mythological and false. The attempt to pick out those sayings which are less obviously objectionable as constituting the real "kernel" of his message will not work, for Jesus' message as a whole presupposed a mythological view of reality. How then can we see him as expressing the basic truth about reality?

5. A fifth problem must be kept in mind while trying to deal with the others. Treating the problems already mentioned with any adequacy will obviously require a rather fundamental re-

construction of the traditional views of Christian theology, for
it is precisely the traditional methods and doctrines which have
led to the problems. But the theological position that results
from this reconstruction must be adequate to support Christian
existence. Christian faith is first of all a mode of existence. The
cognitive beliefs involved in faith are important primarily for
the support they give to this mode of existence. Hence, if the
reconstruction is not such as to support, e.g., a life of self-
transcendence with a freedom from self-preoccupation, a genuine love for individuals as well as a concern for justice, a sense
of both responsibility and peace, then it is inadequate to Christian faith.

Part I

REVELATION IN MODERN THEOLOGY:
PROBLEMS AND POSSIBILITIES

CHAPTER 1

Being-Itself
and Symbolic Language

1. The Rationality of Theology
Based Upon Revelation

Paul Tillich was especially concerned to have Christianity overcome in all areas of existence the fact and the appearance of "heteronomy" in which the autonomy of individuals is compromised by the imposition of some demand from an external authority. The fact that theology's paths of knowledge "seem to deviate radically from all ordinary ways" is a major reason why an epistemological discussion of the relation of reason and revelation must come first in systematic theology. (*ST* I, 71.)

Tillich formulates this relation in the following way: the theologian acts both as a philosopher and as a theologian. As a philosopher he intends, as any philosopher intends, to operate independently of any particular revelation. (*ST* I, 63.) He analyzes the structure of human being in particular and of the rest of being in general. (*ST* I, 67 f.) The philosophy may be "Christian" in the loose sense that all modern philosophy in the West has been influenced by historical Christianity, but not in the narrower sense that the philosopher must subject himself to any principle other than the *logos* of being as it gives itself to him in experience. (*ST* I, 28.) However, this natural knowledge can only raise the question of God. The answer must be given by the theologian. (*ST* I, 119 f.)

As theologian, however, he is passionately committed to a special revelatory experience, and this revelation is the ultimate source of all his theological content. (*ST* I, 67 f.) This content is derived by interpreting the contents of Christian faith in the form of an answer to the question raised by philosophy. Why is this Christian answer, based upon faith, not less rational than purely philosophical answers? For one thing, in all metaphysical views there is implicit some *a priori* of experience and valuation which involves a type of mystical experience. (*ST* I, 8 f.) But this alone would not make philosophy and theology parallel, because the theologian adds to the mystical *a priori* the criterion of the Christian message (*ST* I, 10), whereas the philosopher looks at the whole of reality to discover its *logos,* not at one particular place. Yet the difference even here is more in intention than in execution. For in fact the philosopher's "intuition of the universal *logos* of the structure of reality as a whole is formed by a particular *logos* which appears to him on his particular place and reveals to him the meaning of the whole"; and he also belongs to a special community in which there is an active commitment to this particular *logos.* (*ST* I, 25.) Hence, although the theologian's and the philosopher's intentions are quite different, their actual procedures are comparable. (*ST* I, 24–27; *ST* II, 26, 31.)

The foregoing seems to be Tillich's response to the charge that theology is heteronomous while philosophy is autonomous. Yet in the actual execution of his theology a different way of avoiding a conflict between faith and reason appears, one that puts him more in line with his intellectual ancestor Schleiermacher: there can be no conflict because the Christian faith adds *no additional content* to our view of reality beyond what philosophy gives us. As John Cobb has shown, there is a great difference between the stated and the actual method of Tillich. Rather than simply asking the question, his philosophical analysis prescribes the answer as well.[1]

Tillich himself says that revelation gives us no additional

knowledge about the subject-object structure of reality. (*ST* I, 109.) One might infer from this that it *does* give us additional knowledge about God, who transcends this subject-object scheme. Yet it is philosophy that tells us that God transcends this scheme infinitely, and hence is not *a* being, but being itself. Theology adds nothing to the content of this idea of God. Even the Trinitarian character of being itself is derived philosophically, not from the Christian revelation. (*ST* II, 143.) The theologian does not add to or revise the philosopher's statement of the *structure* of being, but deals only with the *meaning* of being for us. (*ST* I, 22.) He adds nothing to the Trinitarian doctrine except his conviction that the principle of God's self-manifestation was manifest in Jesus as the Christ.

I suggest that Tillich avoids a conflict between reason and faith in the Christian revelation by denying to Christian faith any distinctive ideas regarding reality. The next section will support this assertion.

2. The Content of Revelation

The question in this section is whether there is a cognitive aspect to the Christian faith that is (or ideally should be) the same for all Christians. Is there a cognitive essence of Christianity (abstracting from the question of the possible noncognitive aspects of the "essence of Christian faith")?

The importance of this question was indicated in the Introduction. As a religious being, man has the desire to be in harmony with that which is divine. As a rational being with freedom, he needs some definite idea as to what the divine reality is like, in order to conform to this reality. Tillich, perhaps as much as anyone else in our time, has emphasized the religious nature of man and the importance of worshiping the *true* God. Because of man's irrepressible religiosity there is no alternative between faith or unfaith, but only between true and idolatrous faith. Absence of true faith will create a vacuum into which demonic forces will enter. (*ST* I, 148.)

Tillich stresses that faith has a cognitive side. (*ST* I, 154; *DF*, 10.) He speaks of the content of Christian faith and indicates that we can distinguish between the historic form and the revelatory content of the revelatory event. (*ST* II, 101.) Although one should not speak of revealed doctrines, there are events that can be described in doctrinal terms; although there is no revealed knowledge, there is revelatory knowledge. (*ST* I, 125, 129.) And this revelatory knowledge is, directly or indirectly, knowledge of God. (*ST* I, 131.)

Many of Tillich's statements make clear that it is important that we be able to have knowledge of God. To be an object of man's concern, God must be something that can be encountered, and this means something concrete. (*ST* I, 211.) We must be able to think of him as the "living God" (*ST* I, 242), even as "personal," for man's relation to God is existential, and "an existential relation is a person-to-person relation" (*ST* I, 244). For our religious needs we must be able to speak of God in anthropomorphic terms. (*ST* I, 242.) The ego-thou relationship to God is the central one, and it is implicit even in all the symbols in which it is not explicit. (*ST* I, 289.)

But all our knowledge of God is symbolic. All our concepts are drawn from our experience with finite things and properly refer to them and the relations obtaining between them. (*ST* I, 239.) In order to give content to the cognitive side of revelation, we must use material from this finite realm. (*ST* I, 131.) But since God *infinitely* transcends everything finite (*ST* I, 237), the words cannot apply properly or literally to him. Another way of noting this is to say that our concepts and categories are appropriate to the subject-object structure of reality, in which beings are related to each other. But God is not *a* being, but being-itself, and hence is beyond the subject-object relation. (*ST* I, 214.) Hence, the language suitable for beings and their mutual relations (the only language we have) is not properly suitable for speaking of God and his relation to the world.

But if this be the case, how is any knowledge of God at all

possible? Tillich's answer is that there are concepts which are less universal than being, and yet more universal than those ontic concepts which apply only to one species of beings. (*ST* I, 164.) And since the characteristics to which these ontological concepts refer are rooted in God, as being-itself or the ground of being, these characteristics can be affirmed of him symbolically. A segment of the finite can be used to say something about that which is infinite, since that which is infinite is being-itself, in which everything finite participates. This is the basis for the *analogia entis*, which gives us our only justification for speaking of God. (*ST* I, 239 f.) Speaking of the "divine life" implies that "there is an analogy between the basic structure of experienced life and the ground of being in which life is rooted." (*ST* I, 156.) Because God is the ground of the structure of being, Tillich says we can be certain that the elements of this structure enable us to use symbols that point to God. (*ST* I, 238.)

However, doctrines of analogical or symbolical knowledge of God are always suspect of using terms equivocally. We must look more closely at Tillich's doctrine to see if this is so in his case. It seems clear that the only intelligible difference between analogical and equivocal language is that in the former there is a literal element that can be specified. This has been argued both by thinkers who do and by thinkers who do not think that meaningful language about God is possible.[2] In Paul Edwards' terms, the metaphor, if it is to avoid equivocation, must be "reducible," i.e., it must be capable of translation into a nonmetaphorical statement. This is not to say that analogical language, with its connotative richness, should be replaced by literal language, but only that there must be, among the other elements, a somewhat specifiable literal element intended in every analogical predication.

If this is the correct understanding of meaningful language, it seems that Tillich himself has admitted that his language about God cannot meet the requirements. In the first volume of his *Systematic Theology* he had said: "The statement that

God is being-itself is a nonsymbolic statement." (*ST* I, 238.)
The term "the absolute" seemed to be equally unsymbolic;
and "the unconditioned" seemed (rightly) to be a synonym for
the absolute. (*ST* I, 207 f., 239.) But in the second volume
Tillich says that only statements about our *quest* for God are
nonsymbolic. Any attempt to describe God involves symbolic
elements. This holds true even for the statements that "God
is the infinite, or the unconditional, or being-itself." These
three terms are now given the privileged status of designating
the boundary line which is "both symbolic and non-symbolic."
(*ST* II, 9 f.) But this is not very helpful, since we are not told
what the nonsymbolic element is. However, in order to avoid
circularity Tillich says there is one nonsymbolic assertion about
God that can be made, "namely, the statement that everything
we say about God is symbolic." Whether this is really a statement about God could be debated. In any case it does not
meet the requirement for unequivocal language, i.e., that the
symbolic or analogical terms themselves contain an element
intended literally.

Besides Tillich's own evaluation of his symbolism, an analysis of his doctrines will show that his language about God
cannot avoid equivocation. We have seen that language about
God is said to be possible because ontology is possible. There
are four levels of ontological concepts. The first level is the
basic ontological structure, which is the self-world structure.
This structure is attributable not only to man, and not even
only to living things, but by analogy to all individual *Gestalten*
in the inorganic realm. There is a self-centeredness "wherever
the reaction to a stimulus is dependent on a structural whole,"
as in an atom. (*ST* I, 169.) Each such entity is a "self," which
means it is something for itself; and it has a "world" to which
it belongs. This self-world structure logically precedes all other
structures. (*ST* I, 164.)

The second level of concepts involves the ontological elements. They constitute the self-world structure of being. And
they share in its polar character. The three main pairs are:

individuality and participation (or universality), dynamics and form, freedom and destiny. The first element of each pair expresses the "self" side of the basic structure, and the second expresses the character of belonging to a world. (*ST* I, 165.) The fact that they are polar elements means that neither pole is meaningful except in relation to its opposite.

The third level involves the difference between essential and existential being entailed in finitude. The fourth level deals with the categories, which can also be termed "the structures of finite being and thinking." The important ones for theology are time, space, causality, and substance.

Now, it is primarily the second and fourth levels, the ontological elements and the categories, that are said to provide symbolic material for speaking about God. But how is this understandable? Tillich says the self-world structure in no way applies to God, not even symbolically; it can provide no symbolic material. God cannot be thought of as a self even symbolically, for the notion of "self" has no meaning apart from "world," or that which is not-self. (*ST* I, 244.) This thought is forbidden because it would contradict God's infinity (which is one of the more privileged terms, being on the borderline between symbolic and nonsymbolic). (*ST* I, 189 f.)

But the self-world structure was said logically to precede the ontological elements. And they are simply *elements* of this self-world structure. Is it not contradictory to say that they can provide symbolic material for God if the self-world structure cannot?

Tillich's own assertions support this contention. The first pair of elements is individualization and participation. The question of whether God can be called an "individual" arises in connection with whether God is "personal," since personality includes individuality. But God "transcends" individualization; so God cannot be thought of as *a* person. We are told that man religiously needs to think of God as personal, and that the symbol "personal God" is absolutely fundamental. But then we are told that " 'personal God' is a confusing symbol." God is personal only in the sense that he is the ground of everything personal. (*ST* I, 244 f.)

This twofold type of statement represents Tillich's handling of all the ontological elements. First he tells us that none of the ontological elements can be applied properly to God, since they are taken from the finite world, which is constituted by the self-world structure, and therefore they have meaning only where this structure obtains. They apply properly to living beings and analogically to inorganic individuals. In regard to God their literal meaning must be negated. The terms cannot even be applied analogically to God. (*ST* II, 9.) (Tillich does sometimes equate "analogical" and "symbolic," but his position requires a distinction between them.)

Second, Tillich affirms that the ontological elements can be affirmed *symbolically*, since God is the "ground" of the element or category in question. But this is what Thomas Aquinas called "virtual analogy" and rightly rejected as a sufficient basis for analogical predication, since on this basis alone there would be no reason why some terms more than others are to be applied to God. If one can say "God is good" simply because he is the cause of good things, then one can say "God is a body" since he is the cause of bodies.[3] Tillich himself says that "whatever one knows about a finite thing one knows about God, because it is rooted in him as its ground." (*ST* II, 9.) He of course then adds that these things are known of God symbolically. But he does not explain why it is only terms such as "personal," "freedom," and "love" that he mentions as symbolically applicable to God, when "things," "deceit," "hate," and "mud" are also rooted equally in him as their ground. We will return to this problem in section 5 of this chapter.

We also indicated above that Tillich considers it necessary to use the symbol of the "living God." Tillich rightly says that "life includes the separation of potentiality and actuality" (*ST* I, 246), since "it is the process in which potential being becomes actual being." Therefore, the God who is *actus purus* is not living. (*ST* I, 242, 246.) But then Tillich says that "in God as God there is no distinction between potentiality and actuality." Hence in God the meaning is symbolic: "God lives in so far as he is the ground of life." (*ST* I, 242.)

The attempted application of the other ontological elements to God need not be treated separately, since they all suffer from the same handicap of logically presupposing the self-world structure. Furthermore, each member of the pairs is meaningful only in relation to its polar opposite. Yet Tillich asserts that the distinctions between the two elements in each pair is overcome in God. (*ST* I, 243 f., 247–249.) But there is no difference between saying that the two qualities are "identical" and saying that at least one of them is not present. This means that neither one of them can be meaningfully predicated.

Hence, nothing whatsoever remains of the assertions that Tillich claims are essential for faith. Being-itself cannot meaningfully be said to be "living," for there can be no analogy between it and "the basic structure of experienced life." And since "God" by definition is that which is worthy of our ultimate concern, being-itself cannot be God. For "it is impossible to be concerned about something which cannot be encountered concretely. . . . The more concrete a thing is, the more the possible concern about it." And the individual person is the completely concrete being. (*ST* I, 211.) Since being-itself is not a being, not a self, not an individual, not a person, it is not at all "concrete." Hence "encounter" with it is impossible, as is any ego-thou, person-to-person relationship. And the two main symbols of this relationship, "Lord" and "Father," are left without any basis. And since the ego-thou relation is implied in all the symbols, they are all devoid of any analogical value.

Tillich also asserted that the ontological concepts on the fourth level, i.e., the categories, supply symbolic material. The categories of time, causality, and substance (the category of space can be ignored here) cannot be applied *literally* to God, for they are forms of finitude. This seems to be a modified Kantianism, in that these categories are called the structures of finite being as well as of thinking. (*ST* I, 165.) But they cannot, by definition, be predicated of God, since he is infinite, although the human mind necessarily applies them even here. (*ST* I, 192.)

Accordingly, it would destroy God's infinity if individual substance were attributed to him (*ST* II, 6); this is one way of expressing why God cannot be *a* being, an individual. And to speak of God in temporal terms is to speak in mythical terms. (*ST* II, 29.) Complete demythologization in language about the divine is not possible; but in speaking about the divine, one must remember simultaneously to negate all the terms he affirms. Also finite beings cannot be said to exert any causal influence on God, since he is "the unconditioned" (this being one of those privileged, less symbolic terms). Especially can no emotional effects be predicated of God. (*ST* II, 77.)

Tillich has rejected the charge, made by those who dislike his use of ontological terms, that he has surrendered the substance of the Christian message because he has used terminology that deviates from Biblical and ecclesiastical language. But the problem is really that his continued use of Biblical language partially conceals the degree to which his theology departs from the substance of the Christian faith. For his writings are filled with terms that, if the preceding analysis is correct, can have no meaning whatsoever beyond the purely metaphorical. Despite the fact that God is unconditioned, Tillich speaks of his "hearing" our prayers, and his "accepting" us. Despite the fact that God is not a subject, or a self in any sense, Tillich speaks of his "point of view," of his "image" of our fulfillment, and of his being "a subject even where he seems to be an object." (*ST* I, 263, 280, 282.) Although Tillich says it would be absurd to think of God's omniscience as meaning he knows all objects, since this would mean "subsuming God under the subject-object scheme" (*ST* I, 278), the problem of the relation of essences, universals, and individuals is solved by saying (symbolically) that "in the creative vision of God the individual is present as a whole in his essential being and inner *telos* and, at the same time, in the infinity of the special moments of his life-process" (*ST* I, 255). Furthermore, God is said to "love" man and the universe, even though Tillich has said that "love is absent where there is no individualization." (*ST* I, 280.) And God's love is the character of his "life," which requires a distinction between potentiality and actuality; but God is "beyond" this distinction, so his life is said to be a mystery for finite understanding. (*ST* I, 279 f.) Tillich also speaks of God's "desire" and "longing" for our fulfillment, and quite often of God's "will," although he says that "will implies potentiality" (*ST* II, 22 f.), which God transcends, as he does "the fulfilment and nonfulfilment of reality" (*ST* I, 281). Finally, he speaks of God's "purpose" and of what God "wants" man to be, even though neither selfhood nor temporality can apply to God. (*ST* I, 285; *ST* II, 93.)

The analysis in this section has been carried out in order to see, in Tillich's thought, what possible content there could be to the Christian revelation. Tillich rightly sees that the cognitive side of man's nature needs healing as well as do the volitional and emotional sides (*ST* I, 154) and that faith essentially is concerned with God. And he claims correspondingly that there is a cognitive dimension to revelation, and that this results in knowledge about God. But his basic commitments are such that no cognitively meaningful assertions about God can be made. The only possible candidates are those terms called both symbolic and nonsymbolic, i.e., being-itself, the infinite, the unconditioned. But these notions come from a phenomenological-ontological analysis, not from the Christian revelation, and in any case they provide no basis for a Christian mode of existence. The root of the difficulty seems to be Tillich's retention of the traditional notion that deity must be "infinite" and "unconditioned" *in all respects*. And he sees better than most traditional theologians that this cannot be predicated of an individual being. (*ST* I, 207.)

But the Biblical tradition, despite Tillich's assertion to the contrary (*ST* I, 242), did assume that God was a self and hence *a* being in relation to other beings, in some respect affected by them. This is the basis of the impossibility of joining intelligibly the Biblical language about God with the notion of God as being-itself but not as individual. The notorious result is Tillich's position that we must be able to think of God in a certain way for religious purposes, but that of course God is really nothing like that. This implies a violent split between our cognitive and religious dimensions, precisely the type of split that Tillich was most concerned to avoid.

3. God's Relation to Jesus

We must now look at Tillich's treatment of God's relation to Jesus. As we will see, this relation involves no exception to the normal structure of relations, so it can be understood in terms of the general relation of God to the world. And God *is* said to be related to the world. In fact, "the basic and determinative relation of the ground of being to us" can be described as the content of revelation. (*ST* I, 158.)

The fourth level of ontological concepts, the categories of thought and being, were said to supply symbolic material for speaking of God. For expressing the relation of being-itself to finite beings man is bound to use the two categories of relation —causality and substance. (*ST* I, 237.) We have already seen that the category of substance is not applicable to God. Hence, the category of causality would be the only possibility for speaking at all about God's relation to the world.

And in fact Tillich uses a large number of terms which suggest that God *acts*, and thereby exerts causal influence upon the world. God is called the *prima causa*. (*ST* I, 24.) The formula *creatio ex nihilo* "expresses the relation between God and the world." God "creates" man, and "gives" him power. (*ST* I, 254, 256.) He "drives," "directs," and "lures" his creatures toward fulfillment. Tillich speaks of the way the God of love "acts" and "reacts" in relation to men who resist love. (*ST* I, 264, 283.) And the term "grace" is meaningful, since the power of being is a "gift" from God; in fact, all relations between God and man are "freely inaugurated" by God. (*ST* I, 285; *ST* II, 125.) Finally, the term "Lord" symbolizes God's "governing" of the whole of reality. (*ST* I, 287.)

God's relation to Jesus in particular also seems to be understandable causally. The old Christological concepts of static essences are to be replaced with concepts of a dynamic relation. (*ST* II, 148.) Jesus' revelatory significance will not be due simply to his own activity, but will be rooted in the divine causal activity in him. For Tillich says that the infinite "expresses itself" through the finite. (*ST* I, 218.) The decision at Nicaea made it imperative to affirm the "power" of the divine Logos in the Christ; and this Logos that was manifest in a personal life is the principle of "divine self-manifestation." (*ST* II, 142 f.)

Nicaea has thus affirmed "that God himself . . . is present in the man Jesus of Nazareth." (*ST* II, 144.) But how can this be made intelligible, so that neither God's presence nor Jesus' humanity is sacrificed? If Jesus was truly human, he had to have the finite freedom that all men do; he was no divine-human automaton devoid of temptation, struggle, and error. (*ST* II, 127, 135.) On the other hand his decisions, like all human decisions, stand under God's providence or directing creativity. The same principles apply to Jesus that apply to every man: "Man's destiny is determined *by* the divine creativity, but *through* man's self-determination." The most that can be said is that Jesus' acts constituting him as the Christ are "both acts of decision by himself and results of a divine destiny. Beyond this unity we cannot go, either in the case of Jesus or in the case of man universally." (*ST* II, 130.) Abstract definitions of the nature of the unity of God and man in Jesus as the Christ are impossible. One can protect both the truths involved here by holding simultaneously to the incarnational Christology, which affirms the element of destiny, and the adoptionist Christology, which affirms the element of freedom. (*ST* II, 148 f.)

On the basis of the foregoing it might appear that Tillich simply has the same problem as all traditional Christologies, i.e., how to reconcile the divine causality with the human self-causation, and that he has opted not to try conceptually to solve the relation of the two, but simply to assert that both must be affirmed while insisting on their unity.

And yet Tillich's real difficulty is not how to reconcile Jesus' freedom with God's causality, but how to affirm God's causal influence at all. This conclusion can be based, in the first place, upon the principle, called by Whitehead the "ontological principle," that only that which is an actual being can act. Only that which has the unity of an individual can exert agency, either for itself (self-causation) or for others (efficient causation).[4]

Tillich himself says that God cannot be conceived as an efficient cause. (This is the type of causation at issue here, the influence of one reality upon another. Tillich certainly wants to insist upon the distinction—without a separation—between God and the world.) For as we saw above, causality is one of the categories of finitude that apply to beings in the subject-object structure of the world. To attribute causation to God would bring him into this structure, making him a cause alongside other causes, thereby negating his infinity and hence his divinity. (*ST* II, 6.) And to speak of him as the cause of happenings in time and space would be contrary to his transcendence. (*ST* I, 273.)

How then are we to understand the attribution to God of all those terms with causal connotations? The answer is: in the same way that the ontological polarities were attributed, i.e., symbolically. In speaking of God as related to the world as its ground, both categories of relation, i.e., causality and substance, are to be simultaneously negated (in their proper sense) and affirmed (symbolically). (*ST* I, 209, 237 f.) Also the term "ground," whether in the "ground of being" in general or in the "ground of revelation" in particular, is itself a symbol. Although it suggests both meanings, it can really mean neither that God is the cause of finite beings nor that he is their substance. "It oscillates between cause and substance and transcends both of them." (*ST* I, 156.) Also since "cause" and "substance" are both intended symbolically, rather than categorically, the difference between them vanishes. (*ST* I, 238.)

But if neither of the categories of relation has any literal meaning retained in its application to God, how are we to understand the statement that God is *related* to the world? Again, symbolically. Our relation to God, "in the categorical sense of the word, is not a relation at all." (*ST* I, 272.) There are no "relations of God with something else," since "there is no creaturely independence from which an external relation between God and the creature could be derived." The "unapproachable" character of God means "the impossibility of having a relation with him in the proper sense of the word." (*ST* I, 271.)

My conclusion in this section is doubly negative. First, even if Tillich's language about God's "grace" and "directing creativity" were allowed, he could not give any idea as to *how* the divine and human causations were related in Jesus, especially not how the divine presence was in any way different (even in degree) in Jesus, and certainly not how any such difference could be at all attributable to the divine initiative. Hence, despite Tillich's concern to do justice to the central intentions of the traditional doctrines, his conceptuality gives him no basis for attributing any of the specialness of Jesus to God. But second, Tillich cannot *intelligibly* attribute *any* causal activity to God in relation to the world in general or to Jesus in particular.

4. THE OBJECTIVE AND SUBJECTIVE SIDES OF REVELATION

The preceding discussion of God's causal relation to Jesus will be presupposed in this section. The question here concerns the respective contributions, in a revelatory event, of the subjective response of the believer to whom the revelation occurs, and of that objective element which exists or occurs prior to, and hence independently of, this subjective response. Unless there was something about Jesus himself, independently of my receiving him as God's revelation, that makes it appropriate that I have experienced him as revelatory, the basis for continuing to be a Christian is undercut. If it is *totally* my subjective response that constitutes Jesus as a "revelation of God," then all events are equally qualified to serve as the "objective" side of revelations of deity, and there is no reason whatsoever to encourage others to inaugurate or continue a special relationship to Jesus, rather than to some other object.

Tillich is well known for his emphasis on the subjective side of revelation. Since revelation is by definition a revelation *to someone*, an event must be *received* as such in order for a revelation to occur. (*ST* I, 35.) But he also appears to stress the objective side equally. First, he affirms that in every revelatory event there is a "miracle," which is the objective side of the event, as well as the believer's "ecstasy," which is the subjective side. "These two sides cannot be separated. If nothing happens objectively, nothing is revealed. If no one receives what happens subjectively, the event fails to reveal anything." (*ST* I, 111.)

Second, although anything can in principle become a revelation, some things are better suited for constituting the objective element than others. The more developed the ontological elements in the creature, the better it is for representing the ground of being. Hence, the final revelation could appear only in a person. (*ST* I, 118; *ST* II, 120.) Also, there are some things which are *taken* as expressing our ultimate concern (our God), but which really fail to do so. (*ST* II, 116.)

Third, Tillich insists on the necessity of the *actual fact* to which the name Jesus of Nazareth refers, i.e., a personal life in which perfect unity with God was maintained. (*ST* II, 98.) Jesus became the Christ not only because he was received as the Christ but also because he *could* become the Christ.

"Without both these sides he would not have been the Christ." (*ST* I, 126.)

From these three points it might appear that Tillich does justice to the objective element entailed in confessing Jesus as God's decisive revelation. Certainly this was his intention. But a closer analysis of these three points forces a judgment equally as negative as those in the preceding sections.

One idea in Tillich's thought that apparently gives revelation an objective grounding is his use of the term "miracle." The objective side of a revelation is called a "miracle." But of course Tillich wants to stress that this implies no supernatural interference in natural processes—the rational structure of being is not destroyed. (*ST* I, 115 f.) Hence the term "sign-event," which avoids that connotation, is sometimes used instead. What then makes something a miracle or sign-event? There are three characteristics. (*a*) It is "first of all an event which is astonishing, unusual, shaking." But we are also told that the "extraordinarily regular" can be the medium of revelation; and in fact that *anything* can be. It has nothing to do with any "special qualities" of the thing, but simply whether or not it in fact enters into a revelatory constellation. (*ST* I, 117–120.) Hence, whether or not something is "astonishing, unusual, shaking" must depend totally upon its reception, and not at all upon what it is in itself. (*b*) The second characteristic of genuine miracle is that it "points to the mystery of being, expressing its relation to us in a definite way." (*ST* I, 117.) But this is simply a definition of a *revelation,* and therefore does not help us understand what the objective side in itself is. (*c*) The third condition is that "it is an occurrence which is received as a sign-event in an ecstatic experience." But this simply repeats the purely formal definition of a sign-event, and tells us nothing substantive about it. Accordingly, when Tillich asserts that Jesus became the Christ partly "because he could become the Christ," this does not serve to differentiate Jesus from any other man in any way. Hence, while what is needed is something about the medium of revelation that indicates why men *should* respond positively to it, what is given refers only to the fact that men *have in fact* responded positively to it. While what is needed is a normative statement, or at least a warrant for such a statement, what is given is purely factual and provides no such warrant.

The second idea in Tillich's thought that apparently gives revelation an objective grounding is that some mediums are better than others. And the human being can be the best medium, since only in a person are the polarities of being complete. Being a "microcosmos," he contains the psychological as well as the physical and biological realms, and hence all of the qualities that can point to the mystery of existence, or God. But this does not seem to fit in Tillich's system. The human person would be the best medium only where God is thought of in analogy with the person. And we saw in the previous section that God is in no sense a self, and cannot really be said to embody the ontological polarities. Hence, in Tillich's system the person would be no better medium than anything else. If anything were preferable in this somewhat Neoplatonic outlook, it would seem to be things such as rocks (which are relatively "unconditioned" by other things), oceans, and overflowing fountains.

The differentiation among things on the basis of whether or not they lead to idolatry also fails to provide the type of objectivity needed. The criterion here is whether or not the thing claims holiness for itself as well as for that to which it points, or whether it completely points away from itself to the holy. (*ST* I, 216.) In the former case the faith in that revelation is not true on its objective side, since it does not express that which is truly ultimate (being-itself), but elevates something finite to ultimacy, and hence is idolatrous. For the symbol to be objectively true it must completely negate itself. This is why Jesus as the Christ is the medium of final revelation. (*DF* 96 f.) "The decisive trait in his picture is the continuous self-surrender of Jesus who is Jesus to Jesus who is the Christ." In other words, he gives up everything finite about himself, everything that is "merely Jesus." He thereby becomes "transparent" to that which he reveals. (*ST* I, 133 f.)

But this means that nothing definite in the objective side of the revelatory event is left, according to which to bring one's life into harmony with the divine reality. And Tillich explicitly affirms this, i.e., that we are liberated from the authority of everything finite in Jesus, his tradition, piety, world view, and ethics.[5] Of course, this is what should be expected on the basis of the doctrine of God examined in the preceding section. For if there is nothing *determinate* in God, then nothing determinate in a finite being could especially *correspond* to God's nature. And this connection is also made explicit by Tillich: the cross of Christ is the most adequate symbol, since "it does not accept any truth of faith as ultimate except the one that no man possesses it." (*DF* 98.) This is in harmony with the notion that the only thing we can say about God in a straightforward way is that we cannot say anything about him in a straightforward way.

Tillich's third assertion of objectivity is that there really was a personal life upon which the New Testament picture of Jesus as the Christ was based, and in which perfect unity with God was maintained under the conditions of existence. Van Harvey has shown that Tillich makes some contradictory statements about a personal life *behind* the picture, but also that these are only incidental to Tillich's position, which really rests on the New Testament *picture* of Jesus as the Christ.[6] It is this which he claims as the objective part of true faith in revelation. The ecstatic reception of Jesus (the miracle) by the first believers is called "original revelation," but from then on the Christian revelation is "dependent" revelation. The miracle and its first reception together form the giving side. (*ST* I, 126.) Accordingly, if one wished to deny the reality of a Jesus figure behind the picture, the creation of the picture would itself be the miracle, and its first success would be the original revelation. However, the same questions would have to be raised about the picture that were earlier raised about Jesus, and we would be back to the twofold problem indicated there. That is, a *picture* of a human life is in the same predicament as a human life itself in manifesting being-itself in an extaordinary way. And the only valid part of the picture is its total self-negation; it has no determinate trait which can serve to orient us to the character of deity.

5. THE BASIS FOR CHRISTIAN EXISTENCE

This final issue presupposes a situation in which we are aware of various possibilities of human existence, so that being Christian is merely one of many possible ways of being human. Tillich understands Christian existence to involve, among other things, a commitment to truth, justice, and love. But *why* should a person thus exist? Does Tillich give an intelligible basis for the conviction that one should live this way, as opposed, say, to orienting one's life around the bodily vitalities?

He certainly intends to do so. He has spoken of his "search for absolutes" and says that his theology is based on those he has found. (*MSA*, 124.) He rejects nominalism and believes that values must have a *fundamentum in re*. (*ST* I, 20, 255.)

And his statements about reality appear to provide a support for these intentions. He speaks of the purpose of God's providence as the fulfillment of the creatures, of God's desire for our fulfillment, and of what God wants us to be. Furthermore, God has the character of love, and his love includes his justice, which is a universally valid principle. (*ST* I, 279–283.) The good is not an arbitrary commandment, but is the essential structure of reality. The good-itself and the true-itself are manifestations of being-itself. (*ST* I, 204, 206 f.) Hence, Tillich lists absolutes which transcend the relativities of flux. Given these statements about God's relation to values, Christian existence would seem to have a basis in man's desire to be in harmony with the ultimate reality, to unite his will with the divine will.

However, since there are problems in Tillich's doctrine of God, it is to be expected that there will be problems in his attempt to avoid relativism, since all doctrines are interrelated. The lack of meaningfulness in speaking of God's purpose, will, desire, love, and justice has been explored already. I will therefore turn directly to the notion of absolute values.

The first question to be raised about them is their locus in reality. Where can they be? It is difficult to think of entities such as values as having any reality apart from experiencing subjects. Tillich knows, of course, that much Christian theology has given essences such as values a foundation in reality by seeing them as ideas in the divine mind. And Tillich evidently wants to follow this as closely as he can, affirming that "the essential powers of being belong to the divine life in which they are rooted." (*ST* I, 254.) But the transition from a doctrine of God as *a* being (as well as being-itself), to the Tillichian notion that God is not a being, makes this unintelligible.

Furthermore, even if it were possible to conceive of the reality, apart from a cosmic mind, of essences that transcend the relativities of finite existence, it is not possible to conceive of their being independently efficacious. Tillich rightly speaks of them as having potential, as opposed to actual, being. (*ST* I, 203 f.; *ST* II, 33.) But surely the very meaning of *actual*, that which differentiates it from the merely potential, involves the power to *act*. Only that which is actual can exert any causal influence. Hence, if we ask about the cause of some element in our experience, we must look for an *actual* being. Yet Tillich speaks as if it were meaningful to ascribe the agency behind the ideal element in our experience to the essences themselves. He indicates that they "encounter" us. We *receive* logical and moral imperatives. (*ST* II, 31.) But these come not from a personal God, but from our essential being. We can speak of the "will of God" if we wish, but this is a metaphorical way of speaking of the fact that our potential, essential being "confronts," "commands," and "speaks to" us. (*MSA*, 95–97.)

Within the boundaries of phenomenology it may be provisionally permissible to attribute causal efficacy to essences, or potentials. They certainly *appear* to confront and affect us. One could simply bracket the ontological or metaphysical question as to the source of their efficacy. But Tillich moves beyond phenomenology into ontology, and explicitly denies that the potentials, such as values, are rendered effective for our experience by virtue of God's agency. In so doing, Tillich has rendered the efficacy of essences unintelligible, and thereby failed to give a credible defense of their reality against reductionistic, relativistic explanations of man's experience of ideal values.

There are many ideas in Tillich's thought, primarily formal ones, which I believe to be sound. These include the following ideas: (1) Theology is in principle as rational as philosophy, since each in fact begins with a "revelation." (2) Man is essentially religious, so that idolatry is a greater danger than complete absence of faith. (3) It is necessary for the healing of man to include the cognitive dimension of his existence, and therefore knowledge of God is necessary. (4) The term "God" cannot stand for a reality that is merely one being among others, in the sense of one whose existence is contingent, but rather for a reality that is in some sense being itself and the very condition or ground of all finite beings, and hence the one reality to which we are all essentially related. (5) The relation of God to Jesus cannot be an exception to the normal structure of relations. (6) Revelation always involves a receptive appropriation by the present believer, and is therefore not identifiable with some objective ideas or past events. (7) There is nevertheless a necessity for an objective side of revelation, and some types of events are better suited for this than others. (8) Accepting Jesus as the supreme revelation of God need not mean accepting all his views. (9) Christian existence requires seeing its basic values as rooted in the ultimate nature of things.

Despite the presence of these sound ideas in his thought, Tillich's success in providing substantive ideas corresponding to these formal ones has, in my judgment, been essentially negative. And I have attempted to make clear that the basis for Tillich's failure time after time is his position that "God" can-

not refer to an individual being. Accordingly, the primary conclusion of the present chapter is that, if Christian theology is
to make intelligible the ideas that are essential to faith, it must
have a doctrine according to which God is an individual being
as well as in some sense being-itself. Only on such a basis could
one make intelligible the kind of activity between God and the
creatures that Christian faith requires, the foundation of values
in a reality transcending the temporal flux, and something
determinate in God that something in a finite being might especially reveal. Such a doctrine of God will be discussed in
Chapter 7.

CHAPTER 2

The Relativistic Meaning
of Revelation

1. THE RATIONALITY OF THEOLOGY
BASED UPON REVELATION

The present chapter will examine the position developed by
H. Richard Niebuhr in *The Meaning of Revelation*.[1] In Tillich
the key factor militating against an adequate doctrine of
revelation is a substantive one, the idea of God as being-itself
and not *a* being. In Niebuhr the problematic factor is a formal
one, the relation between reason and faith based on revelation.

Uppermost in Niebuhr's mind is the intention to develop a
definition of revelation that will be adequate to Christian faith,
and yet will avoid any conflict between faith and reason. (*MR*
3.) And here the possible conflict is seen primarily not in
terms of the tension between religious and scientific views of
nature, but that between religious and nonreligious views of
the same historical events. (*MR* vii, 26.) To use the prime
example, the Christian sees Jesus as God's supreme revelation
and thus believes that the most important factor in understanding Jesus was the divine activity in him. The objective
historian, however, does not use the category of divine causation but understands Jesus purely in terms of his historical
context, in terms of the same type of cause-effect relationships

that are used for all historical figures. How are these two pictures to be related? Does allegiance to one of them exclude holding the other? If so, then one would have to choose either Christian faith or the acceptance of the widely accepted methods and presuppositions of modern historiography, i.e., either revelation or historical reason. Theology would have to give up either the idea of revelation or else every pretense of being rational.

Niebuhr's solution is based on a distinction between two types of history, internal and external. External history is "the succession of events which an uninterested spectator can see from the outside." (*MR* 59.) Internal history refers to "the history of selves or to history as it is lived and apprehended from within." (*MR* 60.)

Commentators have pointed out the equivocation in Niebuhr's use of the terms "internal" and "external." The difference between internal and external can refer to the *perspective* of the author, indicating whether or not he shares the faith perspective of the community whose history he is reconstructing. Or it can refer to the *data* treated—internal history dealing with subjects and external history with objects. I will follow Lonnie Kliever in referring to these two meanings as the *epistemic* and the *ontological*, respectively.[2]

Furthermore, "external" in the epistemic sense has two meanings. It can indicate that the author is giving a purely objective account of a series of events, to which historians of all persuasions could in principle agree. Or it can mean that the historian belongs to a *different community of faith*, and hence has a different perspective, than do the subjects of his history. In most cases, his would be no objective, neutral recital of facts, but might well be a highly tendentious reconstruction using the principles of interpretation suggested by his own perspective, e.g., Freudian or Marxist. I will refer to these two types of epistemically external history as *objective external* history and *alien external* history, respectively.[3]

This would seem to require a more complex analysis of the

types of history than the simple division into internal and external. With the three epistemic and the two ontological variables, five or six types would be possible.[4] Niebuhr recognizes that he uses the terms "internal" and "external" to refer both to the perspective of the historian and to the data discussed. But he avoids introducing further distinctions by his assertion that history that is internal epistemically will also be internal ontologically, and history that is external epistemically will consequently be external ontologically. When one speaks of his own community, he will speak of events in terms of their meaning to selves. The data for a nonparticipating observer, on the other hand, "are all impersonal; they are ideas, interests, movements among things. Even when such history deals with human individuals it seeks to reduce them to impersonal parts." (*MR* 64.)

Questions will have to be raised about this neat division, of course. But first it should be seen how necessary to Niebuhr's thesis it is to maintain this simple division.

Niebuhr's thesis is that Christian theology must be confessional in nature. This means that the Christian must be content to express his point of view, to tell simply what has happened to him and how he consequently understands reality. He must not absolutize his point of view, assuming that it is a knowledge of *things as they are in themselves*. Rather, he must humbly acknowledge that his view—as is the case with every human view—is a view of things as they are for him, things as they appear from his conditioned spatio-temporal standpoint. (*MR* 7.) In others words, theology must accept the relativity that characterizes all other human enterprises. (*MR* 8.)

But what of "revelation," the notion to which all fideistic theologies appeal to escape the relativism in all human speculation, which they gladly acknowledge? Niebuhr asserts that it does not allow us an escape. For "revelation" refers, in the first place, to our historic faith, which is one faith among others, and cannot be demonstrated to be superior. More precisely it refers to that part of our inner history which is the primary basis for our point of view. (*MR* 6 f.) It is that part which is intelligible in itself, and makes all the other parts intelligible. (*MR* 93.) Hence, religious relativism and belief in revelation are not antithetical, but belong together. The recognition that all thought is relative is the acknowledgment that all thought must begin with a particular perspective. The Christian community calls that which is the basis of its thought its revelation. And the Christian meaning of "revelation" is a relativistic one. The Christian cannot assert, on the basis of his revelation, that revelation has not occurred in other communities, or that other people *ought* to regard the key events in the Judeo-Christian tradition as the revelation of deity.

Crucial to this relativism is Niebuhr's analysis of the relation of internal and external accounts of the same events. The external account records the outer characteristics of the events. In the language of critical idealism, it is the theoretical, "pure reason" that is operating. (*MR* 65.) In the language of critical realism, the data are the "primary qualities," those which would be available to all human percipients. The internal view deals with the internal world, with subjects. It is the "practical reason" that is operating, and it is concerned with selves and "tertiary qualities," or values. (*MR* 66, 68.) This history is normative, not merely descriptive (*MR* 67). (It is most important for the ensuing critique to notice that Niebuhr's distinction is *not* that theoretical reason is concerned with actualities, while practical reason deals only with norms and values. Rather, the practical reason deals with actualities, i.e., selves, as well as with values.)

Niebuhr insists that we do not need to choose between the internal and the external types of history. They are both valid. The question, then, is how they are to be related. He says that no *speculative* answer is possible. On the one hand, the external cannot absorb the internal history, for an objective picture of the life of Jesus is quite other than acknowledgment of him as the Christ and our Lord, which requires a leap of faith. On the other hand, Niebuhr says that it is impossible to synthesize the two views into a new whole which transcends but does justice to them both. For this would involve determining what the events-in-themselves really are, which means the events as they are for God, and this is impossible for us.

It is this claimed impossibility of a synthesis of the two views which is systematically crucial for Niebuhr's prescription of a relativistic, confessional approach. For if on the basis of our revelation we could show that reality in itself corresponds most closely to the Christian's way of seeing it, we would have a basis for saying that the other philosophies and theologies were less accurate than ours, and we could intend that our central tenets ought to be believed by all men, not merely confess what we believe without implying anything about the truth or falsity of other positions.

According to Niebuhr the correct way to relate the two histories is to be content with "a double and partial knowledge." (*MR* 84.) And this way explains how the Christian can accept Jesus as God's revelation without denying those non-religious pictures of him as a finite, conditioned individual, describable in terms of the same type of cause-and-effect relationships applicable to all men. For these external accounts only give the outer, externally perceivable events and do not penetrate to the other aspect of Jesus, his inner self. This aspect can only be known by another approach, by participation in the historical community emanating from Jesus' personal impact upon his contemporaries. Hence the "two-aspect theory of history" (*MR* 81) is said to allow belief in revelation without any warfare between faith and reason.

In the remainder of this section, and in those following, I will examine whether Niebuhr's own substantive affirmations are consistent with this distinction between external and internal history and the concomitant prescribed confessionalism, and hence whether the relativistic interpretation of revelation is adequate even from the point of view of Niebuhr's own position.

Immediately after stating the impossibility of a speculative solution to the relation of the two types of history, Niebuhr suggests what he calls a "practical" solution. Among the elements involved is the duty to formulate an external history of ourselves. Here "external" has primarily the ontological meaning, since that duty is to try to see ourselves with the eyes of God, to whom we should ascribe a "simultaneous, unified knowledge from within and without." This means that Niebuhr is now exhorting us *not* to rest content with a view of things as they initially appear to us from our finite standpoint, but to seek a knowledge of things as they are for God, which means things as they really are *in themselves.* This knowledge, which is "simultaneous in his case can in a measure be successive for us." (*MR* 88.) Presumably Niebuhr's meaning here is that we can learn to see ourselves from both points of view, but that we, unlike God, cannot understand how the inner and outer views are related. Hence, Niebuhr has not directly contradicted his statement that it is impossible for us to synthesize the outer and inner views into a superior vision, as has been claimed.[5] Nevertheless, this exhortation is in some tension with Niebuhr's relativistic prescriptions, for to attempt to take a number of external views and distill from them *the* external view of ourselves requires a nonrelative criterion for selecting *the* element of truth in each of the views.

It might be objected that Niebuhr's position would be consistent if only this exhortation to try to see ourselves in the reflection of God were removed, and that it well could be removed, since Niebuhr's thought does not require it. In the following sections I will attempt to show that many affirmations which clearly *are* central to Niebuhr's faith and theology also are incompatible with his proposal for a merely confessional theology.

2. The Content of Revelation

As suggested above, there are two sides to Niebuhr's thought. On the one hand, in his formal statements he is highly relativistic; on the other hand, in his substantive statements he makes affirmations that are incompatible with such a relativistic position.

Many passages might suggest that revelation has no ideational content. What is revealed is God himself giving himself in communion, not supernatural knowledge. (*MR* 152.) The content cannot be expressed in terms of ideas or propositions, but only in terms of persons. (*MR* 143, 153 f.) Revelation is not something static that can be possessed, such as a set of doctrines. (*MR* 41.) Faith in the God of revelation is "a personal act of commitment, of confidence and trust, not a belief about the nature of things." (*MR* 154.)

This interpretation would fit with the relativistic emphasis. If the acceptance of revelation entailed no propositional beliefs about God, then nothing would be asserted which would contradict non-Christian ideas about deity. In line with this is Niebuhr's statement that we should keep our focus on God, not on our faith and our theology. (*MR* 27.) Furthermore, theology has learned that it cannot describe God "as he is in himself but only God in human experience." (*MR* 8.) Finally, we are confined by our situation to the knowledge of God that is possible to those who live in Christian history. (*MR* 20.) For "we are in history as the fish is in water." (*MR* 48.)

Niebuhr insists that this relativism does not imply subjectivism and skepticism. Rather, he calls his position "critical realism," which accepts the independent reality of that which is seen from a conditioned standpoint. One who knows that his concepts are not universal does not need to doubt that they are concepts of the universal. (*MR* 18.) Those who participate in the same history are enabled to see the *same aspect* of the universal. The implication is that different communities see different aspects of God. Niebuhr's position seems to be that one community's affirmations do not contradict the affirmations of other communities, since each can be understood as expressing how God is related *to them*, and this involves only *one* aspect of God's nature.

But many of Niebuhr's statements, including ones that are not peripheral to his overall theology, cannot be reconciled with the above restrictions. First, his position involves many propositions about God. Christian faith as well as "critical realism" intends that God has actual rather than purely postulated or ideal existence, and that he really has revealed himself. (*MR* 163, 185.) This God is known as our knower; he is the eternal knower who knows the final secrets of our hearts. As such he is both the universal valuer and judge. (*MR* 152 f.) He is the universal sovereign, an infinite being. (*MR* 40, 151.) He is characterized by an infinite suffering and an infinite loyalty. (*MR* 125.) Despite Niebuhr's apparent deprecation of beliefs about the nature of things, he indicates that we should understand nature as God's garment or body. (*MR* 153, 175.) And he says that belief in God means overcoming the position that this is "a great impersonal cosmos which does not know that we exist and does not care for us," and which would imply that "persons do not belong to the real structure of things." (*MR* 150.) Rather, we learn that there is a great divine dominating purpose in the world, a will directed toward the final unity of all things. (*MR* 124, 183.) Through revelation we learn that "fate" is really a person in community with us. (*MR* 153.) Furthermore, through revelation we learn to correct our previous hypothesis of the unity of deity, as we learn that God is not the unconditioned but the conditioner, not the one beyond the many, but the one who acts in and through all things. (*MR* 183.)

Hence Niebuhr's position must be understood as intending that, although propositional statements about God and the nature of things cannot *adequately* state what we mean by revelation (since valuational confessions must always be included), the content of revelation *involves* such propositions. Niebuhr himself points to this duality in the concept of revelation. There is the idea that God reveals *himself* and the notion that "the will of God and truths about his nature" are revealed. (*MR* 158.) He resolves this by saying that no *explicit* moral laws or doctrines are the _immediate_ content of revelation imparted to men apart from their reasoning, but that God's self-disclosure has implications that supply the basis for our radical reconstruction of our ethical views and our ideas of deity. (_MR_ 171 f., 182–191.)

Although this resolution means that some of Niebuhr's either/or statements should have been qualified, it does overcome any contradiction in his position as to whether revelation has a communicable content. However, the affirmative answer leads to other difficulties. First, the above assertions cannot be understood as only describing God in human experience, and not God in himself. Although a Schleiermachian statement such as "I feel dependent upon God" could be understood as purely relational, all of Niebuhr's assertions cited above imply something about God himself (or else they would have to be interpreted purely symbolically, in a Tillichian sense, which Niebuhr clearly does not intend). To assert that God is a person, that he knows and values us, that he suffers, that he has a purpose, that he conditions all events, is to make affirmations directly about God.

Second, these assertions cannot be understood as merely describing _one aspect_ of God in a way that is compatible with all other assertions about reality. The law of noncontradiction clearly prevents all the above assertions from being true if it be true that there is no eternal knower and purposer, or that there are gods but they do not care for us, or that God is wholly impassible, or that the world's unifying factor does not affect the world.

Hence Niebuhr's proposed relativistic understanding of revelation is inadequate to the content of revelation even as he himself understands this content. And it is clear that most of these assertions are ones that he would not relinquish. (And— to shift momentarily from internal criticism to a normative statement—all or most of these are assertions that Christian faith could not give up and still retain its identity.)

3. God's Relation to Jesus

The next question is whether the presuppositions of Niebuhr's prescribed confessional theology can be reconciled with an adequate doctrine of Jesus' person. In particular the issue is whether Niebuhr's attempt to prevent a clash of faith and reason by radically distinguishing internal and external history allows for an intelligible idea of God as active in Jesus in such a way that the term "revelation" is appropriate.

Niebuhr recognizes that the notion of divine self-revelation entails the idea of divine activity in worldly events. Otherwise one should speak of discovery or vision, instead of revelation. (*MR* 143–147.) And since Jesus Christ is the primary event to which Christians have reference when speaking of revelation (*MR* 93), it would seem that this is the event in which we would believe the divine revealing activity to have been supreme.

But how is the specialness of Jesus in this regard to be understood? The traditional supernaturalistic answer is clearly rejected by Niebuhr. He uses the distinction between internal and external history to formulate the kind of mistake involved in supernaturalism: Christians had located revelation in external history, history known from a nonparticipating point of view. For they had tied it to miraculous events in a sacred history, whose events were said not to be subject to the type of explanation adequate for so-called secular events. Included in this error was the belief that the inspiration of the Scriptures involved a suspension of the ordinary processes of human thought. (*MR* 74–76.)

One should recognize that the events which Christians regard as revelatory can also be regarded from the scientific, objective point of view. Thus regarded they are no different from other events. They can be explained in terms of cause-effect relationships in their cultural, geographic, economic, and political contexts. (*MR* 55.) Presumably Niebuhr would add the physiological and psychological contexts to this list, since he apparently holds to a "two-aspect theory" of the body and mind, parallel to the two-aspect theory of history (*MR* 81); and he includes in objective history the discussion of "general tendencies in human nature" (*MR* 56). The person looking at the central events of Christian history from this point of view has no need for the hypothesis of divine action. (*MR* 55.) He should apply the same laws and principles that he applies to all other events. (*MR* 76.) Looking at Jesus objectively shows him to be a limited, historically conditioned human being. (*MR* 15, 89.)

If the idea is rejected that the normal causal factors were interrupted in the case of Jesus, how is the divine revealing activity in him to be understood? Niebuhr shows no tendency to interpret the notion of divine activity purely symbolically. Nor would he reduce it totally to an existential assertion or a value judgment, in the sense that it would say something only about the believer, and hence would intend nothing objectively about the past event.

Rather, Niebuhr's position is that statements about God's activity *are* "objective" in the sense of really asserting something about the event in question (e.g., Jesus). But they *are not* "objective" in the sense of being appropriate or even possible from a nonparticipating point of view. They are assertions that can be made only about one's internal history. Only the Christian can speak of divine activity in Jesus. External history abstracts from selves, and hence of necessity cannot speak of the divine self, or the meeting of the human and divine selves. (*MR* 74, 87.)

Hence, acceptance of revelation, with its entailed idea of divine activity in history, does not conflict with secular historiography. Assertions about divine activity, being made from the viewpoint of faith, belong to inner history and thereby belong to a different order than assertions of external history. Since external history cannot employ the hypothesis of divine activity, in its own order its explanation of events in terms of immanent causes is complete. This objective account of the basic events in Christian history is entirely acceptable to Christians. That is, it is acceptable as long as totalitarian "nothing-but" phrases, with their claim to tell the whole truth, are avoided; for it must be remembered that this external history only describes the exterior side of the events, and does not permeate to the inside, which can only be described from within, from a participating point of view. (*MR* 85, 181.) Hence by following an approach in line with Schleiermacher's, religious and nonreligious views of the same event in principle cannot conflict. (*MR* 26.)

However, this solution to the problem of faith and history depends on the maintenance of Niebuhr's simple classification of histories into internal and external. That is, history that is external epistemically must also be external ontologically. Only on this assumption would faith find nonthreatening all external histories of Christianity, since they would leave the inner core of the events untouched.

But reflection upon his equivocal use of the term "external history" in the epistemic sense destroys this assumption. As long as epistemically external history means a detached, objective account of the succession of events to which historians of all persuasions could in principle subscribe, it is quite clear that the *data* described will be at a rather high level of abstraction from the concrete decisions and valuations of selves, including all the conscious and unconscious influences and motives. In terms of this definition it makes sense to claim that history that is external epistemically will also be external ontologically, and hence will leave the inner aspect of the events uninterpreted.

But as was seen in section 1 of this chapter, the term "external history" is also used to refer to all histories that are written from foreign perspectives, which I have termed "alien external histories." Examples could be provided by histories

of the events of Biblical and Christian history written from
Marxist and Freudian viewpoints. Here the account would not
be the dispassionate, disinterested account of events that must
be limited to high abstractions and hence externals. Rather,
the account would most likely be dealing with selves, with
their values, their basic motives, the real determinants of their
actions. It cannot be maintained that history which is epistemically external in this sense would also be external ontologically.

Accordingly, the truce claimed between Christian and
secular interpretations of events considered revelatory by
Christians is illusory. For in reality most of the so-called secular
interpretations are not objective, disinterested accounts that
leave the inner core of the events for another approach. Rather,
they are themselves rooted in a perspective which is based
upon faith that a certain aspect of reality gives concepts and
principles adequate to interpret all of reality. The terms "faith"
and "revelation" may be avoided, and the source of the perspective may not even be recognized, but the dynamics are the
same.

Therefore, the Christian interpretation of events is *not* necessarily on a level different from that of "external" histories, as
Niebuhr's reconciliation requires. Rather, it is in *competition*
with other viewpoints, each of which is "internal" in the sense
of having concepts it believes most adequate to elucidate the
most essential factors in the course of events.

Of course Niebuhr recognizes that one who is writing what
he calls external history may try to find the "efficient factor"
among the elements. But he dismisses this by saying that it
"involves the peril of forsaking the objective point of view, as
when a Marxist historian chooses economic elements or an in-
tellectualist regards ideas in the mind as the motivating forces
in history." (*MR* 64.) This statement shows that the ambiguity
in Niebuhr's use of the term "external" has led him to hold up
a false ideal for historians, suggesting that those who are not
participants in the perspective of the Christian community
must *also* be "objective" in the sense of refraining from using

their own categories to interpret Christian history. Of course it is only if all historians would follow these restrictions that Niebuhr's program to avoid a conflict of faith and reason would work.

That this is a false ideal is shown by Niebuhr's own discussion as to how we Christians should interpret the histories of traditions not our own. We are required to regard all events as the workings of the God who has revealed himself in Christian history. Once God has revealed his self and will to us in our inner history, supremely through our memory of Jesus Christ, we must recognize "his rule and providence in all events of all times and communities." (*MR* 87.) Niebuhr calls this a "faithful external history," and sees that "in this sense an external history finds its starting point or impulsion in an internal history." (*MR* 88.) Hence, we Christians are to write other histories, such as the history of Buddhist and Marxist communities, in terms of *our* central category, that of divine providence. Because of the way deity has been revealed to us, as the universal God who is creator of all events, we are required to interpret the events in the lives of other peoples in terms of *this* concept, no matter what central categories those people may use for understanding their own histories.[6]

Niebuhr is surely right here. As long as we are Christians we cannot help believing that our categories of explanation are more adequate than others. But we also must recognize that other people, seeing reality from different faith perspectives, will feel required to interpret *our* history in terms of *their* categories. And since we are engaged in writing a "faithful external history" of them which is ontologically internal, it is irrelevant to point out that their "faithful external history" of us (which we would regard as an "alien external history") is not purely "objective." Also, recognizing that our external history of other peoples has its origin in our internal history should have alerted Niebuhr to the important difference between his two kinds of epistemically external history, i.e., that the one would be ontologically internal.

Once we have seen the true nature of the conflict between Christian and non-Christian interpretations of history, and the inadequacy of a simple division into internal and external, it becomes evident that a confessional solution is not possible. For these various perspectives are not merely different, they conflict. For example, an interpretation which holds that ideas rule history, and one which says that ideas are merely the nonefficient effects of material forces, cannot be reconciled as merely two aspects of the truth. Any reconciliation would involve the total rejection of the one in favor of the other, or the modification of both as partial aspects of a more inclusive view. Thus an interpretation which says that there are no causes of events beyond finite, physical ones cannot be reconciled with a view of God as providentially influential in all events. If the former view is held, the latter is totally excluded. If the Christian holds the latter, he cannot help implying the falsity of the former view, no matter how humble he may wish to be.

To make the relation to Christology explicit, this means that the belief that God was active in Jesus cannot be considered simply compatible with all non-Christian accounts of Jesus on the grounds that these external accounts leave the inner essence of the events constituting Jesus' life to the interpretation of faith. For most of these external histories will be "alien external histories," finding their impulsion in a perspective alien to the Christian faith, and using their categories to interpret the inner essence of Jesus. And these interpretations will in most cases be incompatible with Christology. For example, if the "secular" historian says Jesus was *primarily* motivated by the desire for political or economic power, this is incompatible with the belief that the primary influence on him was the directing activity of God (unless one wanted to claim that God worked by instilling the desire for political or economic power). Or if a physiologist or psychologist said that all of Jesus' thoughts, emotions, words, and outer acts were totally determined by the complex of natural causes exerting influence on him through his five senses, this would be incompatible with the notion that God was a direct influence on him, and that Jesus had chosen freely how to respond to God's will.

It might be thought that Jesus could be understood adequately, both in terms of nondivine causes and also in terms of divine causality, by holding that Niebuhr was presupposing the traditional scheme of primary and secondary causes, which holds to two levels of causation. In fact, Niebuhr's language in one place is reminiscent of this mode of thought. (*MR* 87.) But this would not resolve the difficulties. In the first place, this would again involve a nonrelativistic claim that the ultimate cause of all events is one mind and will. In the second place, one would be involved in equivocation on the term "sufficient cause." For the scheme requires that, from one point of view, the sufficient cause of a given event (B) is a complex of finite events (A), but that from another point of view, the will of God (A') is the sufficient cause of (B). But by definition, there can only be *one* sufficient cause of any event. The claim that this is not the case if the two causes are on different "levels" will not work.[7]

There are two ways to state the conclusion to be drawn from this discussion: First, it is misleading to pose the issue of "faith and history" as if the issue were the relationship between one perspective, "faith," and that of one other perspective, "history." Rather, there is a multiplicity of possible perspectives from which to attempt an accurate historical reconstruction of the events. The question is which of these perspectives—e.g., Marxist, Freudian, behaviorist, or Christian— is the most adequate.

Second, for anyone who rejects supernaturalism, Jesus will have to be interpreted, as Niebuhr says, in terms of the *same concepts and principles used for all events*. The issue is precisely *which* set of concepts and principles is most adequate for interpreting all events, both those that are and those that are not special events in one's own tradition. Especially at issue is whether or not "divine influence" is one of the categories needed. This raises the question of criteria for determining the relative adequacy of the various perspectives, which will be discussed in the fifth section.

4. THE OBJECTIVE AND SUBJECTIVE ASPECTS OF REVELATION

It has been argued that Christology needs to affirm divine activity in Jesus, and that this entails a less relativistic understanding of God and of historical events than Niebuhr's formal proposal allows. But more is required than this. If men are to continue looking back to Jesus as the Christ, as the special event from which we derive concepts for interpreting all events, there must be something special about Jesus in himself which makes this practice appropriate. We must say more than that God was active in him, since we are saying that God is active in all events. If all that can be said is that Christians have *in fact* responded to him as the supreme revelation of God, then to continue advocating that men base their lives on him is purely arbitrary, or at best purely pragmatic. Unless some specialness can be intended about Jesus himself, apart from the response that he has in fact provoked, there is no basis for judging this response as appropriate. Christian faith involves the belief that there is a content there that makes Jesus potentially a better revelation of deity than all the other events in which God is also active.

Niebuhr's position is that, on the one hand, "revelation" is something that occurs in the present. It does not refer to anything that is static and simply objective and that can be possessed, such as a set of doctrines (*MR* 41) or a past event as perceptible to all observers (MR 56 f., 66). Rather, it refers to the illumination that happens again and again to believers through their memory of Jesus Christ. (*MR* 177.)

On the other hand, there is an unchanging element in Christian revelation that *can* be possessed. This is the memory of Jesus Christ. (*MR* 177.) And one can say that God revealed himself in the past as well as that he continues to reveal himself in the present. (*MR* 136.) Present revelation is the repetition and continuation of that moment in the past on which the church is based, in which God revealed himself. (*MR* 133.) And in regard to this objective element in revelation, there can be no progress; we cannot substitute any other moment for it. (*MR* 135.) This clearly implies that Christians must regard that past moment as God's supreme self-manifestation.

Accordingly, Niebuhr's position is that, although "revelation" is not something purely objective—for it does not occur apart from the present believing-valuational response of a subject whereby illumination comes to him—there is nevertheless some objectivity to the total complex. Although Jesus is actually God's self-revelation only to those who call him Jesus *Christ,* he in himself is potentially the best mediator of revelation. It seems evident then that a Christology would have to try to articulate what it is about the external embodiment we have of Jesus (the words and deeds as recorded by the early church) that constitutes it as potentially the most adequate mediator, among all its competitors, of a revelation of deity. I am presupposing, of course, the conclusion reached in the other sections of this chapter, that Niebuhr's substantive position is really not relativistic.

5. THE BASIS FOR CHRISTIAN EXISTENCE

The obvious question that arises when a confessional approach is advocated concerns the possibility of justifying one's beliefs and the life-style implied by them. After coming to an awareness of the diversity of perspectives and of the historical conditionedness of our acceptance of our particular perspective, have we no objective grounds whatsoever for continuing to maintain this faith and for advocating that others accept it?

The complete relativist must give a negative answer. At best, he can argue the necessity of a leap of faith in some direction, precisely because of the lack of objective criteria (along with the necessity for man to have a definite perspective). But he has no grounds for advocating a leap in the direction of Christian faith (except perhaps pragmatic or prudential considerations for one living in Western culture).

Is Niebuhr a complete relativist? Many passages would lead one to think so. He explicitly advocates a "relativistic theology," and says that this relativity is both historical and religious. (*MR* 8, 37.) Not only does the spatio-temporal point of view of the observer enter into his knowledge of reality, so that all his categories are limited (*MR* 7–21), but also man cannot speak of "God" except from the perspective of a particular faith; there is no neutral knowledge of deity with which one's faith can be compared (*MR* 22–38). For example, nature by itself, uninterpreted by our faith, does not point to God. (*MR* 48 f.) We must not absolutize anything relative, and this includes our religion and revelation. (*MR* ix.) We should not try to defend our faith; we cannot prove its superiority to other faiths. (*MR* viii, 18, 38.) And we can only say what revelation means for Christians, not what it *ought* to mean for all men. (*MR* 42.) We cannot say that revelation has not also taken place in other communities. (*MR* 82.) Accordingly, we cannot "prescribe what form religious life must take in all places and all times." (*MR* 17.)

In line with this, Niebuhr sometimes suggests that any "verification" of the Christian's perspective must be strictly internal to the Christian community. An individual's views are to be tested in terms of the experience of those who look from the same standpoint in the same direction, and in terms of consistency with the principles and concepts that have grown out of that community's past experience. (*MR* 21.) Assurance is not to be gained from consultation with those who occupy a different point of view and, hence, look in a different direction. (*MR* 141.)

On the other hand, Niebuhr suggests that Christian faith *can* be justified. It can be justified or proved by its fruits. (*MR* 20, 33.) This suggests that perhaps Niebuhr is not as relativistic as he sometimes sounds. For in order to judge whether or not fruits are "good," it seems that one must have some standpoint that transcends relativism. Of course the relativist, thus challenged, could reply that his value judgments are made in terms of the standards of his own conditioned community, so that he is merely engaged in the circular task of showing that his faith has positive consequences in terms of its own criteria. The question is whether or not that is Niebuhr's position.

The "fruits" of which Niebuhr speaks refer to the success of faith's perspective in giving an adequate interpretation of life. He essentially accepts Whitehead's statement that "rational religion appeals to the direct intuition of special occasions, and to the elucidatory power of its concepts for all occasions." [8] (*MR* 93.) Sometimes Niebuhr paraphrases this in a non-relativistic way: "Revelation means this intelligible event which makes all other events intelligible." (*MR* 93.) But in more careful formulations he makes two limitations. First, the concepts are for the *practical* reason, being applicable only to events as known by participating selves, i.e., moral agents and sufferers. (*MR* 94.) Second, the revelatory occasion gives us concepts for illuminating *our* history. (*MR* 93.) I will discuss the second limitation first.

Niebuhr says that revelation gives us a set of concepts, or better, a dramatic image, that enables us to put meaning into our own history, and, thereby, come to understand it. (*MR* 109 f.) This is the image of the saving work of the one God. (*MR* 135.) In this sense the test of the revelatory power of a revelatory moment is its rationality: it does not replace reason but provides it with the impulsion and first principles by which it can bring rationality or intelligibility into the community's history. (*MR* 109 f.)

But the limitation to our own history is quickly qualified. As we saw earlier, the Christian is required to interpret the history of all communities in terms of the image of the universal God, providentially ruling, revealing himself, and working for salvation. (*MR* 86 f.) While Niebuhr says that revelation makes our past intelligible, "our past" becomes expanded far beyond the Judeo-Christian tradition. The whole past of the human race becomes a unity, including even "the long story of human ascent from the dust." (*MR* 110 ff.) No part of the past is beyond redemption from meaninglessness, "and it is the ability of the revelation to save all the past from senselessness that is one of the marks of its revelatory character." (*MR* 112 f.) Also revelation enables our practical reason to remember parts of the past that we had forgotten because they did not fit into our cherished picture of ourselves, which was based upon evil and inadequate images. (*MR* 113 f.) Further, revelation enables Christians to appropriate as their own "the past of all human groups." (*MR* 115 f.) Christians thereby undergo a conversion, making their own the faiths and sins of their fathers and brothers. (*MR* 117 f.)

This is all possible because in Jesus Christ we get a "more inclusive hypothesis," which shows us both the faith and the sin of man as such, and we learn to see history as a unified affair in light of the great divine, dominating purpose to effect redemption. (*MR* 120, 124.) Without revelation, reason is limited and leads to error. (*MR* 121.) The images it uses to comprehend its brute data, i.e., the affections of the self (*MR* 97 f.), are shown to be evil by their consequences to selves and communities. They result in conflict, the impoverishment and destruction of selves, arbitrariness and isolation. (*MR* 99 f.) They fail to make sense of our life, leaving great areas unexplained. In short, they are inadequate, leaving us ignorant, and they are evil, leading us to destruction. (*MR* 102.) They cannot be overcome by eliminating personal, valuational ideas altogether in favor of impersonal concepts, but only by a more adequate image of the same order. It is Jesus Christ that gives Christians this image which is neither evil nor inadequate. (*MR* 108 f.)

Insofar as the Christian revelation furnishes the practical reason with an adequate starting point, enabling it to turn otherwise arbitrary and dumb fact into related and intelligible fact, it may be said to be validated. (*MR* 138.) Besides giving intelligibility, revelation provides other beneficial fruits. The remembrance of the past overcomes its unconscious, haunting constraint on us. The appropriation of the past of other men is necessary for there to be integrity of the self, and also human brotherhood, which is one of our greatest needs. (*MR* 118–121.)

The point of this summary of Niebuhr's thought is to illustrate how much, as we have seen in previous sections, his substantive affirmations are in tension with his formal relativism. In the first place, one who reads all his statements relating to the "progressive validation" of revelation in terms of the adequacy of the reasoning based upon it can scarcely believe that Niebuhr is a complete relativist, intending his proposed tests for the adequacy of the Christian perspective to be totally circular. Who can believe that Niebuhr intends the terms "error," "impoverishment," "destruction," "arbitrariness," and "isolation" to refer to things which are to be judged negatively only from a relativistic point of view, and that he does not claim that these things are evil in themselves, from the ultimate point of view? Likewise, who can believe that the expressions "intelligibility," "integrity of the self," "brotherhood," and "freedom from unconscious constraint by past errors" are not intended as noncircular criteria which are available to test the relative adequacies of the various faiths in terms of their consequences?

In the second place, the fact that concepts and images derived from the revelation in *our* history are to be employed to interpret all other histories and finally to incorporate them into our history has nonrelativistic implications. For, to repeat the point made earlier, assertions are thereby made about God and the rest of reality in themselves. If the Christian believes that all of history has a unity by virtue of the dominating purpose of the universal God, then he must deny the equal truth of all conflicting views. At best, they could represent subordinate aspects of the truth. They cannot be what they claim to be, the dominant concept or image by which to understand reality correctly. Niebuhr himself talks in this way, saying that inadequate images may be "applicable within narrow limits when they are subordinate to grander hypotheses." (*MR* 102.) And now, rather than speaking relativistically of Jesus as merely giving us one image among others, Niebuhr says that Jesus gives us "a more inclusive hypothesis."

Therefore, to attain consistency (a virtue that Niebuhr by no means eschews), his thought would have to be modified in one of two directions. Either the too-relativistic disclaimers would have to be removed. Or the substantive formulations would have to be almost totally revamped—in order to avoid any assertions that could possibly conflict with those of any other perspective. Faced with this choice, I believe it is clear that Niebuhr would choose the former. Also, I believe it is clear that only this choice is consistent with Christian faith. Finally, I believe that only this choice can be adequate to the nature of man, given his irrepressible desire to be in harmony with reality as it ultimately is. Accordingly, if the word "form" is understood narrowly, we should accept Niebuhr's statement that we cannot prescribe what form the religious life must take in all places and at all times. However, our acceptance should be qualified by a recognition that there are certain basic precepts to which human existence must conform if it is to be in harmony with the nature and purpose of God. Christian existence, broadly conceived, *is* believed to be grounded in the nature of things.

Only brief mention can be given to the other limitation Niebuhr placed on the scope of the concepts derived from the revelatory event, i.e., the limitation to the practical reason. He claims that "the obscurities which it explains are not those which bother us as observers of life, but those which distress moral agents and sufferers." Using Pascal's language, he adds that "it is the heart and not the head which finds its reason in revelation." In using revelation as the basis of our reasoning "we seek to conquer the evil imaginations of the heart and not the [in]adequate images of an observing mind." [9] (*MR* 94.)

But this restriction of the relevance of revelation is rooted solely in Niebuhr's contention that practical and theoretical reason are different in principle, a contention whose problematic status we have already seen. Also, once again Niebuhr's own statements indicate a lack of consistency. On the one hand, he says that it is mythological for impersonal models to be the primary ones used for understanding selves, and likewise mythological for personal images to be used for external objects. (*MR* 99, 104.) This would seem to suggest an ontological dualism between things and selves, which could be used to justify a limitation of the concepts derived from revelation to the realm of selves. On the other hand, Niebuhr says that scientific thought requires that there be no discontinuity "posited at the points where the inorganic merges into the organic, the vital into the mental and the mental into the moral." Events that take place in the brain cannot be regarded as different in kind from other events in the cosmos. (*MR* 144.) Furthermore, it was mentioned above that Niebuhr said that we must consider "the long story of human ascent from the dust." (*MR* 112.) Certainly this involves discussing natural evolution, and this is as "theoretical" or "scientific" as anything could be. Likewise, Niebuhr says that Christian faith entails belief in a universal God who is the creator of all events. It would seem then that theology would have to try to understand God's relations not only to distinctively human events but to all events.

A final point, and one which ties the two previous ones together, is that the criterion of adequacy implies that a putative revelation will validate itself more to the degree that it brings an intelligible unity into all things. This means that we need to try to understand the long process prior to the advent of humanity in terms of the divine purpose. All these considerations suggest that Niebuhr's distinction in principle between the practical and the theoretical reason is an artificial one that needs to be overcome, and that we need to return to Whitehead's more inclusive idea of deriving illuminating concepts for *all* occasions.

CHAPTER 3

Paradoxical Identity
of Divine and Worldly Action

1. THE RATIONALITY OF THEOLOGY
BASED UPON REVELATION

The issue as to the correct way to interpret Rudolf Bultmann is highly controversial. One question involves the consistency of his position. If a negative answer to this is given, then the question concerns the needed corrections. If an affirmative answer is given, then the cause for confusion should be explained. A second issue is his adequacy to Christian faith, in intention and/or in execution. Since most responsible critics will grant that he intends to be adequate, an account must be given of how and why his theology is, or at least appears to be, inadequate in fact.

A plausible contrast of Bultmann's position with the positions of Tillich and Niebuhr on the issue of faith and reason could be as follows: whereas Tillich as theologian makes no assertions about reality that *differ* from those of the philosopher and Niebuhr intends none that could *conflict* with other assertions, *Bultmann intends no cognitive assertions about reality at all.* There are several aspects of his thought that could be used to support this interpretation.

First, Bultmann quite often stresses that demythologization of the Christian message is needed to remove the conflict between the mythological view of the New Testament and the scientific view of modern man. (*JCM* 15.) To require acceptance of the mythological form of the gospel would wrongly require a sacrifice of intellect, thereby reducing faith to works by requiring that one accept a view of the world in his faith that he would deny in his everyday life. (*JCM* 17.)

Second, the Biblical assertions presupposing a mythological cosmology are not even to be reinterpreted in terms of a modern cosmology. For the true intention of myth does not lie in its apparently objective contents, but in the understanding of human existence that it contains. Hence the myths should be interpreted anthropologically, or existentially, not cosmologically. (*KM* 10, 11.)

Third, correlative with this definition of myth is the fact that the most adequate conceptuality available for interpreting myth is said to be Heidegger's existentialist analysis (*JCM* 55 f.), which provides a conceptuality for speaking of man's existence (*Dasein*), but not for God or the world in themselves. Hence, it could not be used to reinterpret the cosmological side of the myths, even if this were thought to belong to their true intention.

Fourth, the understanding of existence contained in myth is an existential (*existentiell*) understanding. Likewise, faith can be described as this kind of understanding. (*TNT* II, 239.) As such it gives answers to questions different from those asked by science and philosophy. (*KM* 104.) One way to interpret Bultmann's meaning here is to say that science and philosophy ask the theoretical question, "What is?" while faith involves the practical question, "What ought to be?" [1] The implication is that faith's answers could not conflict with those of the theoretical reason. Not only does preaching not offer a doctrine that could be accepted by a *sacrificium intellectus,* it does not even offer one that could be accepted by reason, for preaching is addressed not to the theoretical reason, but to the hearer as a self. (*JCM* 36.)

Fifth, even if it is pointed out that faith's understanding does imply some cognitive truths, at least about man, this understanding of existence is said to be the one given with existence itself and, hence, to be discoverable phenomenologically. (*KM* 23–26, 194.)

Much of Bultmann's writing could lead one to believe that the above complex of ideas represents his essential position, and that any apparent contradictions must be seen as statements interpretable in line with this thrust, or else as inconsistencies to be eliminated. According to this position, a conflict of faith and reason would be avoided in principle. The only serious question would seem to be whether it could be maintained that the understanding of existence said to be contained alike in the New Testament and in Heidegger is really the one given with existence itself.

However, to interpret Bultmann in this way would be to relegate to unimportance *a central theme of his thought—the difference between theology and philosophy*. And this is a theme which seems to involve a tension between reason and Christian faith. First, Bultmann says that theology parts company with philosophy by insisting that authentic existence is possible only through an act of God. (*KM* 27.) Although man as man may be able to discover through reflection that authentic existence means a life of self-giving love, Christian faith insists that man cannot free himself from his inauthenticity, but that he can only be freed by being encountered by God's love. This is what the New Testament asserts; however, it cannot prove its case. This is a matter for decision. (*KM* 30.)

Second, this means that faith is always faith in the kerygma or in Jesus Christ. For the love of God that frees man cannot just be an abstract idea based on wishful thinking; it must be a *revealed* love. And it is the kerygma that proclaims the event of Jesus Christ as the act of God that reveals his love. (*KM* 32; *EF* 85.)

Third, this is the true scandal of Christian faith. The whole purpose of demythologizing is not really to make faith acceptable to modern man, but to remove the false stumbling block so that the real scandal will be laid bare. (*JCM* 36.) There seem to be two aspects to the scandal. Bultmann generally stresses that the offense is not to man's understanding, but to his selfish will. (*JCM* 18, 36.) But he also says that modern man has a tendency to regard *any* talk of an act of God as mythological. (*KM* 43.) In any case, the assertion that a strictly human life, explainable in terms of the historian's categories, is God's eschatological act is an offense that cannot be removed by philosophical reflection, but only by faith and obedience. (*KM* 44.)

Fourth, it can thereby be seen that Christian faith does not include only an understanding of oneself (conceived subjectivistically); it simultaneously involves an understanding of God and the world, and also of Jesus Christ as God's decisive act.

Accordingly, it appears that faith in revelation does involve beliefs that could conflict with what many modern men would consider a rational understanding of reality. How then does Bultmann's thought imply that the relation between faith and reason should be conceived? One answer would be that the understanding of God, man, and the world implicit in faith needs to be explicated in terms of a full-scale metaphysics, and one that allows Jesus to be conceptually understood as God's decisive act. A second possibility would be to distinguish consistently between faith and theoretical reason, so that they in principle could not conflict. A third possibility would be frankly to acknowledge that faith in the kerygma involves a nonrational leap of faith, made in spite of all the evidence.

My conclusion will be that, although Bultmann seems explicitly to eschew the first possibility and to favor a combination of the second and third, his substantive intentions, and even essential aspects of his formal position, require the first view. The remaining sections, besides making their own proper points, are intended to support this claim.

2. THE CONTENT OF REVELATION

The issue of the content of revelation in Bultmann's thought has already been introduced. On the one hand, many themes and passages suggest that revelation is contentless, and many interpreters understandably suggest that this is Bultmann's position. On the other hand, faith does seem to involve notions about God, man, the world, and Jesus. And since faith is faith in revelation, this implies that revelation itself involves some content. We must look more closely at this issue, trying to understand both what Bultmann's central intentions require and why his writings have given rise to such divergent interpretations.

We have seen that Bultmann's way of demythologizing the New Testament involves seeing the true meaning of mythical imagery elsewhere than in its apparent claim to "objective" validity. That is, it does not *really* intend to speak about God and his action in cosmic terms. In fact, demythologization could equally well be called "deobjectification." The defining essence of myth is that it speaks of God and his action in objectifying terms, terms which are only appropriate to this world which is properly the object of our theoretical, objectifying thought and language. For to speak in these terms about God is to deny his transcendence, to speak of him as if he were part of this world. (*K* 261; *JCM* 19.)

This is why, to get at its real meaning, the mythology which was used to express the early Christians' faith must be interpreted existentially, as an expression of man's understanding of existence. Faith is not a world view; in fact, faith needs to be free from every world view expressed in objective terms. (*KM* 210.) The corollary is that revelation does not give a world view or any general truths. Rather, revelation is an address,

spoken to the person in the here and now. (*EF* 86.) In line
with this idea is the following famous passage:

> What, then, has been revealed? Nothing at all, so far as the
> question concerning revelation asks for doctrines. . . . On
> the other hand, however, *everything has been revealed, in-
> sofar as man's eyes are opened concerning his own existence.*
> (*EF* 85.)

Also in his interpretation of John, whom he generally regards
as normative, Bultmann says, "Thus it turns out in the end that
Jesus as the revealer of God *reveals nothing but that he is the
revealer.*" (*TNT* II, 66.)

Further support for the view that revelation says nothing
about God can be derived from the fact that Bultmann sees
the question about human existence (and not, say, about the
nature of God) as the right question to ask the New Testament. (*KM* 191 f.) He regards Heidegger's analysis of human
existence as the "right" philosophy with which to explicate the
faith of the New Testament, seeing as no handicap the fact
that this philosophy provides no conceptuality for speaking of
God and his action. (*JCM* 55–59.) This is in accord with his
oft-repeated statement that we cannot, and have no need to,
speak of God in himself, but only of what he does to us.
(*JCM* 43; *KM* 202.)

Bultmann's interpretation of Jesus is in accord with this
line of thought. Jesus "does not speak objectively of the attributes of God," or even in terms of "general truths" at all.
Of course, he did say God was merciful and kind, but this was
said only "incidentally." Rather, Jesus speaks only "in terms of
what God is for man, how he deals with man." (*JW* 151.)

On the basis of these and similar passages, Bultmann has
been accused of reducing theology to anthropology and of
reducing Christology to soteriology, i.e., of giving a sub-
jectivistic interpretation of faith in God and his action, thereby
reducing them to symbols for aspects of experience. Yet such
an interpretation involves two mistakes: failing to take at face

value some statements that should be so taken, and taking certain other statements at face value that should not be so taken.

In the first place, we saw that, although faith can be described as an understanding of existence, even the one given with existence itself, it is also described as faith in the kerygma which proclaims Jesus of Nazareth as God's decisive act. How are these two views of the "content" of faith to be reconciled? One way would be to say that the "kerygma," or "Jesus Christ," could be interpreted exhaustively in terms of an understanding of existence, so that no particular belief about Jesus of Nazareth would be necessarily implied in faith.

But this is not true to Bultmann's intention. And I do not think it is necessary in order to make his position self-consistent.[2] Certainly, the idea that for Bultmann faith should involve no essential reference to Jesus could be inferred not only from his view as to what is the "real intention" of myth and his advocacy of Heidegger's conceptuality for explicating Christian faith, but also from his statement that a theology of the New Testament would be an explication of the existential understanding of God, man, and the world involved in faith. And yet the content of the New Testament is not exhausted by the concepts and images which express this understanding. Rather, Bultmann distinguishes between the *theological thoughts* which arise out of faith's self-understanding, on the one hand, and the *kerygma*, which is the basis of this self-understanding, on the other. True, he says that the distinction is a difficult one to make, since the kerygma itself is never found in some pristine, uninterpreted form but is always found already formulated in theological statements. (*TNT* II, 239 f.) Yet the distinction is essential. Faith does not understand itself as arising spontaneously, but only as the *response* to the kerygma, which tells of God's dealing in the man Jesus of Nazareth. (*TNT* II, 239; *KM* 208.) Hence, the content of faith is not adequately described as an existential understanding of God, man, and the world. Rather, it involves a reference to a particular event. (*EF* 74, 87.) That a clear distinction is intended is also shown by the fact that Bultmann can say that the propositions of theology are not "right teaching," whereas the kerygma is. (*TNT* II, 240.)

This distinction implies that the task of New Testament theology should be reformulated. It must present the kerygma as well as the self-understanding opened up by it. (*TNT* II, 239.) In other words, besides showing that faith is the origin of theological thoughts, it must present the kerygma as the origin of faith.[3] Again, this distinction is said to constitute the crucial difference between Christian faith and existentialism. Whereas the latter can duplicate the New Testament teaching on life before and in faith, the New Testament also speaks of the *point of transition* between the old and new life as an act of God. (*KM* 33.)

This second element in the New Testament's content, the point of transition, raises questions about the above assertions concerning mythology and existentialist interpretation. To make the distinction between myth's true intention (to express an understanding of existence) and myth's *apparent* intention (to express something *objectively* true) is misleading. For Bultmann holds that the event of Jesus Christ is indeed expressed in mythological language, and yet that the kerygma's intention to speak of a unique act of God is not necessarily mythological. (*KM* 15; *JCM* 62.) Accordingly, the intention of speaking of special acts of the divine should be included as one of the possible aspects of the "true intention" of mythology, rather than regarded as always belonging only to the mythological form.

This in turn raises the question as to the adequacy of Heidegger's philosophy as set forth in *Being and Time* to provide a conceptuality to interpret in a nonmythological manner the essential content of the New Testament message. For if part of this content is a decisive act of God in a human figure, then it follows that an adequate conceptuality would have to provide concepts for making intelligible what is meant by "God" and his "action" in man, and even what a "special act" would be. For the present we must examine the question of God himself, leaving the issue of God's action to the next section.

My point thus far in this section has been that, since faith is describable not only as an understanding of existence, but also as faith in the kerygma, and since these two are not totally identical, it involves beliefs that have an objective intent, "objective" in the sense that they directly intend something about a reality beyond the believer's own immediate experience. But even in abstraction from this belief in a decisive act of God in Jesus, there seems to be some cognitive content to faith's understanding of existence.

Bultmann repudiates the charge of subjectivism by emphasizing the *historical* character of man, which is the fact that his existence is constituted by its encounters. Hence an understanding of existence involves an existential understanding not only of oneself, psychologically (solipsistically) conceived, but also of God and the world. (*KM* 199 f., 203; *TNT* II, 239.) In preparation for the crucial issue of God, it is worth noting that faith implies certain cognitive assertions about man and the world. Faith implies that man is free, not totally determined by the conditions out of which his existence arises each moment, as are natural events. Thus Christian faith is not compatible with a materialistic philosophy. (*K* 267.) Also, faith knows the world to be finite, transitory, even ultimately unreal in the face of God's eternity. (*JCM* 23.) Hence, despite the fact that faith is said to give answers to different questions than those raised by philosophy, and though it is often implied that faith does not involve general truths, it does seem that cognitive assertions about man and the world are made which could conflict with certain philosophies.

The same is true in regard to God. Mythology, although it expresses its insights inadequately, is said to speak of the power beyond our calculation and control in which man and the world have their ground and limits. It is in this transcendent reality, beyond the known and tangible reality, that the world has its origin and purpose. (*JCM* 19.) In fact, the "real purpose of myth is to speak of a transcendent power which controls the world and man." (*KM* 11.)

These notions are still valid for faith today. God is beyond the world, and beyond scientific thought. (*JCM* 40.) Although the idea of spatial transcendence is mythological, "the abstract idea of transcendence" is still significant. (*JCM* 20.) And "faith only makes sense when it is directed towards a God with a real existence outside the believer." (*KM* 199.) This God has power over time and eternity. (*JCM* 41.) In revelation we learn to understand ourselves rightly as God's creatures, limited by him and under his claim. (*EF* 86, 88.)

There is even more content given to the idea of the transcendent God. Faith in God's grace is faith that the unseen, intangible reality actually confronts us as love. This God is the one who calls things that are not into being. (*KM* 19.) It is because God is known as creator of the world that we do not consider matter evil, and do not mark off any areas as holy. (*KM* 17, 211.) God is the living God, in whose hands our time rests, and who encounters us at specific moments in our time. (*KM* 206.) God is invisible, and his activity always hidden. (*KM* 210.)

In the light of all these affirmations, which I believe we should take at face value, why could so many critics interpret Bultmann as dissolving all assertions about God into statements about man? The answer to this question is, I believe, twofold. The first major fact has been persuasively presented by Schubert Ogden,[4] and hence need be treated only briefly. This is the fact that the philosophy upon which Bultmann relies for the conceptuality with which to explicate the understanding implicit in faith is inadequate. Although faith is said to include an understanding of God and the world, as well as man, when Bultmann actually carries out his theological program it is in terms of man. No conceptual account of what is *meant* by "God" is given. Also many of Bultmann's formal statements are designed to justify this. For example, he states that for Paul "every assertion about God is simultaneously an assertion about man and vice versa." This *could* mean simply that God and man are internally related to each other. But from the statement Bultmann draws the *non sequitur,* "Therefore, Paul's theology can best be treated as his doctrine of man," although from the premise it should be possible to treat Paul's theology *equally* well as a doctrine of God. (*TNT* I, 191.)

Also, on the basis of the premise that to speak of God means to speak of man, and vice versa, Bultmann maintains that one cannot speak of God *in himself*. Now, there are at least two possible meanings of speaking of something "in itself." In one sense, it would mean implying that the being in question had no real relations to other realities. In this sense one clearly should not speak of the Christian God "in himself." But in a second sense it could mean simply describing what kind of reality the entity in question is thought to be in and for itself, as well as how it appears to others and affects them. The description could well indicate that it was internally related to other entities. Now, Bultmann clearly speaks of man in himself in this second sense. However, he has repeatedly said that we cannot speak of God in himself, but only of what God does to us.[5] (*TNT* I, 190 f.; *KM* 202.)

Bultmann connects this with the assertion that the ground and the object of faith are identical (*KM* 202), which implies that there could be nothing in the description of God as the object of one's faith that went beyond the phenomenological description of that aspect of one's experience (the "encounter") that led one to speak of God. This gives considerable support to those critics who say that Bultmann reduces "God" to a dimension of human experience. And this makes it understandable that some of his followers have done just that, since considerable tension can arise from the awareness that words are being used without any assignable meaning.

Closely related is the question as to whether one can speak of God "objectively." Bultmann's position here is clearly contradictory. On the one hand, he almost always denies that one can make objective assertions about God. The attempt to do so, as we saw, is the defining essence of mythology. God is beyond the world of objectifying thought, and hence his transcendence is denied by objective statements.

On the other hand, Bultmann's position implies that, in one sense of the term "objective," such assertions about God should be possible. Most often Bultmann thinks of objective categories as those which are appropriate for objects known through sense experience, things which are *merely* objects. But he also regards the type of ontological analysis of human existence carried out by Heidegger as "objective," or scientific. And this analysis objectifies the human self in such a way as to show that it is always a subject, never merely an object. Hence this type of objective conceptualization in no way threatens to "objectify" man in the first, negative sense. Bultmann insists that the human self as well as the divine transcends the world of objectivity (in the first sense), and that there is an analogy between man and God. On this basis, it would seem to us that a conceptual account of the meaning of "God," parallel to Heidegger's conceptual account of the meaning of "man," is possible, and even necessary, for theology's explication of the understanding implicit in Christian faith.

The necessity of such a conceptual account can be seen by reference to Bultmann's own statements regarding the fact that the theologian must employ a philosophical conceptuality for speaking of human existence. Without an understandable conceptuality, each of the terms he uses, such as "faith" or "sin," will remain "a mere *x*." (*EF* 98.) Bultmann's lack of a conceptuality for clarifying the term "God" leaves it for the most part "a mere *x*" in his theology.

Although in Bultmann's writings there are occasional signs of his having moved somewhat toward this recognition, he never expressed it in any consistent manner. In 1958 he admitted that we had to use "general conceptions" to speak of God, even though he still maintained that we could not speak of him in "general statements." (*JCM* 66 f.) In 1966 he considered Schubert Ogden's proposal to use Hartshorne's philosophical theology, which asserts that "it is possible to represent the structure of God's essence objectively" without denying that God is always a subject. Bultmann replied that he did not consider such a philosophical theology possible:

> It is only possible to make God the object of conceptual thought in so far as the concept "God" can be objectively explicated. Indeed, that must be the case since theology must be able to say what it means when it speaks of God. Theology must therefore clarify in a conceptual way—for example, the concepts of transcendence, of omnipotence, of the presentness of God, the concepts of grace and forgiveness. This cannot mean, however, that theology speaks directly of God and of his activity. It cannot speak of God as he is in himself, but only of what he does for us. (*K* 273.)

I find the conjunction of the last two sentences with the previous ones totally baffling. Bultmann first seems to agree completely with Ogden's point as to the possibility and even the necessity of giving a conceptual analysis of the meaning of the word "God"; but then he reaffirms his traditional stand against its possibility. In the same volume he says that "any direct speaking of God is mythological, and therefore impossible." He reiterates that *analogical* talk about God *is* possible, the implication being that analogical language is not "direct speaking of God." (*K* 259.) This makes it difficult to understand in what the analogy consists. Furthermore, he rejects the idea of an "ontological basis" for theology, and the idea that theology should "speak in a scientific fashion of the mode of being of God." (*K* 274.) Finally, he considers the suggestion that philosophy could develop a concept of God, even one in terms of which the limits that man experiences through finiteness and the ethical demand could be interpreted. He dismisses this suggestion, even if possible, as being of no importance, saying that philosophy cannot bring about the encounter of man and God—at best it can bring to consciousness the question of God. (*K* 271.)

In the light of his acceptance of a speaking "in a scientific fashion of the mode of being" of man, his vigorous defense of this as a presupposition for making intelligible ontic assertions about man, and his pointing to the parallel between the human and divine transcendence, this rejection is not justifiable systematically but seems explainable only in terms of the biographical fact that Bultmann's theology was formed when the best philosophical resource seemed to him to be Heidegger's anthropology. To this we might add two facts as corollaries: Bultmann was deeply impressed with the dogma of Wilhelm Herrmann that "of God we can only tell what he does to us" (S 196); also, behind all three men—Bultmann, Herrmann, and Heidegger—lies the influence of the Kantian doctrine that one cannot speak of realities in themselves, but only as they appear to us.

Besides the limitations in his conceptuality due in general to Bultmann's standing in the Kantian tradition, and in particular to his acceptance of Heidegger's as the "right" philosophy, there seems to be a second major fact militating against a consistent recognition that Bultmann needs to, and actually does, speak directly of God himself. This is his emphasis on the nature of *true* or *genuine* faith, as opposed to faith as mere assent to propositions. This of course is in line with Luther's attack on the efficacy of mere *fides historica*. Bultmann's emphasis, or overemphasis, on this distinction often leads him to state matters in an either/or way, when his position really requires a both/and.

That is, Bultmann generally gives the impression that faith in revelation does not *involve* a world view, or any general truths at all. The content of revelation is said not to be knowledge about God and the world, but "life," for only this can overcome man's limit, which is death. (*EF* 72.) Revelation does not communicate any doctrines that can then be known once for all, but only opens man's eyes concerning his own existence. (*EF* 86.) Revelation is not the communication of knowledge, but an occurrence. Faith is not the willingness to hold as true some remarkable dogma, but obedience to God. (*EF* 87.)

However, we have seen that Bultmann does give faith and revelation considerable content. Hence his position can only be that *genuine* faith is not *identical* with acceptance of the general truths (and even the world view) which it involves. Several statements indicate this meaning. Faith in God as creator "is genuine only when I understand myself here and now existentially to be the creature of God." (*KM* 198.) "Belief in the almighty God is genuine only when it actually takes place in my very existence, as I surrender myself to the power of God who overwhelms me here and now." (*JCM* 63.) The both/and character is explained:

Theological knowledge always has a "dialectical" character, in the sense, namely, that as a knowledge that is preserved it is always spurious, *however "correct" it may be,* and that it is only *genuine* when the act of faith is realized in it. (*EF* 88; italics added.)

A corresponding theory of how revelation occurs is accordingly held:

The idea of the omnipresent and almighty God becomes *real* in my personal existence only by His Word spoken here and now. (*JCM* 79; italics added.)

If preaching communicates a content, it at the same time addresses us. The both/and character of revelation is again brought out when Bultmann says:

[The eternity of God's Word] is His Word as an event, in an encounter, not as a set of ideas, not, for example, as a statement about God's kindness and grace in general, *although such a statement may be otherwise correct*, but only as addressed to me, as an event happening and meeting me as His mercy. (*JCM* 79; italics added.)

And the Word of God is said to be identical with "the word whose content may be formulated in general statements." (*JCM* 82.)

My conclusions in this section are the following. First, Bultmann's substantive assertions about God, and those formal statements which support these, should be taken at face value, as expressing his central convictions, apart from which Christian faith and theology would seem inconceivable. Second, those many assertions which seem to deny the possibility and necessity of speaking about God should not be taken literally. Rather, they should be seen in the context of the affirmations he does make, and interpreted as one-sided assertions, explainable both in terms of his emphasis upon *genuine* faith as opposed to mere assent, and in light of the inadequacy of his philosophical resources for actually speaking of God in the rigorous, consistent manner possible in the case of man.

Accordingly the content of the revelation in Jesus can be described as the love of God. That invisible power, of which man had some knowledge in the form of a quest for God, is revealed in Jesus of Nazareth, as the kerygma proclaims, as a gracious, loving God who encounters us in time, and hence as *our* God.

3. God's Relation to Jesus

Although Bultmann rejects speaking of God in himself, in favor of what God *does* to us, the latter assertion already implies something about God himself, i.e., that he is the type of reality that can *do* something. And Bultmann clearly intends to affirm that God acts. Faith in the grace of God means "faith that the unseen, intangible reality actually *confronts* us as love. (*KM* 19.) The love of God *meets* man as a power." (*KM* 31; italics added.) In particular, faith knows of a decisive act in Christ. In fact, Bultmann's major complaint against the kind of demythologization carried out by the old liberals and the history of religions school is that it involved a loss of this kerygma. The central question of his programmatic essay in *Kerygma and Myth* is whether the affirmation of a decisive act of God in Jesus Christ can be retained while demythologizing the kerygma. (*KM* 12–15.)

And one should not suppose that demythologizing the kerygma means speaking only of God's *present* act on me here and now. Faith can speak of God's action in the past as well as in the present. (*KM* 31 f.) Faith knows of the same act of God of which the New Testament speaks. And it is Jesus' *person* that is the decisive event. (*KM* 14, 33.) In fact, crucial to the nonmythological character of the kerygma is the fact that it is about a particular human life, Jesus of Nazareth. Although it continues, the decisive act of God occurred in the years A.D. 1–30. (*KM* 43 f., 113.) And the generally normative Gospel of John makes it clear that "when he suffered death, Jesus was already the Son of God." (*KM* 39.)

Hence, although Bultmann will stress that the eschatological act of God in Christ continues, being repeated every time the Word is proclaimed, and that this act can only be *perceived* as God's act when it meets with faith, he by no means intends to limit God's activity to this present event. He means to affirm that Jesus of Nazareth *was* God's decisive act, in which the kerygma had its origin. And he explicitly says that he intends his language about an act of God in its "full, direct meaning" (*JCM* 68); it is to "denote an act in a real, objective sense, and not just a symbolical or pictorial expression" (*KM* 196). And he insists that the notion of such an act of God is not necessarily mythological, at least not in the objectionable sense. (*JCM* 62.)

The obvious question, of course, is precisely how one can

conceive of an act of God that is intended "objectively" and yet is not mythological. Before looking at the ways in which Bultmann attempts to relate God's action to worldly actions, we will look at the ways he explicitly excludes.

The primary notion that he wishes to exclude is that of divine *intervention* in the course of events in the world, so that the natural course of affairs is *interrupted* and natural effects are attributed to a supernatural cause. (*KM* 197.) This is clearly *the* defining essence of myth, that which makes it objectionable; i.e., myth violates both the transcendence of God and the rational order of nature. (*JCM* 19, 37 f.) In the latter, which is presupposed both by scientific thinking and in everyday life, the nexus of natural cause and effect is fundamental. (*JCM* 15.) It is this double violation that serves as the connecting link between the two much-discussed motives for demythologizing, i.e., faith itself, and the modern world view. (*JCM* 83.)

In regard to this definition of mythology, Bultmann makes no distinction between nature and history. They are different, of course, since in history the course of events is affected by the conscious willing of persons, and hence is not determined totally by physical necessity. (*K* 263 f.) But this makes no difference in regard to the question of divine causality. It is just as mythological to speak of the "intervention of supernatural powers in the inner life of the soul" as to speak of such intervention in the course of nature. (*JCM* 15.) Modern man sees himself as a *unity*, not exposed to the interference of powers outside himself, and he is "undoubtedly right" in doing so. (*KM* 6, 120.)

Now, while Bultmann apparently intends to exclude only one idea of God's causal relation to the world, he in effect excludes two distinct ideas. He intends to exclude the supernaturalistic idea of miracle, according to which a certain effect would be thought to have *no* natural cause, but only a supernatural one. Hence the chain of natural cause and effect would be interrupted. This view could be diagrammed thus:

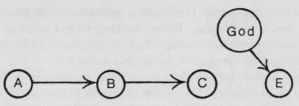

Here B is caused by A, and in turn causes C. But then E occurs without having a natural cause. It is attributed solely to a non-natural cause. If one wants to emphasize the Thomistic idea that God is the "primary" cause of all events, but that sometimes he effects an event without employing a natural (or "secondary") cause, the diagram could be as follows:

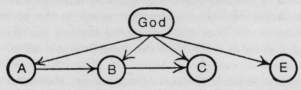

In either case the main point is the same, that some event in the world, whether in man or nature, is thought to occur without any finite causation. This, Bultmann rightly sees, runs counter to the basic presupposition of historical as well as natural science, and hence would force an either/or choice between faith and rationality.

But Bultmann is also concerned to argue that the modern world view provides more the occasion for demythologizing than the central motive. This motive is said to be *faith's* understanding of the transcendence of God. In accordance with this idea he holds that *no* effects in the world can be *directly* attributed to God in *any* sense, for this would make God appear to be not essentially different from natural powers. To speak of God in *any* sense as one cause alongside of others would be to put God within the sphere where subject-object thinking is appropriate. Hence in effect Bultmann rules out a second possible way of conceiving of the relation between divine and natural causation. It can be diagrammed as follows:

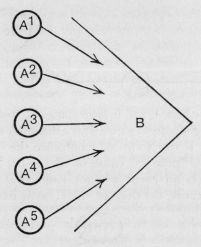

For any given event (B), there would be a multiplicity of causes. God would always be one of these causes (e.g., A^3). Although in some sense he might be a more important cause than the finite events, he would still in a sense be one cause among others. The effect (B) would be a partially self-determining event. Hence, even though God were one of the influences in "the inner life of the soul," the person would not be "handed over to powers outside of and distinct from himself" in a way such that he would not be responsible for his actions. (*KM* 6.)

Bultmann's rejection of the first view of divine influence is stated in such a way that this second view also is excluded. He seems to reject entirely the notion that God may inspire man's thought and guide his purpose (*KM* 1), even though in this second view "to inspire" or "to guide" would not mean "totally to determine."

Bultmann interprets the New Testament idea of "spirit" in line with this understanding of man as a closed unity. He admits that Paul did share the popular belief of his day, which attributed abnormal psychic phenomena to the spirit's agency. But "in the last resort" Paul transcends this view "of the Spirit as an agency that operates like any other natural force," and instead Paul means by Spirit "the possibility of a new life that must be appropriated by deliberate resolve. . . . 'Being led by the Spirit' . . . is not an automatic process of nature, but the fulfilment of an imperative." (*KM* 21 f.) The other possibility, that it might refer to being influenced, though not in an "automatic" way, is not considered.

A third possible view would be to assert a "direct identity" between worldly events and divine activity. But Bultmann also rejects this pantheistic view. (*KM* 197.)

But if God's action, including the decisive act in Jesus, cannot be understood in any of these ways, how should it be conceived? Is there another possible view? Bultmann believes there is. He holds that faith asserts a "paradoxical identity" of worldly occurrence and divine activity. This differs from pantheism in that it is not an anterior conviction, a world view that knows in advance that every event will be God's action since God is thought to be immanent in the world. Faith can see a worldly event as God's act only in the concrete moment and in spite of all appearances to the contrary, since one also sees it in its place in the natural or historical chain of cause and effect. (*KM* 197.) And this view differs from the mythological view by affirming that God's transcendent action does not occur between worldly events, but within them. Faith can see an event as an act of God and still understand it "as a link in the chain of the natural course of events." (*JCM* 61 f.)

Bultmann's meaning can be made clearer by seeing how he understands the problem. On the one hand, both in scientific work and daily living it is necessary to see the worldly events as linked by cause and effect, and "in doing so there remains no room for God's working." (*JCM* 65.) On the other hand, the believer and therefore the theologian must speak of an act of God. Hence the question is "how precisely we abandon natural causation in favour of supernatural explanations." (*KM* 120.) Bultmann's answer is the "nevertheless" of faith, i.e., "that faith 'nevertheless' understands as God's action here and now an event which is completely intelligible in the natural or historical connection of events." (*JCM* 65.) In other words, in faith Bultmann denies "the closed connection of worldly events." He denies this "not as mythology does, which by breaking the connection places supernatural events into the chain of natural events." Rather he denies "the worldly connection as a whole" when he speaks of God. (*JCM* 64 f.)

In application to Christology, this would mean that Jesus' life is in principle "completely intelligible" to the secular historian, who seeks to understand him totally in terms of natural and historical categories. There would not be anything which the Christian historian, believing Jesus to be God's decisive act, would have to add to the objective account. This would mean that none of Jesus' actions or attitudes, not even his faith, could be more adequately explained by adding the element of divine influence. In all objective thought, including the science of history which requires personal categories, there is no room and no need to speak of God's causality. Any attempt to interpret any aspect of Jesus' experience whatsoever as being in the least due to divine influence would be mythological. Rather, in order to speak of God's action, faith must see Jesus totally in terms of the immanent chain of cause and effect and yet simultaneously deny the chain as a whole.

This is a difficult, admittedly paradoxical conception. In the first place, it is hard to know exactly what it would *mean* simultaneously to affirm and deny natural causation. Second, there is the problem of Bultmann's equivocating on the meaning of the idea of "sufficient cause." [6] True, one may claim that Bultmann's position is consistent if it is seen that he is thinking in a Kantian way, in which the world of cause and effect is simply the world as it necessarily appears to the scientific, objective reason. Causality would be a category only of the theoretical reason, and as such, causality would not come into view for the "practical reason," to which "faith" belongs. That Bultmann is thinking in these terms is suggested not only by the fact that he can speak of faith as denying the worldly causal connections altogether but also by his speaking of the closed weft of cause and effect that is "presented or produced by objective observation." (*KM* 198.) Yet when Bultmann in faith denies natural causation, he is not denying the category of causality altogether, which would be required in this view, for he is affirming *God's* causal efficacy. Hence no consistent position is possible in this direction.

Third, as the principal indication in the New Testament itself that it needs to be demythologized, Bultmann cites the contradiction that within its pages human life is seen, sometimes as free, sometimes as "determined by cosmic forces." (*KM* 11 f.) Yet Bultmann's own position involves a contradiction between human freedom and divine determinism. We have already seen that he stresses human freedom and therefore responsibility. But he also affirms that "man in his relations with God is only the passive, the receiving one." (*K* 259.) The apprehension of the love of God "must be attributed to the operation of the Holy Ghost." (*KM* 204, n. 2.) Also, one of his arguments against speaking *about* God is based on God's omnipotence: since "God" *means* "the reality controlling everything," there is no standpoint apart from God from which he could be talked *about.* (*S* 186 f.) This coincides with his statement that the "real purpose of myth is to speak of a transcendent power which controls the world and man." (*KM* 11.)

Fourth, the principal difference between Bultmann's view and that of pantheism seems to be that pantheism thinks of all events as divine actions; whereas faith can only confess particular events as such in concrete moments. (*KM* 197.) Many of Bultmann's statements are in harmony with this view. Yet he quite often suggests that faith knows that *all* events are God's acts. Faith knows our temporality as the relatedness of man to God. God encounters us at all times and in all places (even though he cannot be *seen* everywhere without his Word). Nature and history become, for the believer, the field of divine activity. (*KM* 195, 206 f., 211.) Faith regards God as revealing himself both in nature and in non-Christian religions.

(*K* 262.) Finally, in the light of God's Word the presence of God is said to be discernible in art and in all of man's achievements. (*KM* 121.) Hence, the distinction which he wants to make between his view and that of pantheism is not very clear.

With all these difficulties attaching to Bultmann's view, the question arises as to why it should be held. Certainly if it were the only possible view consistent both with the understanding of God, man, and the world implicit in Christian faith and with the scientific world view, obviously the theologian would have to accept this view (the alternatives being either to give up the idea of divine activity or to give up any hope of showing faith to be compatible with reason). The question, of course, is whether this view of the relation between divine and worldly causality *is* the only one compatible with both faith and science. Several factors indicate that it is not.

First, in regard to the contradiction in the New Testament picture of man, sometimes as completely responsible for his own decisions, sometimes as controlled by a nonnatural spirit, Bultmann opts for the former to the total exclusion of the latter. But is it not more likely that both pictures expressed real experiences of men, and that a more adequate view would see an element of truth in both pictures? As suggested in the alternative view of the relation of divine and natural causality mentioned above, the divine spirit could be an influence on man without destroying his unity and responsibility.

Second, Bultmann is aware that world views can be altered, and also that he is sometimes criticized for still holding to a nineteenth-century view of rigid determinism. His reply is that the details of the various scientific world views are irrelevant to the question at hand. The main thing is the permanent principles of the method of scientific thinking. All scientific views, whether Greek, Newtonian, or twentieth-century, exclude interruptions of the rational, lawful order. (*JCM* 37 f.)

Although modern physical theory takes account of chance in the chain of cause and effect in subatomic phenomena, . . .

modern science does not believe that the course of nature can be interrupted or, so to speak, perforated, by supernatural powers. (*JCM* 15.)

What Bultmann apparently does not see is that the phenomenon of chance at the subatomic level might contribute to a completely new way of conceiving all entities, so that all would be seen as partially self-determining effects arising out of a multiplicity of causes, with God as one of the causes for each event. This would mean that one would not need to think in terms of simple antitheses, i.e., either a natural or a supernatural cause, either free or influenced by God. Hence it need not be the case that in a scientific view, which recognizes the chain of cause and effect, there "remains no room for God's working." Certainly Alfred North Whitehead, who understood the implications of the change from the Newtonian to the twentieth-century physics as well as anyone, did not think so. The alternative view of divine causality suggested above is based on his ideas. He believed that the very idea to which Bultmann appeals, the rationality or lawfulness of nature, is only intelligible if God is conceived as a direct cause on all events. (*AI* 142–147.)

Third, after saying that to speak of God involves denying the closed nexus of cause and effect altogether, Bultmann says that to speak of *oneself* also involves denying this nexus. (*JCM* 65.) Yet in a more careful statement he sees the freedom of the self not as demanding a suspension of natural causation, but as interacting with it. It is important to note that he is speaking in this context of viewing history in an "objectivizing manner" as a chain of cause and effect:

> The causality of this chain is not an absolute, but only a relative determination, because the will and action of men proceed out of their own decisions. These decisions are always conditioned, yet always free—conditioned in so far as they are always grounded in situations which are simply given; free, however, in so far as man is at any time free

to decide what he will allow to be the basis for his willing and acting, unless, of course, one understands history from the standpoint of a thoroughgoing materialism. (*K* 267.)

A finer concise statement of the nature of man's freedom within conditions could not be desired. Bultmann also says that existentialist anthropology does not destroy the connection with nature, but that there is a "reciprocal action" between nature and history. (*K* 267.) The Kantian view of the self as totally free and totally determined, depending on one's point of view, is clearly overcome here. Hence, since the self can be unified and free while being conditioned by various influences, there is no good reason why the self's unity and responsibility would be compromised by divine influence, as long as divine influence were to be conceived as just that, i.e., influence, not total determination. And since the self's subjectivity and transcendence are compatible with the fact that the self is involved in the "worldly" chain of causality, as known to "objectivizing" thought, the same could be true in regard to God. Here "objectivizing" obviously is not used in the narrow sense, referring only to thought based upon categories derived from sense experience alone, but in the broader sense of disciplined, conceptual reflection about realities in themselves, which includes the development and use of the categories (or "existentials") applicable to the human self, or *Dasein*.

Thus far I have suggested that Bultmann's way of speaking of God's activity bristles with difficulties, and also that many of the reasons suggested for the necessity of his view are not convincing. But I think that all these reasons are subsidiary, perhaps being afterthoughts intended to buttress the position. Bultmann's primary basis for choosing this view I believe to lie in the fact that he wrongly thought this ontological position to be required by his *epistemological* position, which in itself is sound.

That is, the principal point that Bultmann wants to make is that God's activity is hidden except to the eyes of faith. (*KM*

197–201, 210 f.) The denial of this hiddenness is what constitutes mythology, i.e., the claim that God's action is such that one can see it from a neutral or "objective" point of view, i.e., apart from faith. Hence his strictures against "objectifying" language about God are, *in the first place, epistemological.* Now, this epistemological position certainly does have *ontological* implications. It excludes the view of supernatural, miraculous interruption of the causal nexus. If a particular event had no natural causes, the nonpositivistic scientist or historian would be practically required to attribute the event to a supernatural cause (unless he wanted to allow for a suspension of causality in regard to this event). Speaking about "God" would not require a particular faith perspective; it would be done with about the same "objectivity" as discussing the cause of a chemical reaction or of the movement of a billiard ball. And the "objectivizing" ontological position that is excluded here does not refer only to the "outer" characteristics of events which are in principle open to sense observation, but also to the "inner" side, for example, psychological motives. No decision can be regarded as *simply* due to God's activity.

However, Bultmann's epistemological position does not have precisely the ontological implications that he apparently assumes it to have. For it forces no decision between his view (paradoxical identity) and the alternative view introduced above. For according to this alternative view, God's activity is also hidden except to the "eye of faith." That is, any event can plausibly be interpreted from any number of viewpoints. Each historian will believe that his own point of view provides him with the most important key. For example, the Freudian and the Marxist will each believe that his perspective provides the essential clue for discerning what is really going on in the events in question. He will believe that those causal factors, e.g., sexual or economic motives, are "objectively" there. Yet what he "sees" there will only be visible with the "eyes of faith," i.e., from the faith perspective of Freudianism or

Marxism. Likewise the Christian, with his faith perspective that God is active in all events, will believe that, *ontologically* speaking, God is "objectively" present as a causal factor in the events in question, even though, *epistemologically* speaking, this is by no means an "objective" fact. Hence, although his view affirming God's activity as an objective fact in the ontological sense is equally compatible with the denial of the visibility or ascertainability of God's action to all men, Bultmann seems to assume that this epistemological position requires the ontological position of paradoxical identity.

I believe that this is the main key to the interpretation of Bultmann, and the source of the chief inadequacy in his Christology. His main point is the epistemological one that the historian qua historian cannot see any activity of God in history. This is held to be true for *all* historians, not only the secular ones, since Bultmann assumes that *the Christian qua historian should not use the category of divine activity.* From this comes the denial "that historical research can ever encounter any traces of the epiphany of God in Christ." (*KM* 117.) Then from this epistemological position he moves to the only ontological position that seems possible to him, that of paradoxical identity, according to which an event can be seen from two perspectives: as totally determined by nondivine causes and, hence, "completely intelligible" within its natural or historical context and also "nevertheless" as totally caused by God. He holds that only this view can protect both faith's understanding of God and science's view of nature and history. This double motive is evident in the following statement:

A miracle—i.e. an act of God—is not visible or ascertainable like worldly events. The *only way to preserve the unworldly, transcendental character of the divine activity* is to regard it not as an interference in worldly happenings, but something accomplished *in* them in such a way that the closed weft of *history as it presents itself to objective observation* is left undisturbed. To every other eye than the eye of faith the action of God is hidden. (*KM* 197; italics added.)

The connection between the epistemological and ontological positions is also evident in many other passages:

> But this is just the paradox of faith: it understands an ascertainable event in its context in nature and history as the act of God. Faith cannot dispense with its *"nevertheless."* This is the only genuine faith in miracle. The conception of miracles as *ascertainable* processes is incompatible with the hidden character of God's activity. (*KM* 199; italics added.)

> Christian faith can only say, "I trust that God is working here and there, but His action is hidden, for it is not *directly identical* with the visible event." (*JCM* 64; italics added.)

> Faith can become real only in its "nevertheless" against the world. For in the world nothing of God and of His action is *visible* or can be visible to men who seek security in the world. (*JCM* 41; italics added.)

Bultmann also implies his rejection of the notion that God's activity could be an "objective" fact in the sense of *one* of the causes of the event which could, even from the perspective of faith, be asserted to be objectively there:

> The *invisibility* of God excludes every myth which tries to make him and his acts visible. Because of this, however, it also excludes every conception of invisibility and mystery which is formulated in *terms of objective thought.* (*KM* 210; italics added.)

> An action of God cannot be thought of as an event which happens on the *level of secular* (*worldly*) *events.* It is not *visible,* not capable of objective, scientific proof which is possible only within an objective view of the world. (*JCM* 61; italics added.)

That God has acted in Jesus Christ is, however, not a fact of past history open to *historical verification.* That Jesus Christ is the Logos of God can never be proved by the objective investigation of the historian. Rather, the fact that the New Testament describes the figure and work of Christ in mythological terms is enough to show that if they are the act of redemption they must not be understood in their *context of world history.* (*KM* 207 f.; italics added.)

Finally at the end of his essay "New Testament and Mythology" there is this most important passage:

> All these [Jesus, the kerygma, the church] are phenomena subject to historical, sociological and psychological observation, yet for faith they are all of them eschatological phenomena. It is precisely its *immunity from proof* which secures the Christian proclamation against the charge of being mythological. The transcendence of God is not as in myth reduced to immanence. Instead, we have the *paradox* of a transcendent God present and active in history: "The Word became flesh." (*KM* 44.)

Of course, showing that Bultmann has made a conversion that is not necessitated does not prove that he should take the other option. But I believe that there are good reasons for choosing the alternative view of God's relation to the world. A first general point to be made is that the alternative view avoids all the difficulties involved in Bultmann's view. (*a*) Speaking of divine causation does not entail any "transcendence" or denial of natural causation. (*b*) There is no equivocation on the notion of "sufficient cause," since God's influence, natural efficient causes, and the event's self-causation would all be factors in the sufficient cause of any event. (*c*) There is no oscillation between seeing human action as free and thereby responsible, on the one hand, and yet as divinely determined, on the other. (*d*) There is no danger of pantheism, for the "substantial independence" of each worldly entity is affirmed, since to each is attributed some power of self-determination, and then some power of other-determination.

A second general point is that this alternative view of God's relation to the world would make sense of the analogy Bultmann affirms as existing between divine and human action. (*a*) Bultmann had asserted that speaking of the self, as well as speaking of God, required transcending the "worldly" connection of cause and effect. Yet we saw that this was not necessarily so, that he could speak of the self as transcendent over the necessities of nature, and yet as being a real factor in the worldly course of events. This reconsideration of the relation of the self to the natural process requires seeing God also as a real factor in the "worldly" chain of cause and effect, if any analogy is to remain.

(*b*) A closely related reason for preferring the alternative view is that it would overcome the equivocation as to whether the self's actions belong to the "worldly" connection of events. Quite often Bultmann speaks as if they do not, so that "worldly" is limited to what can be plainly read off from an event. For example, in contrasting the divine activity with worldly happenings, he says: "Only the so-called natural, secular (worldly) events are visible to every man and capable of proof." (*JCM* 62.) But Bultmann also says that the self "is no more visible and capable of proof than is God as acting." (*JCM* 65.) And this is surely correct. To affirm that the human being is or has a self, a self that is a real agent in the world and not totally determined by natural conditions, is a matter of faith. This humanistic faith may be more widespread and verifiable than is faith in God's providence, and hence not so readily seen to be a *faith* perspective. Yet it does remain one perspective among others. That a certain event is to be explained by reference to a human being's free choice is not "visible to every man and capable of proof." Certainly the materialistic historian cannot see this, as Bultmann knows. And yet Bultmann affirms, from his nonmaterialistic point of view (or faith), that there *really* is a reciprocal action between nature and the partially free self. Hence, to acquire consistency, he needs to differentiate clearly between the epistemological sense and the ontological sense of "worldly" (or "objective") and say that neither the divine nor the human activity is worldly in the former sense, but that both are worldly in the latter sense.

(*c*) Bultmann says that God's action is analogous to man's, that the fellowship of God and man is analogous to the fellowship of man and man. He illustrates man's encountering God in terms of encountering the love of another person (*KM* 200). Now, the love that actually occurs between people has visible consequences in history. The historian who believes in the efficacy of love and is trying to reconstruct certain events accurately would have to report that such and such outer events happened partly because of the love that was experienced by the subjects. Why should the situation be totally different in regard to God? If it is true that God is "a personal being acting on persons" (*JCM* 70), that we have "real experiences of God as acting" (*JCM* 69), that God really encounters us as love, that this is an "encounter which demands my own personal decision" (*JCM* 66), and that this encounter can affect my self-understanding, then it is surely true that God's action can be a causal factor in history, for the change in my self-understanding will lead to my acting differently overtly than I would have otherwise. Hence an accurate historical reconstruction will have to attribute my behavior partly to the act of God which encountered me. The divine activity, if it occurred, is as "objective" a factor in the complex of events as are all the other causal factors (although only those who believe in divine activity will consider it as such). This is required if the analogy between divine and human activity is to have any validity and not collapse into equivocation.

The obvious objection to seeing this alternative view of the divine activity as the right way, in keeping with Bultmann's deepest intentions, to make his position consistent is that it involves a "Christian world view," which he has eschewed. But to this objection several things may be said. (*a*) Part of the reason for Bultmann's depreciating the idea of a Christian world view is his overemphasis on the distinction between propositional belief and genuine faith, which was discussed in the previous section. (*b*) His position itself is a world view. True, it is not "another general world-view which corrects science in its statements on its own level." Yet, he does assert that the scientific view does not give us the whole truth about reality, but must be supplemented, and that this is a *philosophical* issue.[7] (*JCM* 38, 65.) Also the alternative view suggested above can likewise be said not to "correct science in its statements on its own level," for it insists that what are generally called scientific statements are abstractions from the full concrete reality of things, and are correct if not mistaken for this full reality.

(*c*) Bultmann's strictures could be regarded as being directed only toward certain kinds of world views, namely, those that are "objectifying" in the sense of trying to encompass all of reality within categories appropriate only to things as they appear to sense experience, things which are *merely* objects.

> Faith needs to be emancipated from its association with a world view *expressed in objective terms*, whether it be a mythical or a scientific one. (*KM* 210; italics added.)

> Faith itself demands to be freed from any world-view *produced by man's thought*, whether mythological or scientific. For all human world-views objectivize the world and ignore or eliminate the significance of the encounters in our personal existence. (*JCM* 83; italics added.)

Elsewhere Bultmann suggests the problem with world views of the sort that one "possesses":

> It is precisely in such views that man *fails* to understand himself, because he looks upon himself as something simply given and tries to understand himself as part of the world that lies before him. (*EF* 86.)

Now these criticisms are true about many world views. But whether they would necessarily apply to every world view, even a "Christian philosophy" which saw the world in relation to a personal God, and saw every entity as an event that is analogous to a self-determining moment of human experience, is another question, not to be settled *a priori*. That this might be in harmony with Bultmann's intentions is suggested by his comment that "it seems high time that Christology was emancipated from its subordination to an ontology of objective thought and re-stated in a new ontological terminology." (*KM* 209, n. 1.)

4. The Objective and Subjective Sides of Revelation

I have argued in the previous section that Bultmann really does mean to speak of an act of God that occurred in the past and, hence, outside the believer. But because of his somewhat one-sided focus on *saving* faith, and also because of the onto-logical view of the relation between divine and worldly causa-tion that he assumes is demanded by the hiddenness of the divine action, he lacks both the interest and the conceptuality to speak coherently of an event-in-itself, prior to the believer's response to it, as an act of God. Accordingly, the weight is always placed on the believer's present response to the kerygma, leading many interpreters to assume that Bultmann means that it is faith that *constitutes* Jesus as God's decisive act.

To avoid this misunderstanding, Bultmann should have dis-tinguished systematically between "revelation," which requires a subjective appropriation and hence necessarily occurs in the present, and "acts of God," which can refer to past events in themselves. This likely would have led to a more positive ap-praisal of the significance of the historical Jesus for faith.

5. The Basis for Christian Existence

The impression that many seem to have of existentialist theology in general, and of Bultmann's in particular, is that no objective grounds are given upon which one *should* be a Christian. Nothing can be affirmed about the structure of reality as such which shows that through Christian faith one has a greater possibility of being in harmony with "the ultimate reality."

However, the affirmations referred to in the second section of this chapter, plus some others, show that Bultmann is by no means a relativist, and that Christian existence is well grounded in reality. The fact that the world is finite and transitory in comparison to God's majesty and eternity supports the appropriateness of inner detachment from the world. Because God is not only omnipotent judge, but also the Holy One who demands righteousness and love of the neighbor, men are called not only to moderation, humility, and resignation, as were the Greeks, but first of all to responsibility and repentance, to perform the will of God. (*JCM* 26.) The attitude of faith and hope, or openness to the future, is appropriate because God gives the future. An obedient response to the challenge of goodness, truth, and love is known by faith to be obedience to the commandment of God. (*JCM* 31, 39.) The idea of freedom as subjective arbitrariness, which implies relativism, is an illusory idea, for true freedom can come only by recognizing absolute truths and absolute ethical demands which have their origin in God. (*JCM* 41 f.)

Bultmann's notions of sin and righteousness are based on these truths about reality. Sin is the attempt to found one's security on the visible, tangible realm. This is wrong because one is thereby taking for secure and definitive what is really insecure and provisional. It is incongruous with his *real* situation for man to try to achieve his own security by mastering this sphere, for anxiety and destiny will destroy his attempts. (*KM* 18 f.) And man thereby understands himself wrongly, for he has his being from the reality out of which he comes, not from what he makes. (*EF* 83.) Righteousness consists in the reproduction of the original relation of creation. (*EF* 82.) It is life based on the unseen, intangible realities. (*KM* 19.) It involves responsibility to the transcendent power, the God who has power over time and eternity. (*JCM* 41 f.) Far from giving us a picture of an alien or indifferent universe, Bultmann presents us with a natural law theory, albeit a sketchy one.

The New Testament or Christian understanding of man as a

temporal (or historical) being can be affirmed to be man's "natural" understanding of existence. For it is simply restated, for the most part, in Heidegger's philosophy, and this is a phenomenological analysis of the understanding of existence that is given with existence itself. According to this view, man has a past that shapes his character, and a future that brings forth new encounters. (*JCM* 30.) It is these continual encounters that confront him with the necessity to decide, either authentically or inauthentically. Of course, there have been different views, views which have seen man's true self to consist in a supertemporal essence, so that he would find deity by fleeing from his concrete existence in time. (*EF* 67 f.) But these views misunderstand the true nature of both God and man, failing to recognize that man is *essentially* historical and hence constituted by his encounters, and that God encounters man in his daily life, especially in his neighbor. (*K* 259.) It can be shown by philosophical analysis that, if man wants to exist authentically, he must be open to the future in each moment. (*JCM* 77.)

Finally, Bultmann seems to hold, although less explicitly, H. Richard Niebuhr's view that Christian faith is justified by its fruits. We saw in Niebuhr's case that this implied non-relativistic criteria for judging which fruits are good. Bultmann clearly holds freedom, in the sense of openness to the future, to be good. It is shown by philosophical analysis to be an essential feature of man's existence. (*JCM* 77.) But this freedom is not an actual possibility for man apart from faith, only a theoretical one. Although it belongs to his essential nature to know that his life is not authentic, man cannot free himself from his inauthenticity. (*KM* 28–30.) And this is asserted not only on the basis of the New Testament; experience shows it to be true. (*KM* 21.) Authenticity can only come as a gift of God; through the revelation of the mercy and love of God in Christ, man is freed. The forgiveness of sins frees man from himself and makes him free to give his life to others; being met by the love of God, he is freed to love others, since only those who are loved are capable of loving. (*KM* 29, 32.)

Hence, Bultmann seems to claim that, although Christian faith arises out of one tradition among others, it alone corresponds to the true nature of man and meets his need. Only the Christian revelation can illuminate our existence. Through faith in God in Christ we can enter the life for which we were originally created, the life based on the intangible realities. However, because these transcendent realities cannot become permanent possessions, the decision of faith needs renewal in every new situation. (*KM* 21.) Hence there is a structural correspondence in reality between the character of the intangible realities (unpossessable) and the nature of man (ever and again confronted with the necessity for decision). In line with man's historicity, the life of faith is always an imperative as well as an indicative.

The question to be raised, of course, is whether Bultmann's theology provides a sufficiently intelligible basis and context for these nonrelativistic affirmations. I believe it does not. Heidegger's reputed agreement with the New Testament view of man does not show that Heidegger has given a purely phenomenological analysis of man qua man. Although Bultmann wavered on whether Heidegger's *historical* dependence upon the Christian tradition is also a *necessary* dependence, one of his last statements affirmed the latter. (*K* 260.) The claim that Christian existence is that for which we were created would have to be made plausible by a doctrine of God's purpose for the world, or at least for man, which is both consistent and adequate to the facts. And this would require overcoming the hesitancy to speak directly of God himself.

The concept of God, including God's relation to the world, would also have to be explicated rather fully for other reasons. Bultmann seems to hold that the absolute demands of truth, beauty, and goodness are efficacious for us through God's encountering us with them as possibilities for our actualization.

Accordingly, the meaning and the possibility of God's "encountering" man with these possibilities would have to be made intelligible. This would involve, on the one hand, a metaphysical discussion of the relation of God to these possibilities, similar to the traditional discussions as to the status of the "Platonic ideas," and their relation to God. On the other hand, some epistemological discussion would be necessary. Bultmann has indicated that materialism is inconsistent with Christian faith, since it excludes freedom. It is also true that materialism's epistemological correlate, sensationalism, is also incompatible, since it excludes in principle any experience of God and all other nonmaterial ("intangible") realities. As it stands, Bultmann's thought is involved in the inconsistency of denying that "spiritual realities" can causally affect man, yet affirming that God "encounters" man, which surely must make some difference to man's experience and behavior.

Finally, Bultmann's position requires a philosophical context that can render conceivable the freedom of man and the affirmation that God was decisively revealed in Christ. In brief, Bultmann's intentions can only be carried out within the context of a metaphysics, complete with concepts for God and the world, as well as for man.

CHAPTER 4

God's Objective Presence
in Jesus

1. THE RATIONALITY OF THEOLOGY
BASED UPON REVELATION

This chapter presents a critique of the position developed by
Friedrich Schleiermacher in *The Christian Faith*. Schleiermacher has had a seminal influence on the thinking about the
relation of faith and reason in the nineteenth and twentieth
centuries, including that of Paul Tillich, H. Richard Niebuhr,
and Rudolf Bultmann, whose views we have examined. In all
three one can see reflections of Schleiermacher's modification
of Kant's distinction between two kinds of reason in order to
establish the independence of thought arising out of religious
"piety" from the thought of "objective" reason.

Piety belongs to the "immediate self-consciousness," which
is an activity distinct from the "objective consciousness," to
which historical, scientific, and speculative reasoning belong.
(*CF* 5–9.) The essence of piety, which is the same for all men,
is describable as a "feeling of absolute dependence." (*CF* 12.)
This feeling is not derived from objective beliefs; specifically,
it is not conditioned by some prior knowledge about God. (*CF*
11–17.) In fact, it is the business of dogmatics to establish the
independence of the immediate self-consciousness. (*CF* 87.)

Rather, religious doctrines are obtained by explicating the essence of this feeling. (*CF* 77 f., 92, 126.)

This essence of piety is never found by itself, however, so that its explication would constitute a "natural theology." (*CF* 46 f., 124, 261 f.) It is always found within a consciousness that is determined by a particular historical tradition, the originating event for which is called its "revelation." (*CF* 50.) In the Christian form of piety everything is related to faith in Jesus of Nazareth as redeemer. (*CF* 52.) As he is the originator of the Christian community, his saving effects can be described in terms of "revelation." (*CF* 63, 75.) However, the idea that revelation refers essentially to doctrines that operate on man as a cognitive being is rejected by Schleiermacher. Revelation comes through the total impression of a person on our self-consciousness, and involves a communication of redeeming power, which is something quite different from the mere communication of doctrine. (*CF* 50.) The doctrines of a religious community develop *out of* the revelatory experience. The essential doctrinal content thus derived, insofar as it refers to God, is the correlate of the feeling of the absolute dependence of everything finite upon one supreme being, and hence is the idea of God as one, and as omnipotent, exerting absolute causality. (*CF* 17 f.)

As Christian piety or faith is thereby said to be independent of objective beliefs, and "dogmatics" is merely an explication of this faith, the implication would seem to be that dogmatics would be independent of philosophy. And in fact Schleiermacher says that the separation between the two types of propositions should become so complete that, e.g.,

> so extra-ordinary a question as whether the same proposition can be true in philosophy and false in Christian theology, and *vice versa*, will no longer be asked, for the simple reason that a proposition cannot appear in the one context precisely as it appears in the other: however similar it sounds, a difference must always be assumed. (*CF* 83.)

Schleiermacher here seems to be saying that the two types of propositions are different in intention, that they have "different logics," as some would put it today. He further says that, although there can be an awareness of God in the objective consciousness, this should not be used in dogmatics, "for the system of doctrine has as little to do immediately with the objective consciousness as pure science with the subjective." (*CF* 137.) The Christian doctrine of God is not a speculative, philosophical doctrine, but is of religious origin. (*CF* 195.) The complete freedom intended from speculative ideas is shown further by his position that nothing essential would be lost if the section in dogmatics on God and his attributes were omitted, all these propositions being reduced to the "fundamental" form of dogmatic assertions, "the description of human states of mind." (*CF* 126 f.)

The obvious question is whether Schleiermacher was able in fact to keep the two spheres independent more consistently than did his intellectual descendants. In regard to piety, it is important to note first that the feeling of absolute dependence is never the sole content of a moment of experience, but is always contained along with other elements. (*CF* 131.) Although the element of piety is always present, never being totally obscured, its magnitude can vary from the mere disposition to God-consciousness to the constant predominance of it. (*CF* 123.) And the transition from the mere disposition (i.e., from an infinitely small degree of that consciousness) to a definite and perceptible magnitude "is always dependent on some other fact of consciousness." (*CF* 259.) Schleiermacher refers to the ability to discern the "superiority of those states of mind which combine with the God-consciousness without obstructing it" (*CF* 275), and he says that an idolatrous, "anthropopathic" idea of God can constitute an obstructive state of mind (*CF* 277).

In other words, rather than the feeling of absolute dependence being *totally* independent of objective beliefs about God, we find that its *development* into a significant feeling can be obstructed by false beliefs. It is hindered by polytheism, since a developed piety can only coexist with monotheism (CF 35, 133), which means belief in one power which determines all and is not in turn conditioned in the slightest, i.e., belief in God's absolute omnipotence (CF 146, 201, 211–214) and impassibility (CF 14–18, 135, 220).

Furthermore, a development of the feeling of absolute dependence is incompatible with a view which fails to distinguish between God and the world, and which fails to think of the divine causality as absolutely living, but posits a lifeless, blind necessity. (CF 118, 133, 219.) If one posits either a dead mechanism or chance, "the God-consciousness recedes." (CF 139.) Closely related is the fact that piety is only possible if we have a feeling of freedom. (CF 16.) Accordingly, the belief that this feeling of freedom is an illusion would be "destructive of the feeling of absolute dependence." (CF 190.) Having said this, Schleiermacher suggests how we ought to regard nature and man in order best to protect our initial assumption of having freedom. We should not make any absolute distinction between man, or even life, and a "nature-mechanism." For there is "complete absence of freedom only where a thing does not move itself," and "anything which actually has a being for itself moves itself in some sense or other." (CF 190–192.) This is clearly a speculative view, emanating from the so-called "objective" consciousness.

Hence, if certain objective beliefs can be destructive to religious feeling, and if certain others can support it, the religious feeling does not seem to be entirely independent of such beliefs. This would in turn imply that the independence of theology's assertions from philosophy's could not be consistently maintained in such a way that all possible conflict could be avoided. Schleiermacher does recognize that theology is dependent upon philosophy for its conceptuality, but he suggests that this dependence is merely formal. (CF 93.) The highly doubtful character of the claim that the use of a particular philosophical conceptuality will affect only the form and not the substance of the explication of faith is by now widely recognized. The case against such a claim will not be argued here. Suffice it to mention that Schleiermacher himself says that until philosophy provides an acceptable formula for the relation of God and the world, theology will not have an adequate way of expressing the relation of divine and natural causality but will have to oscillate between formulas which approach identifying them and formulas which approach opposing them, both of which are, as we have seen, destructive of piety. (*CF* 174.)

Furthermore, Schleiermacher clearly acknowledges that a real conflict can occur between theology and philosophy, as the "highest subjective function" and the "highest objective function," respectively, of the human spirit. Schleiermacher does say that such a conflict would be the result of a *misunderstanding*. But this is so because both disciplines arise out of the same essential human nature, and hence ought to agree, and *not* because the two types of propositions are different in intention (or "logic") and therefore in principle could not conflict. (*CF* 83.) Accordingly Schleiermacher says that if a conflict does arise, and the person believes the fault to lie on the religious side, he may have to give up his religion. This clearly could not be the case if "religious" and "objective" assertions had "different logics." Schleiermacher still contends that it is not the task of dogmatics to try to reconcile the conflict. Rather, it is the task of that branch of theology called "apologetics."[1] (*CF* 122.)

According to this statement, then, "theology" as a whole is not independent of philosophy. It is only "dogmatics" that is claimed to have this independence. Therefore, the *total* theological task of making clear the nature of faith and supporting its growth would require showing that faith's presuppositions and implications are not contradicted by anything which we must necessarily believe about the world "objectively." Schleiermacher's formal position on faith and reason must therefore be formulated in the following way: The religious dimension of experience is independent of all objective reflection *in the sense* that the relatedness to God is universal, so that an awareness of it can never be totally effaced. But the emergence of this awareness into full consciousness, and in such a way that it could become a dominant factor in one's experience, depends on acquiring beliefs about the nature of God and his causal influence that correspond to reality.

This interpretation is further supported by Schleiermacher's assertions that the awarness of God is first awakened by speech, and that doctrinal preaching is the most important means for promoting it. (*CF* 27, 87.) Although he has stressed that doctrines arise *out of* this piety awakened by preaching, it is also true that the Christian kerygma itself consists in doctrines. (*CF* 77 f.) This means that the birth and development of Christian faith is brought about by doctrines, as well as vice versa. Full recognition of this centrality of beliefs would require that a higher evaluation be placed on the cognitive side of revelation.

2. THE CONTENT OF REVELATION

We have seen that Schleiermacher does not stress revelation in terms of its doctrinal content, especially in regard to ideas about God, but that his position demands it. The question in this section concerns his ideas about God, and what therefore *could* be the doctrinal content about God involved in revelation.

Schleiermacher asserts that we cannot speak about God in and for himself, but only about God in his relation to us. This reflects the essence of human limitedness in relation to him. (*CF* 52.) This means that we can only speak about God's causality on us, not of the being of God in itself, "for the essence of that which has been active can never be known simply from its activity alone." Also, the plurality of divine attributes does not denote anything special in God himself, but only in our relation to his causality. (*CF* 194, 198.)

And yet, precisely in saying that the differentiation in the attributes "can correspond to nothing real in God" (*CF* 198), he does seem to be saying something about God in himself. And he clearly is when he declares that all the attributes in God are identical, and that in God there is no temporal opposition of before and after. (*CF* 203 f.)

Although Schleiermacher says that the attributes of simplicity and unity do not properly arise from the religious consciousness, and that the idea that there is in God "no distinction of essence and existence" belongs to speculative theology (*CF* 229), he does affirm that the feeling of absolute dependence is the awareness of God as "the absolute undivided unity." (*CF* 132.) He also says that the religious meaning of God's simplicity refers to the "inseparable mutual inherence of all divine attributes and activities." Moreover, he declares that there is in God "no distinction between essence and attributes." (*CF* 730.) All of this means that there can be no distinctions in God between possible and actual (*CF* 213), ability and will (*CF* 214–217), necessity and freedom (*CF* 156), causing and permitting (*CF* 326), knowing and doing (CF 225). Despite his claimed agnosticism about God's being in itself, he says that what is fundamental in regard to the divine attributes is "that in the Divine Essence which explains the feeling of absolute dependence." (*CF* 199.) And what *that* is was seen earlier, i.e., the twofold truth of omnipotence and immutability, that everything "has happened only as God originally willed," and that we must not "assume an alteration in God of any kind." (*CF* 177, 206.)

These assertions are doubly significant. First, they suggest that Schleiermacher's claimed source for his doctrine of God, his immediate self-consciousness, is not his actual source. For on the basis of a phenomenological description of his own experience he could not have gone beyond his statement that God is the "Whence" of his consciousness of God. (*CF* 16 f.) He could have described only how "God" appeared to him, or how he was related to God, not what God is like in himself. In his own words, "The essence of that which has been active can never be known simply from its activity alone." That is, it would require *speculation*. Yet in his very definition of God-consciousness as the feeling of *absolute* dependence, he goes beyond this limit and affirms something that can only be affirmed on a speculative basis. That is, the difference between relative and absolute dependence is that, in the latter, that upon which one is dependent is in no way susceptible to counter-influence. (*CF* 13–18.) Hence his attempted separation from speculation breaks down even in his primary theological assertion. For all speculation involves moving beyond description to inference and explanation, and Schleiermacher has posited "that in the Divine Essence which *explains* the feeling of absolute dependence." Accordingly, rather than really basing his doctrines of God on immediate religious experience, it seems evident that he simply takes over the traditional (e.g., Thomistic) doctrine of God, applies it more consistently, and defines the essence of religious experience to conform to *it*.

In regard to most of the personal qualities affirmed by the Biblical tradition, Thomas Aquinas had to see them as "metaphorical." It is widely accepted today that this was due to his beginning with an extra-Christian starting point, a so-called "natural theology," on top of which he attempted to add the doctrines of "revealed theology." Schleiermacher claims that this is not what he is doing, even though he treats the not-uniquely-Christian attributes such as eternity and omnipotence first. He says that these are "abstracted from" specifically Christian doctrines. (*CF* 262, 731.) Yet it is clearly the latter which are made to conform to the former, for the Biblical doctrines, being based on analogy between God and man, are said to be objectionable because of their "anthropomorphic" elements. It is said to be the task of dogmatics to render these elements as "harmless as possible." (*CF* 195.) For example, "mercy" is an "anthropopathic" term to a preeminent degree, suggesting "a state of feeling specially evoked by the sufferings of others." (*CF* 353.) Also the "holiness" of God cannot consist in his being "well-pleased with what is good and displeased with what is bad," for that would imply passivity and reciprocity. "A divine state would then be determined by human action." (*CF* 341.) In accord with this exclusion of all passivity, the divine love is then interpreted in a purely active way, as the divine nature's self-impartation. (*CF* 727–730.)

Schleiermacher's assertions about God in himself are also significant in that they show that the problems with speaking about God do not really arise from the "essence of human limitedness in relation to him." Rather, the real difficulty arises from *what is thought to be known* directly about God's essence. As was the case in Tillich, the privileged attributes are such that nothing else can be said about God.

3. God's Relation to Jesus

In the previous sections we saw that Schleiermacher's position on faith and reason had to be modified to be consistent, and that, even if the need were recognized to define revelation as involving cognitive content about God, nothing could be said about God beyond his absolute causality and immutability. But what is perhaps Schleiermacher's most important, and generally overlooked, contribution to Christology is his attempt "to define the mutual relations of the divine and the human in the Redeemer." (*CF* 397.) He pointed the way to solving the traditional problem as to how God could be objectively present in Jesus in a unique way without vitiating Jesus' humanity and unity.

The incarnation does not threaten Jesus' full humanity, in the first place, because God is said to be *formally* present in Jesus in the same way in which he is present in all men. That is, God is present in all men insofar as they have a feeling of absolute dependence.[2] (*CF* 126, 252, 387.) And in fact "the realization of oneself as absolutely dependent is the only way in which God and the ego can co-exist in self-consciousness." (*CF* 133.) Accordingly "to ascribe to Christ an absolutely

powerful God-consciousness, and to attribute to Him an existence of God in Him, are exactly the same thing." (*CF* 387.)

In the second place, this doctrine implies that God is objectively present in Jesus, not subjectively. In other words, God
is present not as an experiencing subject, but as felt, or apprehended. Schleiermacher's somewhat ambiguous term "feeling" not only refers to the subjective form of a response, but
also indicates an apprehension of some reality beyond the self.
This is why a feeling of oneself as in relation to God is also a
presence of God in the self-consciousness. Conceiving of God's
presence in Jesus in this way avoids the problems that arise
when one thinks of a trinity of three persons, and of the "second
person" as incarnate in Jesus, a view which Schleiermacher
eschews. (*CF* 392–395, 399.) From that traditional starting
point one cannot avoid either mixing the two natures, or making one less important and limited by the other, or neglecting
the unity of the person. For example, if there be two complete
natures, each must have a will and a reason. But it is

> unthinkable that a divine reason, which as omniscient sees
> everything at once, should think the same as a human rea-
> son, which only knows separate things one after the other
> and as a result of the other, and that a human will, which
> always strives only for separate ends and one for the sake
> of the other, should will the same as a divine will, whose
> object can be nothing but the whole world in the totality of
> its development. (*CF* 394 f.)

Schleiermacher avoids these problems, since for him God is not
said to be present in Jesus' self-consciousness as a personal
subject, with a reason and a will, but only as apprehended. God
is incarnate in that his causal influence is felt. (*CF* 402.)

This approach protects Jesus' full humanity while affirming
the presence of God in him by seeing this presence as not
ontologically different from God's presence in all men. But how
then is Jesus unique? Schleiermacher says that we must think
of him as having an "exclusive and peculiar superiority" over
us, even an "essential distinction" from us, as well as an "es-

sential likeness" to us. (*CF* 99, 396.) Jesus differs in that the God-consciousness in him is clear and absolutely powerful, not obscure and weak as is the case in all other men. (*CF* 397, 402.) In other men there is a struggle between the sensuous self-consciousness and the higher self-consciousness, which is God-consciousness. (*CF* 55, 272.) But in Jesus the God-consciousness dominates every activity and every perception in every moment of his existence. (*CF* 378, 383.) Hence, only in him is there "an existence of God in the proper sense." And only in him is there an absence of conflict, and, hence, perfect unity. The "perfect indwelling of the Supreme Being [is] His peculiar being and His inmost self." (*CF* 388.)

Accordingly, it can be said that Schleiermacher does posit a difference in kind between Jesus and other men. For the difference between "some" and "all" must be said to be a difference of kind, not merely a difference of degree, if that distinction is to have any meaning. And in other men the God-consciousness is at best *sometimes somewhat* dominant, whereas in Jesus it was *always totally* dominant. Hence his consciousness of God, the presence of God in him, constituted his selfhood. All his activity proceeded from his apprehension of the divine causality.

Schleiermacher has suggested a way in which Jesus can be thought of as the supreme act and incarnation of God, in an important sense different in kind from other men, and yet as a fully human, unified person. Yet he himself did not develop this suggestion into a coherent position. Although in this century he has generally been criticized from the other direction, the crucial problem with his Christology is that he failed to hold to the full humanity of Jesus.

Of course, Schleiermacher certainly intended to affirm this full humanity. We have already seen evidence of this intention in the way the existence of God in Jesus is defined. And Schleiermacher says that Jesus' perfect God-consciousness is not an absolutely supernatural occurrence, but only a *relatively* supernatural one. (*CF* 62–65.) It is only relatively supernatural because of two factors that make it a *natural* fact. First, the possibility of taking up the restorative divine element into itself resides in human nature; this power need not first be given to it. (*CF* 64.) Elsewhere, where he is being more careful, Schleiermacher says that the human nature cannot have been active

> in such a way that (to put it so) the being of God in Christ was developed out of the human nature, or even in such a way that there was in the human nature a capacity to draw down the divine to itself; only the possibility was innate in it (and must have remained in it intact even during the dominion of sin) of being assumed into such a union with the divine, but this possibility is far from being either capacity or activity. (*CF* 400.)

Second, even though the actual implanting of the divine element is a divine, eternal act,

> the temporal appearance of this act in one particular Person must at the same time be regarded as an action of human nature, grounded in its original constitution and prepared for by all its past history, and accordingly as the highest development of its spiritual power. (*CF* 64.)

If the act were not thus *conditioned,* it would be "an arbitrary divine act that the restorative divine element made its appearance precisely in Jesus." (*CF* 64.) Schleiermacher, in saying that the act was conditioned or prepared for by history seems to refer to the fact that the redeemer should spring from a monotheistic people, and that the Hebrews' monotheistic faith was only fully developed after the exile. Also, by the time of Christ the Greek and Roman world had been prepared for monotheism. (*CF* 37, 60.) Hence, Schleiermacher says that "the Redeemer could appear only at a particular time and out of the midst of this people." (*CF* 417.)

Yet despite all this "naturalness" of Jesus' God-consciousness, it must be called *supernatural.* This follows from Schleiermacher's doctrines about human sinfulness and Jesus' sinlessness. Sin refers to the condition in which one's God-consciousness is not the dominating factor in his experience. (*CF* 54 f., 366.) Accordingly to say that Jesus had an absolutely powerful God-consciousness is to say that he was sinless. (*CF* 272.) But Schleiermacher sees that it is difficult to understand how this perfection appeared "in a truly historically-conditioned individual." (*CF* 380.) For human sinfulness has been so defined that every activity of a historically conditioned individual is inevitably involved in sin. (*CF* 361.) Of course, sin is not essential to man; to maintain that would be Manichaean, and would imply a docetic Christology. (*CF* 100, 278.) And yet, apart from a redeemer, man has a complete incapacity for good, i.e., incapacity to be determined by the God-consciousness. To assert otherwise would be Pelagian, and would imply an Ebionite Christology. (*CF* 100, 282 f.) This incapacity arises from outside ourselves, from the society into which we are born and educated. Man inherits from the actual sins of others a persistent inward ground, from which his own actual sins proceed unfailingly. This voluntary actual sin then increases his original tendency to sin, and also is inherited by the succeeding generation as a bent toward sin. (*CF* 286 f., 304 f.) Hence there is a condition of universal sinfulness. Original sin is common to all; it is a corporate act. The whole human race is included in this sinful corporate life, in which sinfulness sin propagates itself naturally. (*CF* 288, 365.) It is in this context that the question arises:

If sin is posited as a corporate act of the human race, what possibility then remains that an ideal individual could have developed out of this corporate life? (*CF* 380 f.)

The difficulty is fully revealed by Schleiermacher's argument that it cannot be the case "that the ideal might be produced by human thought and transferred more or less arbitrarily to Jesus." Since "there is a natural connexion between reason and will," the condition of universal sinfulness means there could have been no "room in human nature before Christ, and apart from him, for the power of producing within itself a pure and perfect ideal." (*CF* 380 f.) Hence, if man could not *conceive* of a perfect ideal, due to the effect of his sinful will upon his reason, it seems impossible that a human being could *actualize* the ideal.

Schleiermacher's position is that Jesus "must have entered into the corporate life of sinfulness, but He cannot have come out of it, but must be recognized in it as a miraculous fact." (*CF* 381.) Schleiermacher adds here that "miracle" must be understood in the way he has defined it, i.e., in the relative sense, in line with certain analogies. That is, the special endowment of any man who manifests originality in any area, such as art, science, or religion, can never be *explained* in terms of the condition of the circle in which he appears (although the more limited in influence the man's expressions are, the more they appear *conditioned* by the immediate context). (*CF* 63, 386.) Rather, they must be attributed to a power of development that resides in human nature and expresses itself in particular men at particular points, according to laws of divine arrangement, in order to secure progress in the human race. (*CF* 63.) In other words:

> The origin of every human life may be regarded in a twofold manner, as issuing from the narrow circle of descent and society to which it immediately belongs, and as a fact of human nature in general. The more definitely the weaknesses of that narrow circle repeat themselves in an individual, the more valid becomes the first point of view. The more the individual by the kind and degree of his gifts transcends that circle, and the more he exhibits what is new within it, the more we are thrown back upon the other explanation. This means that the beginning of Jesus' life cannot in any way be explained by the first factor, but only and exclusively by the second. (*CF* 388.)

Schleiermacher is speaking here, of course, not of Jesus' language, race, physical characteristics, etc., but only of his perfect God-consciousness, and therefore of his essential sinlessness. He continues:

So that from the beginning He must have been free from every influence from earlier generations which disseminated sin and disturbed the inner God-consciousness, and He can only be understood as an original act of human nature, *i.e.* as an act of human nature as not affected by sin. (*CF* 388 f.)

Unlike other men, Jesus "cannot have entered life as one for whom the foundations of sin had already been laid before His being began to be manifested." (*CF* 388.) This requires that, although it is superfluous and inadvisable to suppose a virgin birth, we must nevertheless posit a "supernatural conception." For there had to be a

higher influence, which, as a creative divine activity, could alter both the paternal and the maternal influence in such a way that all ground for sinfulness was removed. (*CF* 405.)

Schleiermacher's justification for the claim that Jesus' self-consciousness was *not at all conditioned* by the sinful influence that infects every other man from the beginning is that Jesus' effects will be unlimited spatially and temporally, as he is destined to quicken the whole human race (see the parenthetical comment in the preceding paragraph). (*CF* 63 f., 386.) The question of the logic of this argument can be left aside. What is crucial here is that Jesus' full historicity, and therefore his full humanity, have been denied. Full humanity demands full historicity, being conditioned (though not totally determined) by the historical context in which one appears. Full humanity is not preserved by the fact that Schleiermacher removes this conditioning only from one aspect of Jesus, his God-consciousness, just as the docetism of some early theologians was not overcome by their assertion that Jesus was fully human except for his rational soul.

Schleiermacher quite often (and justifiably) says that Jesus' sinless God-consciousness cannot be *explained* by the human environment. (*CF* 50, 61, 380.) But this is true of any partially self-determining event. It is quite a different matter to say that it is not at all *conditioned* by it, that Jesus' spiritual originality

is "set free from every prejudicial influence of natural descent."
(*CF* 389.) He claims that,

> since we can never properly understand the beginnings of
> life, full justice is done to the demand for the perfect his-
> toricity of this perfect ideal, if, from then on, He developed
> in the same way as all others. (*CF* 381.)

But the fact that we "can never properly understand the begin-
nings of life" is not relevant to the point, which is that mankind's state of sinfulness has been so *defined* by Schleiermacher
himself that no human being could possibly respond *directly*
(i.e., apart from a historical redeemer) to God's grace in such
a way that the divine impulse in him could become dominant.
Hence he had made it impossible for the redeemer himself to
be a human being (and therefore, by Schleiermacher's own
dictum, really to be a redeemer). (*CF* 99, 397.) He has fallen
victim to the dilemma he himself described—he avoids Pela-
gianism only to fall into docetism. (*CF* 100 f.)

Nor is this docetism overcome by the assertion that Jesus'
God-consciousness, like that of everyone else, began only as a
germ, and had to develop gradually. (*CF* 381.) For in Jesus it
began as a germ of a perfect, clear, absolutely powerful God-
consciousness, while in us it began as a germ of an imperfect,
obscure, powerless one. (*CF* 367, 402.)

Finally, this conclusion is not affected by the fact that
Schleiermacher says that the "supernatural conception" of
Jesus, i.e., the new implanting of the perfect God-consciousness
in him, goes back to an eternal divine decree and forms, in a
higher sense, part of a "natural system." (*CF* 389.) The absolute supernaturalism involved in a phenomenon totally unconditioned by its historical context cannot be defined away.
Schleiermacher's claim that only a *relative* supernaturalism is
involved in his position was based on the notion that the incarnation of God in Jesus was "natural" in that it was conditioned by the history leading up to it. Yet we have seen that it
was, in its essence, not historically conditioned at all. The con-

nection of the appearance of the redeemer with "that which precedes" it "is to be found only in the unity of the divine thought." (*CF* 365.) On this basis any type of miraculous interruption of the finite causal nexus could be called "natural." Schleiermacher has clearly violated his own principles. For he has said that

it can never be necessary in the interest of religion so to interpret a fact that its dependence on God absolutely excludes its being conditioned by the system of Nature. (*CF* 178.)

Not only the objective consciousness, but also piety assumes that all things are conditioned by the interdependence of nature. (*CF* 174.) For an interference by God would mean that there was some imperfection in his work or in him, i.e., that something not ordained by him could offer resistance to him. (*CF* 179.) Schleiermacher further says that one cannot defend miracles as necessary to restore the order that was destroyed by free causes, for they too are part of the world that is absolutely dependent on God. All free acts of human beings are as completely ordained by God as events in the so-called "nature-mechanism." (*CF* 179, 189–192.)

Yet Schleiermacher defends the mission of Christ as the "one great miracle," by saying that it

has, of course, the aim of restoration, but it is the restoration of what free causes have altered in their own province, not in that of the nature-mechanism or in the course of things originally ordained by God. (*CF* 180.)

But *all* things were "originally ordained by God." The province of free causes was not excluded. Even the *self-consciousness* belongs to that "universal system which is the essential indivisible subject of the feeling of absolute dependence." (*CF* 189.)

Schleiermacher's other defense for this miracle is that the free cause performing the restoration does not "have a different relation to the order of nature from that of other free causes."

(*CF* 180.) But that is contradicted by his essential point, i.e, that Jesus' God-consciousness was not at all conditioned by his environment. Schleiermacher himself provides the best argument against the possibility of this unconditionedness.

> The event in which a miracle occurs is connected with all finite causes, and therefore every absolute miracle would destroy the whole system of nature. . . . Since . . . that which would have happened by reason of the totality of finite causes in accordance with the natural order does not happen, an effect has been hindered from happening, and certainly not through the influence of other normally counteracting finite causes given in the natural order, but in spite of the fact that all active causes are combining to produce that very effect. Everything, therefore, which had ever contributed to this will, to a certain degree, be annihilated. (*CF* 181.)

Hence the distinction between an absolute and a relative miracle collapses, since the reason Jesus was not affected by inherited sin was "not through the influence of other normally counteracting finite causes."

Closely related to this issue is another doctrine which denies Jesus' humanity. Since sinlessness is simply the reverse side of perfect God-consciousness, it is clear that Jesus never sinned, and, therefore, that he had the possibility not to sin. And this formula (*potuit non peccare*) by itself is said to assert the essential preeminence of Christ. For all other men "can never not-sin." Yet Schleiermacher says that we must also say that Jesus did not even have the possibility of sinning (*non potuit peccare*). The reason is that,

> where the inward possibility of sinning is posited, there too is posited in addition at least an infinitely small amount of the reality of sin, in the form of tendency. (*CF* 414.)

Hence the fact that Jesus' likeness to us includes his being tempted in all points cannot mean "that there was even an infinitely small element of struggle involved."

Now, Schleiermacher claims that, since sin is not *essential* to man, "the possibility of a sinless development is in itself not incongruous with the idea of human nature." (*CF* 385.) And he further says that in his Christology "the only thing that could be regarded as docetic is that in the Redeemer the God-consciousness is not imperfect." (*CF* 398.) The implication is that no Christian would want to call his concept docetic, thereby implying that Jesus' relation to God was imperfect, hence surpassable. But the problem is not the idea that Jesus' God-consciousness was *in some sense* perfect. The problem lies in precisely how Schleiermacher defines "perfection," i.e., as necessarily excluding even the possibility of sin. For although sin as such may not be essential to the definition of "fully human," the *possibility* of sinning certainly is.

The question to be raised about the inadequacy of Schleiermacher's Christology is this: If it is the case that his approach could have resulted in a way of speaking of God's supreme presence in Jesus without involving docetism (as well as Nestorianism), why was this not achieved? Of course, some of the reasons were doubtless biographical, and as such will not come under discussion here. Rather, the question concerns systematic reasons, a discussion of which will entail suggestions as to needed corrections.

One of the two restrictions of Jesus' humanity was that his essential sinlessness was said to exclude the possibility of sin. Why does Jesus' "perfection" have to be thus defined? The answer to this seems to lie in the fact that Schleiermacher has *only one variable* with which to contrast Jesus and other men. That is, the *way* God is present in Jesus is equated with the *strength* of his God-consciousness, which is equated with *sinlessness*. (Every Christology defines Jesus as being perfect, or final, in some sense. For, as Schleiermacher points out, if one can conceive of a greater actualization in regard to the characteristic in question, the standpoint of Christian faith has been left.) (*CF* 387.) Since Schleiermacher has only this one variable, Jesus' sinlessness must be defined in the highest terms

conceivable. And the impossibility of sinning apparently
seemed to Schleiermacher to be a more perfect sinlessness than
merely the possibility of not sinning.

The meaning of this argument can perhaps be made clearer
by using for contrast a possible view in which there would be
two variables with which to compare Jesus and other men in
regard to their relation to God. Besides differing in the *degree*
to which their apprehension of God's causal influence on them
was the source of their activity, they could be thought to differ
also in regard to the *content* of the divine causality upon them.
If this were the case, the specialness of Jesus' person, which
provides the ground for his significance for others, would not
have to rest solely upon his sinlessness, i.e., the *degree* to which
he lived in terms of the divine influence. Rather, his specialness
could be conceived partly in terms of the content of the divine
presence in him. And if this were the case, the demand for
perfect "sinlessness" in the former sense might be relaxed somewhat. It could be a matter of relative indifference whether
Jesus' apprehension of God was always, from birth till death,
dominant over or identical with, his own wishes. The important
thing would be the way God's reality came to expression in his
words and deeds, especially during his active ministry. Of
course, this might imply, in order to be made intelligible, that
the divine impulses were extraordinarily dominant in Jesus'
case, and even that they came to constitute his selfhood. But
even this would not necessarily mean that he never acted in a
contrary way (since the man who identifies his selfhood with
his reason, for example, sometimes acts irrationally, saying in
retrospect that he was "beside himself").

The fact that Schleiermacher could only have one variable,
and therefore could not develop such a view, is in turn rooted
in his doctrine of God. As we saw, he insists on the absolute
simplicity of God. There is no real distinction between any of
God's attributes, e.g., between his love and his causality. And
since the favored way of speaking of God is in terms of his
causality, all the "other" attributes are said to be merely dif-

ferent ways of describing this causality. Another way of defining "simplicity" is to say that there is no distinction in God
between an essence (unchanging) and an actuality (changing).
Hence, simplicity and immutability imply each other. If there
were a distinction between God's essence and his actuality,
then it would be conceivable, even probable, that *some* of the
acts of God's full actuality (made in response to concrete situations in the world) would better express some aspect of his
essence than other acts. But Schleiermacher, in line with the
classical tradition, allows for no such distinction. God's essence and his causality are identical.

In view of this, no distinction between worldly events, such
as the one suggested in the previous paragraph, would be intelligible. That is, the only difference between men in relation
to God would be the *degree* to which they are conscious of
his causality. There could not be differences in the content of
the divine causality in various events such that some of them
might better express some *other* attribute of God's essence,
e.g., his love or his purpose.

The other restriction on Jesus' full humanity was the claim
of a "relatively supernatural" origin of his God-consciousness,
in the sense that his self-consciousness was not at all influenced
by the sinfulness permeating society that affects all other men.
This doctrine also can be seen as necessitated by the fact that
Schleiermacher has only one variable for the God-man relation. For the revelatory power of the existence of God in Jesus
is identical with his sinlessness. Accordingly, since the influences inclining one to sin are so described that some degree of
involvement in sin is inevitable, the distinctive spiritual life of
Jesus had to be severed from any connection with the spiritual
condition of his cultural context, in order that he could be
thought to have "everything that we need." Only if the basis of
Jesus' significance for us were not defined primarily in terms
of his sinlessness could one see the divine creative activity in
relation to him as not absolutely different in kind from the
divine activity in relation to all men. That is, one could posit

the need to struggle to overcome real temptation, and still attribute "finality" to him in respect to what we need, e.g., a manifestation of the purpose and love of God for us. Hence the divine causality would not have to be thought of as miraculous, as setting aside the normal effects of the finite efficient causes.

4. The Objective and Subjective Sides of Revelation

Part of Schleiermacher's positive significance in Christology is that he overcame the separation between the "person" and "work" of Christ that had developed, especially in Western theology. That is, the juridical doctrines of atonement made the incarnation quite externally related to the saving efficacy of Christ. Schleiermacher's Christology represents a return to the close connection of the two that is typical of Eastern Christianity. It is Jesus' own relation to God which effects salvation in others, insofar as this relation is communicated to them. But this does not mean that the person of Jesus is simply identified with his "benefits." Rather, after recognizing the benefits that have been received from him, "the dignity of the Redeemer must be thought of in such a way that He is capable of achieving this." (*CF* 377.) And despite what critics may have claimed, the procedure of moving from soteriology to Christology does not mean an indifference to the historical actualization of that ideal which is posited. Schleiermacher says that it could not have been the case that the picture of God-consciousness was arbitrarily attributed to Jesus; it could not have been "faith that made Jesus the Redeemer." The faith that has been communicated through the centuries is only understandable on the assumption that it was Jesus' perfection itself which effected its recognition in others. (*CF* 362 f.)

Hence, the proper criticism of Schleiermacher's Christology is not that he does not give enough weight to the "objective" side, but that, as indicated in the previous section, his way of stating the objective side loses Jesus' full humanity.

5. THE BASIS FOR CHRISTIAN EXISTENCE

Schleiermacher's doctrine of God is such that most of the criticisms directed toward Tillich's language would apply to him as well. That is, the Biblical attributes that ground the appropriateness of Christian existence are so subordinated to alien metaphysical presuppositions that they cannot be affirmed in any significant way. Since this has already been discussed at length, I will deal here rather with Schleiermacher's treatment of the ideas of freedom and sin, which he rightly sees to be necessary presuppositions of the Christian life. For example, he says that if the consciousness of God were incompatible with freedom, then morality and religion would be antithetical. (CF 193.)

But how is freedom in relation to God possible, and therefore, how is sin possible, since Schleiermacher tells us repeatedly that everything, including every "free" decision, is eternally ordained by God? He even specifically says that sin is ordained; to say otherwise would be "to assume that divine action can be limited by what does not depend upon divine action." It would be Manichaean to say that the human will is sufficiently independent of the divine will to be the ground of sin. (CF 329, 335.)

He examines the position that makes a distinction between God's "commanding will" and his "efficient will" on the grounds that sin is only possible if man can act against the divine command. This doctrine holds that the two wills are not identical, and that sin involves disobedience to the commanding will, which does not of itself secure obedience. (CF 332.) But Schleiermacher cannot accept this way out, since he has allowed no distinction between what God thinks and what he effects, and no validity to the traditional distinction between the "antecedent" and the "consequent" will of God. Even if one tries to make the distinction, the lack of conformity to the commanding will is itself brought about by the efficient will. (CF 216, 333.)

Schleiermacher's position is that sin is ordained by God, but not in itself, so as to preserve it, but only in view of its being overcome through redemption. (*CF* 324, 337 f.) But even so, why was it ordained? He rejects the view that sin was an indispensable means to a higher achievement, for the antithesis of means and end cannot exist for omnipotence. Rather, "the merely gradual and imperfect unfolding of the power of the God-consciousness is one of the necessary conditions of the human stage of existence." (*CF* 338.) But the idea that a gradual development is "necessary" would only make sense if the human will could be recalcitrant in relation to God and could hinder his will. Hence, Schleiermacher does not answer his own question:

> If there are divine attributes related to sin, indeed, but not in the way of giving it persistence and confirmation, how should even that, which from its very nature ought not to continue, have come into being in association with all that owes its being to the eternally omniscient divine omnipotence? (*CF* 269.)

The idea that sinfulness is somehow necessitated by worldly conditions is unintelligible in the context of divine omnipotence, as indicated by Schleiermacher himself: "For if the divine will without any such latent strain were wholly directed against sin, the latter of necessity would vanish altogether and at once." (*CF* 327.)

Hence Schleiermacher's position, like all those that affirm unqualified omnipotence to God, cannot avoid being rendered unintelligible by the problem of evil. For if God is love, why does he not eradicate all evil? Furthermore, why did he cause it in the first place? Why does his perfect will have a "latent strain" which prevents him from eradicating it?

Of course, these questions cannot finally even be asked within the context of a doctrine of divine simplicity. The very idea of a "latent strain" is unintelligible in this context, as is the assumption that God could have done otherwise. Although

Schleiermacher understandably wants to avoid saying that God's creating this world was necessary (*CF* 156, 216 f.), no other conclusion is possible. For God's essence is eternal and immutable, and his knowing and will are both identical with it and with each other. Accordingly, since that which is eternal is necessary, God's knowing and creating this world, with all its details, is necessary. Therefore, since Christian existence presupposes freedom, at least one of the prerequisites of Christian existence is denied in Schleiermacher's position.

CHAPTER 5

Pointing a Way Forward

THE MAIN PURPOSE of this chapter is to summarize the conclusions to be drawn from the previous chapters. However, whereas those chapters were primarily critical, focusing on the *problems* in modern theological thought about revelation, this chapter focuses on the *possibilities* present in it, at least implicitly, for developing an adequate position. Hence, the purpose of this chapter is to point forward—by indicating a way to surmount the various impasses encountered in modern theology's attempt to make sense of the belief in Jesus as God's decisive revelation, and at the same time indicating the tasks of the following chapters.

1. THE RATIONALITY OF THEOLOGY BASED UPON REVELATION

In regard to the relation between faith (based on revelation) and reason, the twofold conclusion reached seems to pose a dilemma. On the one hand, if theology is to be rational it cannot submit to a "revelation" in the sense of doctrine that is to be accepted because of its alleged origin. And, partly due to this necessity, and partly due to historical studies and the resultant awareness of the gulf separating us from the formative centuries of Christianity, theology can no longer speak of "revealed doctrines." Hence, insofar as theology develops doctrines about the nature of reality, it cannot be construed as differing in method from philosophy. This must be the case not only if theology is to have self-respect and to make its appeal to modern man in good conscience, but also because its own self-criticism of its history demands relinquishing the notion of a set of doctrines that are simply divinely given.

But, on the other hand, the explication of Christian faith requires a full-fledged metaphysical conceptuality for speaking coherently about God, man, and the world, in themselves and in their interrelationships. And the conceptuality to be used by theology cannot be derived from a "natural theology" in the sense of philosophical doctrines that are based on some supposedly neutral starting point. As we saw, this is the major source of difficulty in the actual practice (as opposed to the methodological prescriptions) of Tillich and Schleiermacher in regard to the doctrine of God, and in Bultmann in regard to the notion of worldly events. As Niebuhr has seen, the ideas about reality that are employed must themselves be based on, or at least radically reformed by, Christian presuppositions. Otherwise no position can result which is both self-consistent and adequate to Christian faith.

The requirement of rationality seems to imply that theology cannot be based on revelation, while the requirement of adequacy to Christian faith demands that it must be. However, a way to solve this apparent dilemma has also been suggested. Tillich has seen that every philosophical position is based upon a value judgment. Some limited aspect of reality is taken to be the most important clue to understanding all of reality. Accordingly, a philosophy that takes personal relations, and hence temporality and events, to be fundamental would not thereby be less rational than a philosophy based upon a judgment as to the higher cognitive value of other dimensions of reality. This would be a Christian philosophy. It would be "Christian" in that it is based upon judgments made under the impact of the long acceptance of the claim that the Biblical events in general, and the Christ event in particular, have mediated the decisive revelation of reality. It would be "philosophical" in the sense that it would ask for acceptance not because of its claim to be derived from revelation, but because of its superiority measured in terms of the philosophical criteria of consistency, adequacy to the facts, and illuminating power.

Of course, after we have said this, the task remains of showing how the "revelation" with which a Christian philosophy begins is to be conceived, such that it does not consist in revealed doctrines, yet supplies a distinctively Christian starting point. This is the task of Chapter 6. Also we must sketch a philosophical position that is "Christian" in the requisite sense and which provides a context for handling the above problems. This is the task of Chapter 7.

2. The Content of Revelation

In regard to formulating the content of revelation, it has been seen that a philosophical conceptuality for speaking directly of God must be presupposed. The inconsistency between Niebuhr's formal and substantive assertions results from his partial acceptance of the Kantian dictum against speaking of "things in themselves." And insofar as Bultmann applies this dictum to God, his term "God" tends to remain "a mere x."

And as was seen, this relationship between faith and philosophy is a reciprocal one, since the philosophical doctrine of God must itself be informed by Christian faith. As Niebuhr, Bultmann, and Schleiermacher say, man does have some knowledge of God prior to faith. This is rooted in the fact that God is universally active, as Augustine stressed. But as Niebuhr has seen most clearly, this prior understanding of God must be radically reformed under the impact of the Christian revelation. If this is done, then extra-Christian ideas about God, such as his infinity, omnipotence, impassibility, simplicity, and transcendence, will not be allowed to dominate, thereby reducing the specifically Christian notions to a merely metaphorical, symbolic status. The critiques of Tillich and Schleiermacher, respectively, showed the necessity for a doctrine in which God really acts in the world, on the one hand, yet is not the total cause of worldly events, on the other.

In regard to the question whether revelation involves any cognitive content, the separation between revelation of God *himself* and ideas *about* God cannot be maintained. Bultmann and Niebuhr both presuppose that revelation results in some cognitive knowledge about God, however much they want to stress knowledge by acquaintance. The content of this revelation is most often expressed in terms of God's nature (his love, or his valuation of us) and God's will or purpose. The Christian doctrine of the Trinity was originally designed to distinguish that aspect of God (the Logos) which was manifest in Jesus from that aspect which was not; a contemporary Christian doctrine of God likewise needs to include this kind of distinction. Another need is for a distinction between God's full actuality and his essence, which means a further rejection of the traditional idea of simplicity. In order to correspond to the distinction between the object of faith (God himself) and its content (the nature and purpose of God), a distinction is needed between the subject of revelation (God himself) and the content (that part of his essence which is revealed). A doctrine of God that meets the above requirements will be suggested in Chapter 7.

3. God's Relation to Jesus

At first glance it may seem that theology's speaking about God's special presence in Jesus constitutes a fundamental difference between theology and philosophy. For it is generally held that philosophy does not speak of particular, ontic events, but only of the general, ontological features of all events. Yet part of the philosophical task is epistemological. The philosopher must show how, if things are the way he says they are, it is possible for him to know this. Accordingly, since the Christian theologian explicitly recognizes those events which he takes as providing the decisive clue to the nature of things, it is incumbent upon him to explain how these events could have this revelatory significance.

Hence the claim by some theologians—that it is unnecessary to discuss *how* God could have been present in Jesus in a unique way—cannot be sustained. The assertion that Christians know it was possible since it was actual presupposes an authoritarian situation that no longer exists. Nowadays the credibility of Christian faith rests only upon its intrinsic coherence, adequacy, and illuminating power. In this context, to use Niebuhr's terms, the event from which concepts are derived to make all other events intelligible must itself be shown to be intelligible in terms of those concepts.

The necessity of Christology proper can also be formulated in terms of the demand for meaningful use of language. Unless the special activity of God in Jesus implied in the assertion that he is God's supreme revelation can be shown to be a possibility, the *meaning* of the assertion is itself doubtful. That is, unless the assertion that Jesus was fully human, although God was uniquely present in him, can be shown not to be a self-contradiction, then no real assertion has been made at all; only a meaningless combination of words has been uttered.

Showing this assertion to be a possibility involves, in the first place, avoiding any suggestion of a miraculous interruption of the normal relations of cause and effect. This demand was really implicit in the early insistence on Jesus' full humanity, but it has been made more pressing by our modern understanding of nature, which makes any such interruption unthinkable. Some have thought that this made all talk of God's activity in the world impossible. Acquiescence at this point would mean an end to Christian faith. Others have tried to make both science and faith autonomous by distinguishing between two different aspects of events and/or two different ways of regarding the events. But as we have seen in Schleiermacher and his descendants, these attempts break down in inconsistency and equivocation.

The only possible solution seems to be on the basis of a Christianized ontology, in which God is conceived as active in *all* events. In such a view, asserting God's activity in Jesus would not require implying an interruption of the normal course of events and thereby a denial of Jesus' full humanity. The question would only be how to think of God's activity in Jesus as special. Now the nature of this specialness need not be bound to previous assumptions about it. Every doctrine of Jesus' person is to be judged in terms of its *adequacy* to the *Scriptures as currently understood*, and to the *particular doctrine of Jesus' saving significance* with which it is combined.

For example, the Christology in the present essay, if measured against the traditional orthodox view, would most likely be considered Ebionite, since it does not identify Jesus' selfhood with a preexistent divine person. But that traditional view clearly presupposes an outdated conception of the Bible, seeing it in terms of inerrant inspiration and verbal revelation. Also this traditional view was designed to support a quite different soteriology than is proposed in the present essay. Because of this twofold relativity, there is no reason to try to reconcile our modern knowledge of the Scriptures with the traditional doctrine of the subjective presence in Jesus of "God the Son," as some have done, by emptying this doctrine of all meaning through a doctrine of radical *kenōsis*. Besides its lack of necessity and meaning, the doctrine that God is subjectively present in Jesus necessarily involves an ontological difference between Jesus and other men, and thereby denies his full humanity.[1]

In the present essay the specialness of God's presence in Jesus will be described in a way that is both consistent with our understanding of the Scriptures and explanatory of how he could have the saving significance that is here deemed central, i.e., being God's decisive revelation to man. Schleiermacher provided the first step in this reconstruction by conceiving of

God's presence in Jesus as objective, as it is in all men. Jesus differed from others only in the degree to which this objective presence of God in him dominated his being. But I have argued that an adequate Christology would also need to distinguish between Jesus and other men in terms of the *content* of this objective presence, as well as the degree.

A second step has been provided by John Baillie's stress on the fact that the specialness of an act of God also depends upon the free response of the person in whom God is acting. Although the initiative is always with God, God's "second move" depends upon the person's response to the first.[2] And this idea is only intelligible if the traditional views of God's omnipotence and immutability are rejected.[3] In fact, even Schleiermacher's views would be more intelligible within a modified doctrine of God's power, for his own doctrine of omnipotence makes unintelligible the variations in the degree to which the presence of God is an effective force in men. This variation would be understandable if man's free self-determination could limit God's effectiveness in him.

Schleiermacher and the other most influential Protestant theologian of the nineteenth century, Albrecht Ritschl, have provided two aspects of a third step. Many have stressed that for a man to serve as the decisive revelation of God, there would have to be the greatest possible unity between God and this man. For example, John Baillie says the human nature would have to provide no hindrance to the divine self-manifestation other than that which is inherent in human nature as such.[4] In Tillich's language, the man would have to be "transparent" to God. Ritschl has suggested a way of conceiving this unity by rejecting any antithesis between a person's essence and his will.[5] A person's will, or life purpose, could be thought of as constituting the central factor in his essence. Hence a unity of will between Jesus and God would constitute the highest possible personal union. Within such a framework, the traditional distinction between a "substantial union" and a mere "moral union" would be overcome. Schleiermacher has seen that there are different ways for one's psyche to be ordered, depending upon which of the elements in one's experience dominates the others. That element which is the organizing center can be said to constitute the person's "self." In Jesus the dominant element was the awareness of God, so that the objective existence of God in him constituted his selfhood. In Chapter 9 a doctrine of Jesus' person along these lines will be developed, on the basis of the process conceptuality sketched in Chapter 7.

Thinking of God's special presence and activity in the world in the above way, on the basis of a Christianized ontology in which all events are acts of God to some degree, makes it possible to speak of God's special acts and yet to follow the demand of Niebuhr and Bultmann that these events be interpreted in terms of the same principles used for all other events. And this can be done without radically opposing "faith" assertions to "historical" ones. Rather, it should be recognized that all historical reconstruction that deals explicitly or implicitly with causal factors is based upon some perspective. An ontology based upon Christian belief in God's providential activity is one among the possible perspectives. Hence there is no reason *in principle* why the Christian qua historian could not speak of God's causal influence in certain events, especially if his ontology allows for the divine influence to be more important in some events than others. Of course, for practical reasons one might wish to make a distinction, as is done in the present essay, between the "historical Jesus," meaning Jesus insofar as he can be described in terms to which historians of all persuasions could in principle agree, and the "Jesus of faith." This second category would include statements about God's special presence or activity in Jesus, as well as the "historical" assertions. But the two sets of assertions would not be related as "objective" and "subjective" so that the "historical Jesus" would be taken as, in principle, giving a totally adequate account of the causal factors on Jesus. Rather, they would be related as the less and the more complete descriptions. The assertions that are more distinctively made from the perspective of Christian faith would be intended to correspond to "objective facts" just as much as do the so-called "historical" statements. In Chapter 8 the different levels of assertions about Jesus will be more fully discussed.

4. THE OBJECTIVE AND SUBJECTIVE SIDES OF REVELATION

In the previous studies of the objective and subjective sides of revelation, two distinct aspects of the objective side emerged, due to the provisional distinction allowed between the "historical Jesus" and the "Jesus of faith." One aspect of the objective side of revelation, the special presence of God in Jesus of Nazareth, was discussed in the previous paragraph. The subjective side refers to the fact that for a special act of God to become a "revelation" a present response to it is required.

The other aspect of the objective side concerns the "historical Jesus," as this term has been conventionally defined. Jesus as knowable according to recognized historical principles must be *compatible* with faith's interpretation of him as incarnating God. Of course, that God was actually efficacious in Jesus' ministry is not something that can simply be read off from the historical facts, e.g., from the fact that Jesus claimed to be God's decisive agent. This judgment depends upon the person's faith that he has come to know God through Jesus. Yet it must be a *plausible* judgment in the light of a responsible historical reconstruction of Jesus of Nazareth.

In Chapter 8 a historical interpretation is given of Jesus which is intended to be historically responsible as well as compatible with faith's interpretation of Jesus. The interpretation is carried out in terms of Bultmann's insight that a methodological distinction needs to be made between the surface meaning of a religious text's time-conditioned conceptions, on the one hand, and the underlying understanding of God, man, and the world expressed therein, on the other. Bultmann himself

gave such an interpretation of Jesus in *Jesus and the Word,*
but he resisted seeing this as theologically relevant, due to his
desire to avoid every suggestion of seeking to "legitimatize" the
kerygma (the Christian proclamation of Jesus as God's decisive act) through historical research. But the proponents of the
"new quest of the historical Jesus" have rightly distinguished
between legitimatizing the kerygma as *kerygma* (i.e., as God's
word) and legitimatizing it *as an interpretation of Jesus of
Nazareth.* In this second sense, grounding the Christian message historically in Jesus' own underlying understanding of
God, man, and the world is seen to be both legitimate and
necessary, i.e., insofar as we do have historical knowledge of
Jesus.

In the present essay this underlying understanding is termed
a "vision of reality." The distinction between it and the conceptuality in which it is expressed is discussed in Chapter 6.
Then in Chapter 8 some of the results obtained by those engaged in the historical quest for Jesus will be employed, although the emphasis will be on the character and purpose of
God rather than on the understanding of human existence, as
is the case in Bultmannian circles.

5. The Basis for Christian Existence

Our examination of the basis for Christian existence in the
theologians we have discussed has been far from adequate.
Fully to explore how the ideas based upon revelation are seen
as supporting a Christian life-style would have involved a too-
lengthy examination of each theologian's total theological position. Instead, only very selective treatments have been given.
Our purpose has been to bring out some of the elements necessary to support Christian existence. To support Christian existence we need (1) a means of judging the Christian view of
things as essentially true, so that a complete relativism can be
avoided; (2) a way of speaking of the reality and efficacy of
those values fundamental to Christian existence; (3) a way of

conceiving the reality of human freedom in relation both to
other finite causes and to the divine causality; (4) a way of
conceiving God's power so that the fact of evil does not falsify
the Christian evaluation of God's character and purpose; (5)
a way of conceiving God's power so that, further, the gradual-
ness and particularity of God's self-revelation does not falsify
the Christian evaluation of his character and purpose.

The first of these elements will be discussed in Chapter 6,
which follows. We will discuss the second, third, and fourth
elements in Chapter 7. Chapters 9 and 10 will touch on the
fifth of these elements in relation to God's character, purpose,
and mode of activity. The more general focus of Chapter 10
will be the relation between faith in Jesus Christ as God's decisive revelation and the universal saving activity of God as
Holy Spirit. Otherwise expressed, the issue is the relation between religious belief and Christian existence under God.

Part II
REVELATION
AND REASON

CHAPTER 6

Vision of Reality
and Philosophical Conceptualization

CERTAIN FORMAL CONCLUSIONS have been reached thus far in regard to theology's speaking of Jesus as God's decisive revelation. First, since revelation always includes a subjective or receiving side as well as an objective or giving side, nothing about Jesus himself can be simply designated as revelation. The question, rather, concerns how to understand Jesus as having expressed a *potentially* revelatory content, i.e., something which is both (1) true and (2) the result of God's special activity and therefore can be *appropriately received* as revelation. The question of God's special activity is the topic of Chapter 9. In the present chapter the concern is with this potentially revelatory content itself and its truth.

Second, even this potentially revelatory content cannot be identified with any explicit doctrines. For every formulation of a doctrine presupposes some particular imagery or conceptuality, and, thereby, a particular understanding of reality. As Whitehead has said, "You cannot claim absolute finality for a dogma without claiming a commensurate finality for the sphere of thought in which it arose." (*RM* 126.) Hence no set of Jesus' teachings can be seen as providing the potentially revelatory content for Christians of all centuries. Also, beginning with explicit doctrines, e.g., the incarnation or the resurrection, would make the theologian guilty of that irrational heteronomy of which he is often charged by the philosopher. For he would not simply be starting with convictions rooted in his immediate experience.

Third, the potentially revelatory content must nevertheless provide the theologian with a *distinctively Christian starting point* for all his reflection. Otherwise all the problems associated with the idea of a purely natural theology arise. Formally, the problem is that the employment of a non-Christian philosophical position to verify the Christian revelation actually means a denial of the revelatory character of the Christian content. For if the non-Christian knowledge is used to judge the truth of the Christian faith, then this other knowledge is taken to be a higher knowledge. It is this realization that has led some to reject the idea of allowing philosophical reflection any place in theology.

Substantively, the problem is that the results of the so-called natural theology are in considerable tension with the basic notions of God, man, and the world implicit in the Biblical tradition in general and Jesus' message in particular. Besides the tensions we have seen in Tillich, Schleiermacher, and Bultmann, a most striking example is provided by the eleventh-century theologian Anselm, who had accepted the essentially Greek philosophical assumptions about God's total impassibility. In the form of a prayer, he says:

> But, although it is better for thee to be . . . compassionate [and] passionless, than not to be these things; how art thou . . . at once compassionate and passionless? For, if thou art passionless, thou dost not feel sympathy for the wretched; but this it is to be compassionate.[1]

Anselm's answer is that God is compassionate in the sense that the wretched experience the *effect* of compassion, but that God himself is "affected by no sympathy for wretchedness." This provides another reason why the revelatory content cannot be identified with particular doctrines. Besides being less explicit than particular doctrines, the Christian revelation must be understood as being *much more fundamental*. The theologian cannot simply add the content of revelation to some doctrines derived from another source. *All* his reflection must be rooted in a distinctively Christian perspective.

Implicit in the foregoing is a fourth point, that the revelatory content must be a *cognitive* content. That is, it must affirm something about reality which could in principle be thought to be true. This is required if Christian thought is to have a distinctively Christian starting point. It is also required if the Christian revelation is to be susceptible to some type of verification, which earlier we saw to be necessary.

The manner in which the Christian revelation can be conceived so as to meet these requirements has already been suggested. The requirement of rationality can be met by the recognition that every conceptualized understanding of reality is based upon some nonrational starting point. This starting point can be termed a "vision of reality." [2] This refers to a preconceptual way of seeing things, of structuring one's experience prior to any conceptualization of it. This vision of reality is nonrational in that it is not argued to, but is itself the basis from which one's rational judgments are made. It is not "irrational," however, for that term would imply that there is something about beginning with such a preconceptual basis that is contrary to the essence of human reasoning. It would suggest that there is some other way to proceed. But that is not the case. The human thinker necessarily begins with some intuition as to what is real and important, whether this be called a "model," "root metaphor," "existential self-understanding," "blik," or "vision of reality." That this is the case is one of the great discoveries of modern thought. The thinker's metaphysics is an attempt to develop a conceptualization of reality that both embodies his preconceptual vision and is self-consistent and adequate to all the facts of experience.

Once this is recognized, any difference in principle between the philosopher and the theologian disappears. Both have received a way of seeing things from some tradition. The vision of reality common to a tradition can be called its "faith." Hence, the philosopher and the theologian each come out of a community of faith, and their thought is an explication and at the same time a defense of the faiths of their respective communities. The difference becomes merely formal, and a matter of degree. The one whom we call a theologian is more consciously aware of his indebtedness to his tradition for his own faith perspective.[3] And because of this he will give explicit attention to those events which are central to his community's perspective. Also, the theologian will focus primarily upon matters of "ultimate concern," while the person whose self-image is that of a philosopher will more likely spread his reflection over a wider range of issues. However, this is only a generalization, since there are some philosophers who speak primarily about matters of ultimate meaning and destiny, and since it is doubtful whether there are any philosophical issues that do not somehow have bearing on the more distinctively theological issues.[4]

Accordingly, if the Christian revelatory content is understood as the Christian vision of reality, the charge of theology's irrationality is overcome. The theologian, in beginning with revelation, is not subjecting his thought to some heteronomous authority, but is simply reflecting upon reality in terms of the way he himself *sees* reality. His reflection, carried out in terms of the Christian vision of reality but also informed by scientific, historical, and axiological beliefs, may lead him either to disagree or essentially to agree with his community's past formulations of its faith.

It should be stressed that this is not a form of the *tu quoque* ("you also") argument, which William Bartley has rightly criticized. The *tu quoque* is an argument based on a recognition of the fact that rationality can never fully justify a starting point. In this argument the theologian says to the philosopher, "You too must begin with an irrational commitment, so my own faith commitment is not to be criticized." Bartley counters this by distinguishing between being *convinced* of a position's truth, and being *committed* to it, so that one intends to hold to it, regardless of the arguments that may be marshaled against it. The difference is that one who is convinced but not committed can continually allow his position to be subject to criticism.[5] Bartley's proposal, following Karl Popper, is that we modify the modern idea of what constitutes a "rational" position. To be rational a position does not have to be fully justifiable. It must only be open to maximal criticism. The position advocated here is that (ideally) the Christian theologian is not committed to the truth of the Christian vision of reality. He is convinced, as long as he remains a Christian, that his starting point is the best one, but (ideally) he allows it to be subjected to all types of relevant criticism. In other words, the question of a possible conflict between his commitment to Christian faith and a commitment to truth does not arise. He is committed to seeking truth, and he is convinced that his Christian perspective points him in the right direction.

Thus far I have discussed how theology can be based on revelation and still be recognized as a rational enterprise. Another basic question regarding the Christian belief in Jesus as God's decisive revelation is how Jesus can be understood by us as expressing the essential truth about reality, in view of the unacceptability of the explicit imagery he employed, based as it was upon an outdated world view. The identification of the objective or giving side of revelation with Jesus' underlying vision of reality points to an answer to this question. It is the vision of reality expressed through his imagery that is of decisive importance. Whereas no finality can be claimed for Jesus on the level of the history of ideas, it is possible that his expression of a vision of God, man, and the world, and of their interrelatedness, might be unsurpassable.

The distinction intended between the two levels at which Jesus' message can be interpreted can perhaps be clarified by comparison with another view. Adolf von Harnack is famous for his distinction between the "kernel" and the "husk" of Jesus' message. He meant thereby to answer the question as to "the essence of Christianity" by specifying that element in all forms of Christian thought that is "common to all the forms" and is of "permanent validity."[6] Thus expressed, his distinction sounds similar to the one in the present essay. However, in regard to Jesus, it becomes instead the distinction between that which Jesus shared with his contemporaries, and that which was peculiar to him. Hence, in regard to the message of the coming of the Kingdom of God, the "husk" was the traditional idea that the Kingdom would come in the future, in an external way. The real "kernel" was the idea that was original with Jesus, that the Kingdom is already here, and that it comes internally, to the person's soul.[7]

Rather than distinguishing between two different levels in Jesus' message, Harnack distinguishes between two sets of ideas on the same level. One set of ideas is said to be obviously mythological and erroneous, but the other set is thought to be directly valid for men today. This type of distinction ignores the fact that all of a person's thought expresses the conceptions of his time, as Bultmann has said. Here Bultmann's procedure is more valid. We are not simply to eliminate the obviously mythological elements, but to interpret them. Rather than making arbitrary selections, we need a methodological distinction. The real core of Jesus' message is not a set of ideas that stand alongside his mythological conceptions, but the vision of reality that is expressed *through* these conceptions. The task of indicating the content of this vision of reality is reserved for Chapter 8. For the present the question is the formal one as to how such a vision of reality could be held to be true.

A vision of reality is a cognitive matter. It is a "meaning," which can be true or false.[8] But, being preconceptual, it could never be examined for its truth value simply in and of itself, since it can never be thus communicated. It can only be expressed in terms of an explicit conceptuality. Hence, different visions of reality cannot be directly compared with each other in order to judge their relative merits. Rather, they can only be judged indirectly, by comparing the various conceptualizations of reality in which the various visions of reality are embodied.[9] The comparison is made in terms of the philosophical criteria of consistency, adequacy to the facts, and illuminating power. This third criterion, illuminating power, is really a dimension of adequacy, yet it deserves special emphasis, since a really good description of reality should not merely be such that we would grudgingly admit that it is compatible with the facts of experience. Rather, it should become self-evidencing as it helps us to see facets and dimensions of reality that we had not noticed before, thereby giving us the conviction that we are seeing things truly for the first time.

Accordingly, to the degree that a philosophical conceptualization of reality that embodies and explicates the Christian vision of reality can be judged superior on these grounds to rival metaphysical positions that embody other visions of reality, the cognitive essence of Christian faith can thereby be said to be verified, and Jesus can thereby continue to be regarded as having expressed the basic truth about God, man, and the world.

Of course, the task of verifying a vision of reality is not as simple as the above statement seems to imply, due to a circularity inherent in the criterion of "adequacy to the facts of experience." [10] Along with the discovery that every explicit outlook presupposes a vision of reality comes the awareness that what the "facts of experience" are for any person is at least partially determined by his preconceptual perspective, for it involves a way of structuring experience. It is this awareness that has led to much relativism, as it is held that there is no way to verify or falsify visions of reality: "There is no arguing about 'bliks.'" [11]

But against this total relativism of perspectives it has been pointed out that the paranoiac also has his "blik," and few of us hesitate to call it wrong. This is admittedly an extreme case. But it points out that we assume that there is a distinction between the way things *really* are outside the person, and the way they *appear* to him. The fact that the paranoiac may perceive his wife and doctor as plotting to kill him does not mean that they in fact are. In other words, when speaking of something as being adequate to the facts of experience, we presuppose a distinction between the facts *in themselves,* independently of their being experienced by the person in question, and the facts *as* they are experienced by him. This does not mean a dualism between "facts" and "subjective experience." The person's experience of the facts is itself a new fact, and as such it is to be distinguished from the way the facts are experienced by someone else, or even by the person himself in a later moment.

This commonsense distinction implies a realist position. This realism means, first, that although our preconceptual perspective may structure our experience, it does not constitute the reality of that which is experienced. The facts that enter into any act of experience have their reality prior to, and, therefore, independently of, that experience of them. Second, this realism means that even the facts as they are experienced by us are not *totally* structured by the perspective we bring to the experience but are partially determined by their own inherent characteristics. Accordingly, the recognition of the influence of one's vision of reality upon what he judges to be the facts need not lead to total relativism. The irrepressible objectivity of reality will survive all inadequate perceptions of it, and will continue to impose itself on experience, so that a felt tension between reality and appearance will never be totally lacking. Although the drive for truth may be "the weakest of all passions," it is nevertheless a passion, and it will finally not let us rest content with this felt tension. Also, to the extent that our perceptions of things are inadequate to the things themselves, the behavior of the things will run counter to our expectations —a fact that has rightly been stressed by the pragmatists.

Accordingly, although the verification of visions of reality is no simple matter, it can in principle, and therefore to a degree in fact, be carried out. The facts to which the rival theories must be adequate do have objectivity, despite the partial distorting and blinding caused by certain perspectives. Furthermore, to introduce the other side of the coin, man is able to some degree to transcend his own perspective. He can, through discipline, learn imaginatively to participate in other visions and thereby learn to lift his own to consciousness, making it one among others. Because of this dual transcendence, the transcendence of the facts over our perspectival perception and the transcendence of man over his own perspective, a certain degree of objectivity in the evaluation of competing visions of reality is possible.

Thus far I have suggested that the identification of the Christian revelatory content with a preconceptual but cognitive vision of reality avoids the objections raised by the idea of revealed doctrines, and it nevertheless provides theology with a distinctively Christian starting point. It also offers a way in principle of seeing Jesus as having expressed the basic truth about reality, and allows an indirect way of testing the truth of this content which Christians consider revelatory. This way of conceiving the relation between faith and reason also overcomes the justifiable formal and substantive objections many have raised against the use of philosophy in theology. For if the philosophy that is used is itself based upon the Christian vision of reality, it is a Christian philosophy. Hence, using it to verify the truth of the Christian vision of reality does not mean a denial of the revelatory character of the latter by judging it from an alien perspective which is thereby itself implicitly accepted as the highest revelation. Rather, the Christian vision of reality is allowed to prove itself, as every claim to truth finally must, by being self-authenticating. It authenticates itself by giving rise to a conceptual understanding of reality which is judged superior in terms of the criteria of consistency, adequacy, and illuminating power. The use of these criteria to test the veracity of all reputed revelations is not objectionable in the way that the use of a natural theology is, since they are purely formal in character, and can be said to belong to rationality as such.

In the present essay, the philosophy whose excellence is appealed to is the process philosophy inspired and largely developed by Alfred North Whitehead. It has rightly been said to be a "Christian philosophy" in the broad sense in which the term is being employed here.[12] Because of this, the use of this philosophy to explicate Christianity's underlying vision of reality will not lead to the distortions that were produced by the use of philosophies which were not at all, or at least not fundamentally, affected by the Biblical vision of reality. In the Biblical vision of things, the person is the locus of the real and the valuable. The supreme reality is a supreme person. The world is the creation of this personal, purposive God. Hence the world is finite on the one hand, yet good and purposed on the other. And God is interacting with his creatures, working in terms of his purpose for them. Hence, history is important, being the locus of the interaction between God and man, of man's obedient and disobedient responses to God's action, and of God's responses to man's responses.

Traditional Christian theologies had trouble with these notions. Anselm's difficulty in reconciling the Biblical idea of God's compassionate response to man with the Greek idea of divine impassibility provides a classic example. Schleiermacher had to see the idea of God's "mercy" as more fitted to homiletics than to dogmatics. In fact, most of the history of theology can be read as the history of the tension between the Christian vision of reality, which the theologians derived from the Bible and the liturgy, and the alien philosophical assumptions in terms of which they tried to conceptualize this vision. In the program of "faith seeking understanding," the "understanding" reached often involved the recognition that much of the "faith" was to be taken as merely figurative.

But with the process philosophy of Whitehead and Hartshorne there is no such dilemma of trying to reconcile doctrines of God's interaction with the world, his purposiveness, sympathy, and even displeasure, with a conception of God as totally immutable. The Greek stress on immutability is not given precedence over the personhood of God, but is relegated to the status of mere abstraction. Nor is there the problem of reconciling man's freedom and sin with God's eternal omni-causality. God is a causal factor in all things, but never the total cause of anything. In short, there is not the problem of trying to explicate a *vision* of reality as dynamic within a *conceptualization* of reality as static. Process philosophy emphasizes as primary the notions of history, becoming, novelty, purposiveness, freedom, response, and mutual involvement that reflect the impact of the Judeo-Christian vision of reality upon Western man's sensibilities and thought.

Because of the canonization of the Scriptures, and because of their use in the church, this vision of reality was preserved and allowed to ferment in men's minds, even in the minds of the sophisticated few who knew the official theologies. With the elevation of the importance of the Bible in the Reformation, and with the criticism of the scholastic theologies, the way was opened for the Biblical vision of reality to have more far-reaching effects. The philosophies of Leibnitz and Hegel, with their attempts to give more weight to becoming, represent important steps in this regard. Many others followed. But it can be said without exaggeration that Whitehead's philosophy represents the major breakthrough thus far in Christian faith's search for a metaphysics that would explicate its fundamental notion of reality.

Whitehead himself described Christian faith in this way, i.e., as "a religion seeking a metaphysic." It could develop, because "it starts with a tremendous notion about the world . . . derived . . . from our comprehension of the sayings and actions of certain supreme lives." In regard to Jesus in particular, the record indicates that he carried out a revision of the Jewish religion based upon a "first-hand intuition into the nature of things." But Jesus did not give us formalized doctrines. Rather,

"Christ gave his life. It is for Christians to discern the doctrine." (*RM* 50.) These and other passages (e.g., *PR* 520 f.; *AI* 211–218) indicate that Whitehead saw his own philosophy as providing the most adequate approximation thus far to that metaphysics for which Christianity has been seeking to explicate the "tremendous notion about the world" inherent in faith's acceptance of Jesus as the Christ.

This chapter began with a number of factors that an adequate doctrine of revelation would have to embody. The conformity of the present account to these requirements has now been discussed. However, a few additional comments may serve to make the position clearer.

The identification of the content of revelation with the Christian vision of reality is also a statement as to the essence of Christian faith on its cognitive side. Some have recently despaired of finding a cognitive essence of faith, of finding any aspect of the *fides quae creditur* that is the same for all centuries. Accordingly, they have either rejected the idea of an essence of Christianity altogether or tried to identify it with a certain mode of existence, a *fides qua creditur*. But unless there is an essence of Christianity that can be indicated, it would not be meaningful to apply the adjective "Christian" to Paul, Origen, Augustine, Aquinas, Luther, Ritschl, Bultmann, and the brothers Niebuhr. Yet we sense that this is meaningful. Hence it is a historical as well as a theological task to indicate what all these men, with their diverse theologies, have in common. And to see the common element solely in terms of a recommended mode of existence would be inadequate. It would not do justice to their own self-understandings, as they all believed the Christian life to be rooted in distinctively Christian beliefs. And it would be inadequate theologically. As Frederick Ferré has pointed out, even if the emotional and volitional value of one's vision or model of reality is in some sense more central, this value will nevertheless be lost if the model's cognitive value cannot continue to be affirmed.[13]

The best way to grasp the Christian vision of reality is to

compare the formulations of theologians such as the above, on the one hand, with religio-philosophical systems of other traditions, such as Greek, Hindu, and Buddhist, on the other. That which Jesus and all these Christian theologians have in common over against the other imageries and conceptualities, will indicate what is meant by the Christian vision of reality.

Of course, this procedure is complicated considerably by the fact that the influence between a vision of reality and a philosophical conceptuality is not only a one-way affair, from the former to the latter. Rather, the conceptuality, if it is somewhat inappropriate for articulating the underlying vision or model, can alter the vision itself.[14] And this happened in Christian theology, almost from the beginning, as theologians tried to explicate the Christian faith in the available Greek philosophical conceptuality. This conceptuality had by no means merely a formal significance; it was itself rooted in a vision of reality. Hence, insofar as the acceptance of the conceptuality entailed the acceptance of the vision underlying it, the Christian theologians were caught in the conflict not only of trying to express the Christian faith through an alien conceptuality, but of trying to reconcile two different visions of reality. Insofar as the alien conceptuality and its underlying model relegated the Christian vision to the status of the merely figurative, to this degree this vision itself was in effect denied.

Accordingly, to say that the Christian vision of reality—for which Jesus' message is normative—is the self-identical cognitive essence of the Christian faith down through the centuries is first of all a normative statement. It affirms that this vision of things should have, and in principle could have, remained essentially the same through these twenty centuries, even with all the changes that would have been inevitable at the doctrinal level. Although we can be grateful for the job the formative theologians performed in reconciling (Biblical) "faith" and (Greek) "reason," which was a necessary condition for the survival of Christianity, we can still maintain that they could have allowed their faith that (the Hebrew) Jesus was the de-

cisive revelation of reality more radically to inform their thinking. The reconciliation could have involved quite radically re-
vising the formulations of the insights of the Greek experience,
rather than primarily taking these formulations as the limited
but valid conclusions of "reason" as such. In particular, the
reconciliation could have involved allowing Jesus to revolu-
tionize the philosophical concept of God, rather than reconciling their assertions about Jesus to this non-Biblical idea of
God. Thus from the very beginning the tension between "faith
and reason" could have been considerably less.

Nevertheless the identification of the Christian vision of reality with that which provides the common element in Christian
thought is also a descriptive statement. For through the life of
the church this vision had been communicated to the theologians prior to and alongside their exposure to Greek thought
and the theology informed by it. Hence, its influence remains
in their thinking, providing the motive force of their construc-
tions and ever again causing inconsistencies in their thought,
insofar as they attempted to be adequate to the Biblical and
liturgical roots of their thought.

This fact, that the Christian vision of things was not totally
distorted by its subordination to an inappropriate conceptuality, shows the importance of theology's continually returning
to its roots. As Whitehead says, "Religions commit suicide when
they find their inspirations in their dogmas," rather than in "the
primary expressions of the intuitions of the finest types of religious lives." (*RM* 138.) And he says that "the essence of
Christianity is the appeal to the life of Christ as a revelation
of the nature of God and of his agency in the world." (*AI* 214.)
The present essay agrees with the advocates of the "new quest,"
over against most of Bultmann's explicit statements, that it is
the vision of reality that came to expression in Jesus himself
that is normative for Christian faith. This is implicit in the
basic Christian confession that Jesus is the Christ, that it is in
him that saving knowledge of God was and is revealed.

The idea of a preconceptual but cognitive vision of reality as the essence of Christian faith on its cognitive side also allows us to indicate that which grounds the appropriateness of Christian existence, and thereby to specify the task of Christian theology in each generation. James M. Robinson has observed that the early Christian belief in Jesus as cosmocrator meant existentially that to be a Christian is to be "in step with the universe." [15] The task for contemporary theology is not to try to hold to as many of the early Christian formulas as possible through ingenious reinterpretations of their meaning. Rather, the task is to formulate a conceptuality of God, man, and the world that will be compatible with our modern knowledge and relevant to our sensibilities, that will have the same significance for men today that the New Testament formulations had for first-century men.

And the idea of Jesus as cosmocrator obviously could not have had any existential significance unless it had been believed to be cognitively true. Hence if the present-day theologian is to show that Christian faith puts one "in step with the universe," his reconceptualization of faith's underlying grasp of reality cannot be simply anthropological, as Bultmann advocates, but must also be theistic and cosmological. Also, the theologian cannot simply describe what beliefs must be held if Christian existence is to be possible, and then inform us that these things are not really true, as Tillich does. Man cannot base his existence on notions that he is trying to hold "as if" they were true. As Whitehead says, men's character and conduct will be shaped by "intimate convictions" that are "sincerely held."

It is the formal thesis of the present essay that Whitehead's metaphysics provides us with a conceptuality never before equaled in its combination of appropriateness to the Christian faith and intrinsic excellence as measured by the normal rational and empirical criteria. In the following chapter this conceptuality will be sketched. Those previously unfamiliar with process thought should be able to form a provisional judgment as to the consistency and adequacy of the scheme, even from this highly inadequate account. However, the concern of the explication will be primarily to exhibit the appropriateness of this conceptuality to the Christian faith, and to stress those features which are most essential to the later chapters. A more definitive judgment as to the philosophic excellence of process thought can only be based upon more adequate secondary studies and upon the writings of Whitehead and Hartshorne themselves.

CHAPTER 7

A Process Conceptualization of Reality

THE PRESENT CHAPTER is designed to fulfill two purposes. First, it is intended to present process philosophy as a coherent explication of the Christian vision of reality. However, it fulfills this first purpose only to an extremely limited extent. It is primarily intended to provide concepts for the task of conceiving God's relation to the man Jesus. Accordingly, only selected aspects of process philosophy are emphasized. For example, whereas I spoke at the close of Chapter 2 about the need to develop concepts for illuminating *all* occasions, rather than only human ones, the focus in this chapter's discussion of the world is primarily on man. However, enough is said about nature in general that the reader can infer, e.g., what type of theology of ecology could be developed along process lines.

I will try to introduce the concepts essential for the remainder of this essay in such a way that the reader previously unfamiliar with process philosophy can understand them. However, because of limitations of space, I can offer little explanation, few examples, and no arguments.

Actual Entities as Actual Occasions. In the first place, Whitehead understands every actual entity to be atomic. It has long been accepted that the ultimate building blocks of the universe are spatially atomic; but Whitehead also means that they are *temporally* atomic. Each actual entity is an event, an occurrence, a happening, an occasion. Whitehead often calls them "actual occasions."

Experience and Subjectivity. Every actual occasion can also be called an "occasion of experience." This does not mean that all occasions have consciousness. By far the majority of the actual occasions in the universe do not. But it does mean that there is no such thing as "vacuous actuality," i.e., no individual actuality which is "merely matter," merely an object to be experienced by other actualities. Rather, every actual entity is a pulse of experience which is "something individual for its own sake." (*PR* 135.) It is a throb of emotion, a brief moment of self-enjoyment. This means that every occasion is a subject, something for itself, not merely an object, something for others.

Prehension, Objective Datum, and Subjective Form. An actual entity's subjectivity involves its "prehension," its taking account, of other entities. Except that Whitehead prefers the term "prehend" to Berkeley's term "perceive," he would agree that an actual entity is one whose essence is to perceive. There are two aspects to every prehension, besides the actual occasion that is the subject of the prehension. There is the content of the prehension, termed the "objective datum." And there is the "subjective form" with which it is felt. The term "feeling," which is synonymous with a positive prehension, carries this double connotation: *something* is felt, and it is felt *in a certain way.* For example, when I prehend my mother-in-law, the content of what I prehend is the objective datum (my mother-in-law *as she appears to me*), and this datum is felt with some emotion.

Subjects and Objects. After an actual occasion is a subject, it becomes an object. When its brief moment of immediacy or subjectivity is past, it is an object to be prehended by others. *Then* it is an object, whose essence is to be prehended (although it is prehended as having-been-a-subject, which distinguishes it from possibilities that are merely objects). There is no ontological dualism within the actual world. An actual occasion in the mode of being present is a subject; in the mode of being past it is an object. For example, a moment of one's own past experience is no longer a subject; it is only an object to be prehended by the present. Actual occasions come into being as subjects, then pass from subjectivity into objectivity as they are prehended by new subjects.

Enduring Objects and Corpuscular Societies. Of those individuals which endure through time, such as an electron, a proton, an atom, a molecule, or a mind, each consists of a series of actual occasions. Each member of such a series is, in its moment of immediacy, a subject that prehends the past members of the series and repeats certain structural characteristics common to all of them. This new member then becomes an object for the occasion which follows after it, and so on. All these things are routes of actual occasions, and as such they endure through time and are called "enduring objects."

Those things which are big enough to activate the human senses of sight and touch are composed of myriads of these enduring objects. These large bodies are not themselves actual entities, but are "corpuscular societies." Some of these have no subjectivity of their own. They are termed "democratic societies" because none of the enduring objects that compose them exercises a dominating influence over the rest. Examples are rocks, sticks, and plants. It is not a mistake to think of them as objects with no subjectivity. The only mistake is to think of them as the finally real things, or to think of the finally real things in analogy with these gross objects.

Living Persons. Some corpuscular societies have a "dominant" member. These corpuscular societies we call animals. Whitehead's technical term for them is "monarchical societies." There is one enduring object in the society which has preeminence over the rest. The other enduring objects are structured in such a way that the dominant member receives information from them, and in turn exercises a rather decisive controlling influence over them. This is especially the case in animals with a central nervous system. By virtue of this dominant member's influence, the monarchical society is a real individual, whereas the democratic society (e.g., the rock or the plant) is not.

This special type of enduring object, normally called a mind, or psyche, is technically called a "living person." This term is not reserved only for the mind or psyche of a human being, but applies to the psyche of all the higher animals, for it is used for any enduring object with sufficient complexity and novelty to merit the term "living." Whitehead also refers to the living person as a "soul." He says that "it is not a mere question of having a soul or of not having a soul. The question is, How much, if any?" (*AI* 267.) Correlative with the amount of complexity, freedom, and novelty of which an actual entity is capable is the degree of self-value its experiences can have. That is, the more complex an entity is, the more variety it can unify into a harmonious experience, and therefore the more intensive its experience can be. And it is the combination of the variety, harmony, and intensity of an experience which is the measure of its felt value. (*AI* 324.)

Actual Entities Present in Others. An actual occasion is a process of becoming. In this process, several prehensions of past actual entities are brought into a unity of experience. Each of the prehensions includes a past entity (or group of such), so that the past occasions are present in the becoming occasion. (*PR* 33, 35, 323.) This means that the old substance philosophy is radically rejected. In that philosophy an actuality was called a "substance," and a substance was defined, most clearly by Descartes, as "that which required nothing but itself in order to exist." In Whitehead's philosophy, an actual occasion is *constituted* by its prehension of other actual occasions. Hence a relation to others belongs to the essence of an actual entity, not merely to its accidental features, making this a social philosophy *par excellence*. Whitehead even sometimes calls an actual occasion a "superject" instead of a subject, to stress that it is not *first* something in itself which only secondarily takes account of other entities. (*PR* 234.)

Efficient and Final Causation, and Subjective Aim. To speak of the present entity's prehending a previous entity is simply one way of speaking of the previous entity's causal influence on the present occasion. This is Whitehead's doctrine of efficient causation, of how the past affects the present. The past occasion exerts its causation simply by being there to be prehended, hence, by being what it was.

In many philosophies, efficient *causation* has been interpreted to mean *complete determination*. Hence, the past was understood as totally determining the present, and of course, the present was understood as totally determining the future. Freedom in any real sense was denied. But, for Whitehead, to say that one entity has causal efficacy for another is not to say that it completely determines it. There are two reasons for this. First, there is never simply one past entity acting as the efficient cause of a becoming occasion. There is always a multiplicity of causes. In fact, no absolute line can be drawn between those past entities which exert an influence and those which do not. By the principle of relativity, in some way the whole past conspires to create the present. (*PR* 33, 340.) Second, even the totality of efficient causation does not exhaust the causality involved in an actual occasion. For each occasion is to some degree *causa sui*, i.e., self-caused. This is another way of saying that each actuality has some degree of freedom. This can be expressed by speaking of the final causation of the occasion. It has some degree of power to determine what it will be, what possibility for its own being it will actualize.

Belief in both efficient and final causation is possible in the following way: Efficient causation is what occurs *between* occasions, in the process of transition from one occasion to another. The new occasion must take account, in some way, of the occasions in its past. Final causation, on the other hand, occurs *within* the actual occasion, in the process of concrescence, of becoming concrete. *That* the past be prehended is necessary; but precisely *how* it will be responded to is finally decided by the occasion itself (even though in low-grade actual entities this freedom or self-causation is insignificant). The final causation of the occasion is its aim toward an ideal of itself. It is this "subjective aim" which determines exactly how the past will be received into the present experience.

Objective Datum and Initial Datum. The relation between a present, becoming occasion and a past occasion has been termed both efficient causation and prehension. It is also called "objectification." The past occasion is objectified by the present one when the latter prehends the former. We have already seen that this means that the past actual occasion is present in the prehending occasion. *But it is not present in its subjective immediacy,* as we have also seen. It is present as an object. This is brought out by saying that it is objectified.

But there is another way in which the past occasion is generally not present in its fullness in the occasion prehending it. Objectification by finite entities always involves *abstraction.* The former occasion is prehended by the present one in terms of one of the former occasion's prehensions. That aspect of the past occasion that is objectified by the present entity belongs to the latter's "objective datum." The past occasion as it was there and then is termed the "initial datum." To use Kant's terminology, the objective datum is the "phenomenon." This is the past occasion functioning as object for another. The initial datum is the "noumenon," what the entity was "in itself."

Hence, according to Whitehead's metaphysics one can say formally what something is "in itself," for every actuality in itself is a subject, an occasion of experience. Even though one could never conceptualize the full actuality of any particular entity in itself, one can at least say what he *means* when making a distinction between what something was in itself (in its moment of subjectivity) and what it is now (in its effect upon others). What it is now, as objective datum, is an abstraction from its subjective significance for itself, and also from its full content.

Truth. The notion of truth is central to this essay, but I have not yet given any definition of it. This has been possible because Whitehead's understanding of the meaning of "truth" corresponds closely with what is normally understood by this term. Generally, when people ask about truth, they are asking whether a certain statement is true. Or, to be more precise, they are asking whether a certain "proposition," which is a *meaning* that a verbal statement attempts to articulate, is true. When a subject entertains a certain proposition, he is making a supposition about certain actualities. He is connecting a definite predicative pattern (a set of possibilities, or "eternal objects") with a logical subject (an actual entity, or a nexus of entities). (*AI* 312 f.) For example, if I say, "Smith is angry," I am postulating that a certain actuality, termed "Smith," is embodying the subjective form "anger." If that is really the case, then the proposition is true—there is correspondence between the proposition and reality.

This correspondence theory of truth is not intended as a means for verifying propositions. It is a statement of what conditions must exist for a proposition to be true. Also it should be obvious that for a proposition to be true does not mean that it totally describes the initial datum. It only means that the proposition states something correct about at least one of the prehensions of the actuality that is the logical subject of the proposition. For example, to say that at 3:00 P.M. yesterday Smith was angry with his son does not exhaust the content of his experience. He may also have been angry with his wife, hungry, and anxious to play golf. But if he really was angry with his son, the statement is true, even if it is not the total truth. It correctly describes the subjective form (anger) and objective datum (his son) of one of his prehensions.

Furthermore, to speak of "correspondence" between a proposition and some actuality is not to speak of *identity*. For there is obviously no identity between the proposition, "Smith is angry," and Smith's actually being angry. One of these is merely a meaning, possibly true, and the other one is a stubborn fact. The difference is that in the proposition the actuality and the predicate are together only in the *mode of abstract possibility*, whereas in the actuality they are together in the *mode of real-*

ization. (*AI* 313 f.) For Smith to contemplate the possibility of himself embodying anger is one thing; to actualize this is quite another. Yet there is a correspondence; for the same actuality (Smith) and the same possibility (anger) are together.

Subjective Aim and Ideal (*Initial*) *Aim.* The notion of "subjective aim" has already been introduced. The actual occasion decides how to respond to the past in terms of its subjective aim. But what is the origin of this aim itself? It is at this point that the discussion of Whitehead's understanding of God must begin. His notion of God was introduced into his philosophy because his analysis of experience and the world demanded an actuality having many characteristics in common with "God" as traditionally understood.[1] Although no real explanation can be given here, the main ideas can be indicated. Whitehead was led to affirm the existence of an actuality who served as an explanation both of the order and the novelty in the world. I will discuss only the latter.

When new possibilities are actualized in the world, this is not explainable in terms of the efficient causality of the past actual entities in the world; for they had not actualized these possibilities. And by the "ontological principle" that only actual entities can act, the ingression of new possibilities into the world cannot be explained by the causal action of the possibilities themselves. Hence the fact that novel possibilities do sometimes exert an influence on emerging occasions can only be explained by an actuality whose nature it is to envisage unrealized possibilities and to exert an influence (efficient causation) on worldly actual occasions to actualize them. It is because Tillich does not speak of God as an actuality, and because Bultmann will not venture to indicate what type of reality the term "God" designates, that neither one can render intelligible the assertion that we are confronted by normative values, essences, or possibilities.[2]

This influence of God on actual entities Whitehead called the "ideal aim" of an occasion; he also called it the "initial aim."

These two terms express the fact that it is an aim at an *ideal* with which the occasion *begins*. Hence every actual occasion begins with a prehension of God. God himself is the initial datum of the prehension, and the occasion's initial aim is the objective datum of the prehension.

But if the occasion begins with an aim which is supplied by God, is not its freedom denied? No, because the occasion has the power either to actualize the highest aim presented by God, or to choose some other aim which is a real possibility for it. That is, the occasion has, within the datum of its prehension of God, a gradation of possibilities. At the top (one could say) is the ideal aim toward which God is luring it. But there are also lesser possibilities associated with it, and one of these can be chosen in its process of self-creation. The occasion finally decides its own ideal of itself toward which it aims. When this decision is made, the change from "initial aim" to "subjective aim" has been effected.[3] Insofar as the subjective aim is directed toward a lesser possibility, this transition corresponds to the "fall" from essence to existence of which Tillich speaks. It is because of this freedom (however negligible it may be in the most primitive entities) to make this change that the past actual world of an occasion, including God's purposes for it, cannot completely determine exactly what it will be.

Anticipation. The subjective aim of an actual occasion is a certain possibility for its own existence that it is aiming to actualize. The final phase of an occasion is termed the "satisfaction," since it brings its moment of subjective immediacy to a close, and since a degree of self-value has been achieved. Every actual occasion, as stated above, has some significance for its own self. There is no actual occasion totally devoid of self-value. An occasion experiences its own existence as intrinsically good: life in the present has intrinsic value. This is clearly in line with one side of Jesus' vision of reality, which will be discussed in Chapter 8. That is to say, the Reign of God—the experience of that which is the final good—is already in the present. Whitehead states this in somewhat poetic language: "There must be some immediate harvest. The good of the Universe cannot lie in indefinite postponement. The Day of Judgment is an important notion; but that Day is always with us." (*AI* 346.)

But Whitehead also says that the subjective aim does not only refer to the present moment; it also anticipates the relevant future. The final phase of an occasion can also be called the "anticipation." (*AI* 248.) Now it is very important to see exactly what is meant by "anticipating" and what the "relevant" future is. "The relevant future consists of those elements in the anticipated future which are felt with effective intensity by the present subject by reason of the real potentiality for them to be derived from itself." (*PR* 41.) Hence, in making my present decision, I anticipate that this decision will contribute to the future. That part of the future which is effectively taken into consideration (perhaps unconsciously) is the *relevant* future as far as that occasion of experience is concerned. Of course, more of the future will probably be affected than I anticipated. An outsider might well think that I should have included more of the future in what I considered relevant. But the relevant future of any actual occasion is defined as that part of the future which *it* considers relevant.

The main point is that, although every occasion's aim is to actualize a certain possibility that will be immediately experienced as good, included in this aim is also a reference to the future.

The point to remember is that the fact that each individual occasion is transcended by the creative urge belongs to the essential constitution of each such occasion. It is not an accident which is irrelevant to the completed constitution of any such occasion. . . . It belongs to the essence of this subject that it pass into objective immortality. Thus its own constitution involves that its own activity in *self*-formation passes into its activity of *other*-formation. . . . The final phase of anticipation is a propositional realization of the essence of the present-subject, in respect to the necessities which it lays upon the future to embody it and to re-enact it so far as compatibility may permit. (*AI* 249, 248.)

Hence it is clear that for Whitehead there is in the present an anticipation of the effects of the present on the not-yet-actual future, and that this is an essential aspect of every moment of experience.

This issue is central for the question as to how the future is to be interpreted in Jesus' vision of reality. In the interpretation given in Chapter 8, God's purpose, as derived from Jesus' preaching of the Reign of God as present and future, is understood as referring to the not-yet-actual future as well as to the present. In Bultmann's interpretation of Jesus, to illustrate by contrast, reference to the future in this sense is not seen as essential. That is, Bultmann discounts the temporal future and speaks only of "futurity" which is an aspect of the present moment of experience. The reason for this is that the analysis of human existence which he accepts (Heidegger's) does not include the element of anticipation in Whitehead's sense.

To be sure, Heidegger speaks much of anticipation. But for him this refers not to what the present can contribute to the future, but to what the anticipation of the future (finally, one's own death) contributes to the quality of the present moment— i.e., it frees one from illusions.[4] Bultmann replaced this notion of Heidegger's (anticipation of death as that which limits man) with the notion of encounter by the word and the neighbor. For Bultmann this is the "futural" element in each moment of experience. A possibility for my present existence can be said to come to me from the future since it comes toward me in the encounter with the word and the neighbor.[5] This possibility coming "from the future" determines my present existence; for it constrains me to decision. On this basis, Bultmann says that for Jesus

the future of the Kingdom of God, then, is not really some-thing which is to come in the course of time. . . . Rather, the Kingdom of God is a power which, although it is entirely

future, wholly determines the present. . . . Future and present are not related in the sense that the Kingdom begins as
a historical fact in the present and achieves its fulfillment in
the future.[6]

Hence in Bultmann's radically anti-social-gospel interpretation
of the underlying meaning of Jesus' message, there is no reference to the effects of present decisions on the temporal future
and no reference to God's purpose for the future toward which
present activity might contribute. This follows naturally, since
in Bultmann's analysis of human experience there is no mention
of this type of anticipation as being an essential ingredient.
Obviously an analysis of the essential meaning of Jesus' message will not include an element which is not thought to correspond with some essential aspect of human existence. The
difference between Bultmann's analysis of Jesus' message and
the one in the present essay illustrates Bultmann's own point
about the effect of a philosophical preunderstanding on historical interpretation, and thus emphasizes the importance of
the question of what philosophy theologians, including Biblical
scholars, presuppose. The results are not merely academic but
have ramifications for the understanding of the relation of
Christian faith to the problems of society.

*Human Experience: Causal Efficacy and Presentational Im-
mediacy.* Much modern theology has been prevented from
talking about God's causal influence on man, at least in any
clear way. This has been in part due to a mechanistic notion
of the world's causal nexus, such that there was no room for
God to act. But it has also been partly due to the pervasiveness
of the sensationalist epistemology. According to this doctrine
of knowledge, man has experience of realities beyond his own
subjective states only through his five senses, if at all. The only
objects of experience, then, especially since sight and touch
have been taken as the privileged senses, would be material
objects (however these be defined). Accordingly, even if God's
reality were allowed, he could not be a possible object of experience.

Whitehead rejects the notion that perception in the "mode of presentational immediacy," which can here be treated as synonymous with sense experience, is the only type of experience of realities beyond the human experiencer. In fact, it is not even the primary mode. Of course, it is prior in the sense that we become conscious of it first and most clearly and distinctly. Temporally, however, it is not the first element in experience, but the last. Experience in the first place is perception in the "mode of causal efficacy" (which is simply a synonym for "prehension").

In the first phase of an occasion of experience there are direct prehensions of all the actual entities in the occasion's past world. In this phase, termed the "causal phase," there is an immediate but generally vague awareness of these past entities as exerting causal efficacy on the present subject. The causal influence consists in the fact that the present occasion must take account of these other actualities in some way, and that the subjective forms of the past feelings that are appropriated impose themselves on the first phase of the present occasion. The first phase is therefore also called the "conformal phase."

Since God is everlasting and omnipresent (cf. our discussion of "God's Infinity," below), he is in the immediate past world of every actual entity, and hence is prehended, or perceived in the mode of causal efficacy, by every occasion of experience. Of course, God will never be "seen," since it is only corpuscular societies (what are normally called "material objects") that become objects of perception in the derivative mode of presentational immediacy.

The World as Incarnating God. As indicated above, when one entity is objectified by another, it is present in the latter. Of course, it is not present in its subjective immediacy, for the moment of subjectivity must pass for the entity to be objectified by another. Since God is the one actuality which is objectified by all other entities, he is present in every actual entity. (*RM* 91, 149.) Whitehead directly speaks of the experience of ideals as being the experience of deity (*MT* 141), and writes of "the actual ideals which are God in the world as it is now" (*RM* 152). He even says that "the world lives by its incarnation of God in itself." (*RM* 149.) He believes that the early Christian theologians made a fundamental metaphysical advance on Plato. Plato had said that the world included "only the image of God, and imitations of his ideas, and never God and his ideas." As for the theologians, "they decided for the direct immanence of God in the one person of Christ. They also decided for some sort of direct immanence of God in the World generally." (*AI* 215 f.) However, Whitehead points out, they made assumptions about the nature of God that prevented this insight from being incorporated into metaphysical views of the world. It is clear that he intends his own philosophy to explicate this notion that God as Holy Spirit is present in the world generally. Hence the problem for a Christology based on Whitehead's philosophy will be to understand, not how God could be present in Jesus, but how God could be present in him in a special way, so that Jesus would be especially revelatory of God's nature.

Man as Significant for Himself and for Others. As is the case with all other actual entities, there is a difference between man's experience in and for itself, and the way it is significant for others. To speak of man's experience in itself is to speak of an actual occasion, or a series of such occasions. Adequately to describe this would mean referring to the many, many prehensions involved, their objective data and subjective forms, and the way these prehensions were brought into a unity. This would entail speaking of the decisions made; and one of these decisions would be that of responding to God's initial aim (even if it is not thought of as such by the person). And as indicated above, each occasion of experience achieves a certain "satisfaction," which means that there is always an element of self-value, or significance for itself.

To speak of a man's significance for others is to speak of the way in which his experience has been objectified by others. In the first place, this would mean how his psyche was objectified by the various entities constituting his body. But in the more customary sense the question is how his bodily action has been objectified by another person—the bodily action usually being taken as expressing accurately the feelings and intentions of the psyche. Obviously, one person can be significant for another person in all sorts of ways. Someone may be seen as expressing love, hate, or indifference toward me. He may be seen as exemplifying the depravity or the glory of man. Or he may be experienced as expressing the love of God to me and all men.

Each of these objectifications of another person involves entertaining (perhaps unconsciously) a proposition about him. Now each propositional feeling implies something about the person himself; i.e., the predicate of the proposition is assumed really to correspond to the logical subject of the proposition, the person's psyche. If I react to a certain action of yours as expressing your hostility toward me, my interpretation necessarily is that you really have hostile feelings toward me, and that your action expressed it. Hence, the question of truth is implicit in every response of one being to another.

God as a Living Person. In the above discussion I have used the term "actuality" for God, since I use this term to designate either an actual entity or a temporally ordered society. Whitehead himself spoke of God as an actual entity. But it has been argued, cogently I believe, that it is much more consistent with Whitehead's principles to speak of God as a living person.[7] This means that God is thought of, in analogy with the human psyche, as a strand of occasions of experience. Accordingly, God's relations with other actualities can be understood as exemplifying the general principles applying to all such relations.

God as Dipolar. Many of the traditional attributes are applied to God by process thinkers. But also many things are affirmed of him that were not affirmed by classical theists. In fact, at first glance it may seem as if contradictory predicates are asserted. For example, it is said that God is both eternal and becoming, both absolute and relative, both independent and dependent. How can this be?

Here the thought of Charles Hartshorne, who has worked out the implications of Whitehead's suggestions about God much more closely than Whitehead himself did, will be followed primarily. A fundamental doctrine of Hartshorne is that God is dipolar—i.e., there are two poles to God's full reality. One pole is the abstract one. It is God's unchanging essence, those characteristics which God always embodies. In this respect God is strictly eternal, unchanging, absolute, and infinite—for those characteristics which constitute God's deity or divine essence could not possibly change, or God would not remain God. But this aspect of God is merely an abstraction from God. It is not concrete or actual, just as a man's "character" is not an actuality, but only an abstraction from his full concrete reality. To speak of a man's "character" is to speak of a set of characteristics which are embodied in each (or most) of a man's concrete experiences.

The other pole is the concrete one. This refers to God as actual. God's concrete experience in each moment is more than that in him which is absolute, his abstract essence. For example, God's omniscience belongs to his absolute character, his abstract essence. But to refer to God's omniscience is not to refer to his concrete experience, but only to the fact that, whatever has happened, God knows it. Analogously, one can designate something about man's essence in regard to knowledge by referring to that part of the light spectrum which man can see. To say that it belongs to my essence to be able to see such and such frequencies states something true and important. But it states nothing about the actual content of my present experience, e.g., whether I am now seeing yellow objects or red ones. Nor does it say anything about the subjective form with which I prehend these objects, e.g., delight, disgust, or apathy. Hence one can say that God is omniscient and thereby designate what types of things, if they occur, God can experience

—i.e., *every* possible type. But this merely states an abstraction; *what* God is concretely experiencing depends on what has happened.

Therefore, by speaking of God in dipolar terms one can predicate things of him that would have been impossible and contradictory in terms of classical theism, with its doctrine of God's simplicity. According to that doctrine, there was no distinction between God's essence and his actuality. In traditional terms, there were no "accidents" in God, i.e., no experiences which did not belong to his essence. In the dipolar view, there are accidents in God. For example, *that* God will experience every event is essential, but all those experiences that God actually has are accidental, i.e., they are not part of his essence. He would still have been God had he not had just those experiences (that is, of course, if different things had actually happened). Analogously, I would still be the same person if I were experiencing the books in the other room instead of the ones in front of me. My concrete experience would be different, but the same abstract essence would be embodied in an alternative set of experiences.

In terms of this doctrine of God, one can say that God is constantly changing. For the content of his concrete experience is constantly changing, since new things are always happening in the world, which he knows infallibly. God as concrete is perfectly relative, affected by everything.[8] God is unchanging, if one is speaking of his abstract essence. Nothing can affect this abstract essence, so it is strictly absolute, eternal, immutable. Also belonging to God's essence is his eternal purpose or subjective aim; this purpose "changeth not." But God's purposive action is always changing, for he does something new in each moment, responding to the world's decisions and then influencing it in line with his eternal purpose.[9]

Also, this dipolar view allows one to maintain a correspondence between faith and its object. Some have said that, since faith is essentially trust, it must be directed toward God himself, and not toward some idea about God, for this would reduce faith to propositional belief. But, as was argued earlier, faith does involve propositional beliefs, even though it is not exhausted by them. The dipolar view of God allows one to hold to the insight that faith is directed toward the living God, and yet to indicate that aspect of God which corresponds to the beliefs inherent in faith. That is, the total act of faith is directed toward God himself, in his full (and mostly mysterious) actuality, whereas the beliefs refer to God's abstract essence. Hence there is a distinction between the object of faith and the content. Correspondingly, there is a distinction between the subject of revelation (God himself) and the content (that part of his abstract essence best called his "character and purpose").

God as Categorically Unique. One of Whitehead's most famous statements is: "God is not to be treated as an exception to all metaphysical principles. . . . He is their chief exemplification." (*PR* 521.) This statement sums up both how God is similar to human experience and how he differs from it. God is similar in that he exemplifies all the categories that apply to all other actualities, e.g., prehension, subjective aim, anticipation, subjective form, etc. Hence, since God is structurally the same as human experience, language which applies to the latter can also be used to apply to God.

But God is categorically unique in that he actualizes the categories in a perfect way, while all finite actualities exemplify them in a very meager way. For example, we prehend other entities; but of the totality of actual entities in our past worlds we significantly prehend only the most meager part. But God prehends completely, i.e., he fully prehends all the actual entities there are. The difference between our exemplification of the category of prehension, then, and God's must be described as a difference in kind. Likewise, to prehend others with the subjective form of sympathy—in other words, to love others— is something we exemplify, but again in a very inferior way. But God loves fully; he prehends all actual entities with the subjective form of love. Here again, God exemplifies this category one hundred percent; our exemplification of love for other beings, while real, is extremely meager. Likewise, we have a certain amount of power to influence others. But the scope within which we have any significant effect in the universe is quite small, while God's influence extends over all areas equally. Likewise, man exists; but he has come into existence at a certain time, and the threat of nonbeing always faces him. God is the one actuality which has always existed and always will. There is no possible state of affairs with which he could not exist. Hence God's perfect exemplification of these categories puts him in a class by himself, even though it is possible to use language literally for speaking of him.

God's Subjective Aim. God's eternal subjective aim is that all the entities of the world experience existence as good, and that they constantly experience it as better. All experiences have some intrinsic value, but they differ in degree. Those with greater harmony, variety, and intensity are experienced as intrinsically better than those with less. God's aim is for the entities in the world constantly to experience greater value. The prerequisite for greater value is greater complexity, for as a greater variety of data can be synthesized into a harmonious unity, a greater intensity of feeling is possible. A few of the most important thresholds in the ascending complexity of finite existence were life, the psyche, and consciousness. These novel possibilities were able to emerge because of the complex order that evolved. Life could only emerge out of very complex ordering of molecules; and a psyche, especially one with consciousness, could only emerge out of an extremely complex order among the living cells. Hence, the fact that the direction of the evolutionary process is toward ever-increasing complexity is illuminated by the idea that God's aim is toward higher types of values being experienced by his creatures. This implies that, for one to be in harmony with the will of God, he must will the good of all of God's creatures. And this involves willing those structures and processes that make possible the enhancement of the quality of life at all levels.

God's Omniscience. Some of the traditional attributes can be used for speaking of God, as indicated above, but their definitions must be carefully observed. God is omniscient; but this means that he knows things as they are—he knows possibilities as possibilities, and actualities as actualities. This means that he does not know exactly what will actually occur in the future, for the future is still indeterminate and is not "there" to be known. Theologians have always agreed that God cannot do things that are impossible in principle. For example, he cannot make a round square, or change the past. If the future is still indeterminate, then it is impossible in principle for it to be known. Hence the fact that God cannot know it does not mean that he is finite or limited in comparison with some other conceivably more perfect being.[10]

God's Transcendence. God is transcendent, but this does not mean that he is totally "above" the world in the sense of not being in any way affected by it or dependent upon it. In the first place, God transcends the world in that he is not merely the sum of its parts, nor merely an aspect (e.g., the "being," or the "depth") of its parts, but is a unique individual who experiences the world. In the second place, God transcends the world in that he is an agent. He not only prehends all the experiences of the world, but he in turn acts upon the world, as we have already discussed in dealing with initial aims and God's subjective aim. In the third place, God transcends the finite world in that he is not dependent upon it for his existence. As implied in the paragraphs on God's dipolarity and omniscience, he *is* dependent upon the world for part of his actuality, the concrete experiences that he is having. If the world were not just the way it is at this moment, God would not be having just these experiences. But his existence, the fact that there is some embodiment of the divine essence in every moment, could not be threatened by any possible state of affairs. This gives God a type of transcendence not shared by any other actuality.

God's Perfect Power. God can be called "omnipotent," if this does not mean that he has a monopoly on power. For "to be actual" means "to have power." Hence, if God had all the power, he would be the only actual being. This not only contradicts our immediate knowledge of our own actuality and power. It is also contrary to the Judeo-Christian view of the world as creation. God's omnipotence, if that term is to be used at all, means only that God has all the power that any one being could possibly have. But it is less confusing to speak simply of God's "perfect power." As Hartshorne puts it, "His power is the absolutely maximal, the greatest possible, but even the greatest possible power is still one power among others, is not the only power." And as Hartshorne stresses, this doctrine should not be spoken of as a "limitation" of the concept of God's power. "To speak of limiting a concept seems to imply that the concept, without the limitations, makes sense." God's power, rather, is not "less than some conceivable power." [11]

Also, from what has been said, it is clear that God's power is persuasive, not coercive. Coercive power is the kind that one *corpuscular* society has over another, such as the power of one human body over another when an arm is twisted. But that is a secondary, indirect, derivative type of power. It always presupposes the primary type, persuasion, which is the type of power exerted directly by one actual entity on another. For example, the human arm is activated only by the persuasive power of the psyche over the brain cells, and the latter's effect on nerve cells, and so forth. Since God in each moment is an actual occasion of experience, his power is the primary, persuasive type. Hence it can never be said that God completely determines an event (which is the notion usually conjured up by the term "omnipotence").

God's Infinity. Speaking of God's infinity is as ambiguous as speaking of his omnipotence. There are certain senses in which it is meaningful and appropriate. "Infinity" can be used to refer to the fact that God is unlimited temporally—there was no time when he was not, and there will be no time when he is not. Here the term "everlasting" is better than "eternal," since the latter has connotations of timelessness. As indicated above, God's essence is eternal, but God himself is becoming. Also, the term "infinity" can be used to indicate that God is unlimited spatially—there is no place to which he is not immediately related. Here the term "omnipresent" is less ambiguous than infinity. The term "infinity" can also properly refer to the fact that God embodies the realm of possibility, together with the urge toward its actualization. Since this realm is infinite, his subjective aim for its realization is infinite.[12]

However, there are senses in which it is inappropriate to speak of God as infinite. To say that God is actual and infinite, in the strict sense of infinite, would entail that God is literally everything. This would entail pantheism, and be contrary to the Judeo-Christian vision of the world as creation, i.e., as finite but real. And this would involve the denial of the freedom either of God or the creatures. For if God is thought of merely as the sum of the parts of the world, then he lacks any transcendence, any individuality, and hence any power to act. Or if the entities of the world are thought of as *merely* parts of one individual, then they are not individuals with any power to act. In the pan*en*theistic doctrine the world is *in* God, but only in his experience, not in his essence. Hence God includes everything, but everything is not God. Within this view, which can either be called panentheism or dipolar theism, the simple alternative, either infinite or finite, is misleading.[13]

There is another sense in which it is inappropriate to speak of God as infinite. This would be the notion that for God the infinite realm of possibility is already actualized, so that he already possesses all the possible value. On this assumption (made by classical theism) the world would mean literally nothing to God, it would be of no value to him. The notion of "serving God," or of doing something "for God's sake," would be meaningless. Also, the idea of an infinite actuality in this sense is of doubtful meaning. For all actualization is the realization of some possibility, and this means that some other possibility has gone unactualized. Hence there is limitation—this has been experienced instead of that. Limitation means finitude: one value has been realized instead of others that might have been. In this sense, God's experience is not meaningfully called infinite.

God as Personal. In regard to the four preceding characteristics of God, the ways in which their traditional explanations must be qualified has been emphasized. However, some of the traditional perfections that classical theism affirmed of God only in an equivocal way process theology can attribute to God in a straightforward way. One of these is the idea of God as personal. In the ordinary understanding of this term, to be personal is to be a conscious being. It is to respond to others with feeling. It is to have a certain character or personality which is reflected in different actions. It is to have a certain underlying purpose in life in terms of which one actualizes himself in different situations, responding now to this event, and now to that. And it is to have freedom to choose how to carry out this underlying purpose. Process theism can affirm all of these things whereas classical theism could not, due to its ideas about God's impassibility, simplicity, and immutability.

God as Loving. God is also said by process thinkers to love in a literal sense. This central aspect of the Christian vision of reality was seriously truncated by classical theism. That this was the case has already been suggested by the paragraphs on God's infinity and personhood. According to classical theism, the values achieved in the world were not values to God, and he could not be affected by anything that happened in the world. But to love someone in any real sense means to be affected by their experience. What could it mean to say that a father loved his son if he did not share his son's triumphs and tragedies with him, rejoicing with him, suffering with him? But according to the tenets of classical theism, Jesus' picture of the father rejoicing over the return of his son could be no real analogy, but merely a metaphor. God's "love" was said to contain no passivity, but only activity. God was said to love us in that he gives good things to us.[14] Now this is certainly a necessary aspect of God's love. It has been spoken of here in terms of God's initial aims for his creatures. If that is all it is, then the analogy is with the wealthy father who gives his son all the money and material things he can use but is indifferent to the son's feelings about the gifts, and in fact does not choose the gifts in terms of a response to the son's feelings and real situation.

In the panentheistic view, all beings are internal to God's experience, so that he literally shares their experiences with them. Analogously, the experiences of the cells in the hand are internal to the psyche's experience. Hence, the psyche does not impassively view the bleeding hand, but experiences the pain, and does what it can to remedy the problem. In this way the experiences in the world are internal to God. Hence what we do "unto one of the least of these," we do unto him—we crucify him daily. Yet daily we bring him joy.

God as a Trinitarian, Dipolar Unity. The idea that God is a trinity, somehow being a unity of threeness, is traditional Christian doctrine. There have been unitarian protests against this doctrine, especially its formulation in terms of three "persons," on the grounds that it implied tritheism and was contrary both to rationality and Biblical monotheism. Others have said that it makes sense to speak of a duality in God, but not of a trinity. For example, some way of speaking both of God's immanence and transcendence is needed.[15] Others have maintained that it is necessary to continue speaking in trinitarian terms.[16]

On the basis of the process conception of God, an element of truth in all three positions can be seen. The unitarian protest against the trinity was correct insofar as that doctrine had suggested that there were three aspects or beings in God which were all on the same level of concreteness. The Father, Son, and Holy Spirit were understood by many as if each of them were a center of consciousness. Against this implication the stress on God as one concrete individual is certainly correct.

But those who have seen a need to speak of a duality in God are also correct. For some way is needed to speak both of God's immanence and of his transcendence in the requisite senses.

The Christian vision suggests that God is related to the world, yet that he is transcendent in the sense that he retains his own self-identity. How can this be conceptualized without contradiction? Here Hartshorne's dipolar doctrine is needed. God as concrete is related to the world. He is affected by the world (as well as affecting it), and therefore changes. But God's abstract essence is strictly absolute, being affected by nothing. Hence God as an individual retains his self-identity.

Finally, it is also necessary to make a distinction between two aspects of God's abstract essence. On the one hand, there are those attributes which distinguish God categorically from all other actualities. That is, while all other actual entities manifest the metaphysical categories in a very meager fashion, God manifests them perfectly in each moment of his existence. These can be called his "metaphysical" attributes, for they describe his metaphysical uniqueness. One can then distinguish between these and God's "personal" attributes (although these belong to his metaphysical essence as much as do those that I am calling "metaphysical" in a narrower sense). To speak of God's personal attributes refers to the *content* of his purpose (technically, his eternal subjective aim), and his character (technically, the general subjective form with which he responds to his creatures).

The difference between the metaphysical and the personal attributes is analogous to the difference between the attributes that describe a man as a member of the species *homo sapiens*, and those qualities that describe what *kind* of man he is. Reference to a person's character or personality, and his basic life-purpose, indicates that which distinguishes him from other men. The analogy is not perfect, since there is *ex hypothesi* only one God and therefore there are not a number of beings belonging to the genus "deity" which are differentiated from each other by their "personal" characteristics. Yet on the basis of the analogy we can make a distinction between God's basic character and purpose and those attributes which constitute his metaphysical uniqueness. The latter attributes indicate God's unique relation to the world, and hence these could not be shared at all by another being, whereas a finite being could to an extent embody the same character and purpose. Of course, the infinity of the divine subjective aim belongs to God's metaphysical uniqueness, as does the fact that God's significant subjective response to others is not limited in range. Nevertheless one could conceive (even if not with complete coherence) a being who was everlasting, omnipresent, omniscient, omnipotent, and infinite in purpose, and therefore deserving of the name "God," yet who was different in character and purpose from the God conceived of here. Hence the distinction between the metaphysical and the personal attributes, although not clear-cut, is intelligible.

On the basis of these distinctions many of the valid intentions of more traditional doctrines can be affirmed. God's abstract essence is absolutely immutable, impassible. God's metaphysical attributes clearly indicate his uniqueness. Insofar as this aspect of God corresponds to what some of the early theologians meant by "God the Father," the rejection of Patripassianism is intelligible. The second or personal aspect of God's essence compares to the Logos, through which God created all things, for it is on the basis of God's character and purpose that he has brought our world into existence. And it is this which Christians believe to have been expressed through Jesus. Finally, God as concrete corresponds to God as Holy Spirit, God as he is immediately present to and in us, God as he experiences us and is experienced by us.

Part III
JESUS CHRIST
AS GOD'S DECISIVE REVELATION

CHAPTER 8

Christology
and the Historical Jesus

IN THESE FINAL CHAPTERS process concepts will be used to attempt to show the intelligibility of the claim that Jesus is God's decisive revelation. The present chapter will attempt to point to the vision of reality expressed by Jesus. But first a terminological discussion is needed, in order to distinguish the various levels of discourse about Jesus, and to clarify the relations among them.

1. TERMINOLOGY

a. *Jesus of Nazareth.* This term refers to Jesus as he really was. All statements which attempt to say something true about Jesus himself, i.e., statements which fit under the second and third categories, are true if they correspond to this past reality, although they will necessarily be great abstractions from it.

b. *The Historical Jesus.* This category includes all statements about Jesus which can be made with reasonable probability on the basis of historical research. Recalling the ontological meaning of "internal" and "external" in Chapter 2, the focus in this essay is on internal data. Futhermore, Bultmann has distinguished between two levels of such data—explicit conceptuality, and the underlying "understanding of existence" expressed therein. In the present essay this latter term is replaced with "vision of reality." This change reflects the fact that the focus here is more on God—his character and purpose —than on man, and that the element in experience referred to is more decidedly cognitive.

c. *The Jesus of Faith.* This category differs from the previous one in scope, but not in kind. It includes all assertions regarding the historical Jesus, but goes beyond them by speaking of God's actual relation to Jesus. As discussed in Chapter 5, this convention of excluding all statements about divine causality from historical reconstructions is arbitrary. For example, no Freudian would consider distinguishing "the historical Lincoln" from "the Lincoln of [Freudian] faith." He is convinced that his categories of explanation serve to bring out the actual dynamics involved in the past subject. Despite its arbitrariness, this convention has been followed in the present essay in order to facilitate comparisons with other discussions, and also because a higher degree of probability is obtainable for statements falling under the second category (the historical Jesus) than for those under the third (the Jesus of faith).

d. *Jesus as the Christ.* This category includes the assertions belonging to the previous two, but goes beyond them by speaking of the saving significance of Jesus. Hence it is fundamentally different. For the previous statements intend to say something directly only about Jesus of Nazareth as a past figure, while the statements belonging distinctively to this fourth category intend to say something directly about the subjective form of the speaker's apprehension of Jesus. Hence, statements in this category refer to the present as well as the past, while the intention of those in the second and third categories is to refer only to the past.

On the basis of these four categories, the causes for some of the controversies revolving around different terms for Jesus can be examined. A major issue has been the relationship of the Jesus of history to the Christ of faith. Some make a strong distinction between these. For example, Emil Brunner has said,

"Faith presupposes, as a matter of course, *a priori,* that the Jesus of history is not the same as the Christ of faith." [1] Others declare that the Christ of faith *is* the Jesus of history. In view of the fact that both of these terms are ambiguous, it is not surprising that there are apparently wide differences of opinion among theologians. *The Jesus of history* can be understood as referring either to "Jesus of Nazareth," or to "the historical Jesus." And *the Christ of faith* can be understood to mean either "the Jesus of faith" or "Jesus as the Christ." (In these paragraphs, the terms considered ambiguous are italicized, while the technical terms being proposed are put in quotation marks.)

If *the Jesus of history* is taken to mean "the historical Jesus," and if the notion is accepted that the science of history excludes all talk of God's action, then the Jesus of history will be contrasted with the Christ of faith, regardless of how this latter category is understood, for it will include a reference to Jesus' relationship to God. (This understanding of *the Jesus of history* is presupposed in Brunner's statement quoted above.)

But if *the Jesus of history* is taken to mean "Jesus of Nazareth," then the relationship to *the Christ of faith* depends upon how this latter category is understood. If it is understood as "the Jesus of faith," then the Christian will say that the Christ of faith *is* the Jesus of history. This need not mean that the latter is completely exhausted by the former, for the predicate of a proposition never exhausts the actualities designated by the logical subject. But it means that faith statements about Jesus say something true about Jesus of Nazareth, and in fact it means that faith's picture of Jesus is the most accurate one that can be drawn.

However, if *the Christ of faith* is understood to mean "Jesus as the Christ," then there is again a difference in principle between the Christ of faith and the Jesus of history (even when this latter term is taken to mean "Jesus of Nazareth"). Statements about Jesus' significance refer not only to Jesus himself but also to his reception by others. Without this reception he would not be "the Christ" for them. This fact lies behind Bult-mann's arguments against the importance of the historical Jesus for faith in Christ. He associates any theological interest in Jesus himself with the illegitimate effort to prove the *kerygma* proclaiming Jesus as the Christ. This effort is illegitimate be-cause whether Jesus is the Christ cannot be proved by any amount of historical data, since it is (partly, at least) a ques-tion about how men in the present understand themselves.

The relationship between categories three (the Jesus of faith) and four (Jesus as the Christ) must be closely defined, especially since there is a difference between their epistemo-logical and their ontological relationships. As a preliminary statement, to be qualified below, it can be said that, in the order of knowing, the fourth category precedes the third. That is, Jesus is experienced as soteriologically significant, as "the Christ," before the question of his special relationship to God is raised. For it is only out of the experiences of Jesus' media-tion of a new relation of God to men that they have any reason to ask what relationship Jesus himself had to God. And the apprehension of Jesus as the Christ provides not only the *mo-tive* for reflecting about Jesus' relation to God. It also influences the *form* and therefore the *content* of this reflection. As Schlei-ermacher said, Jesus' person must be thought of in a way that explains how he was capable of achieving what he did. In this sense, soteriology (the statement about Jesus as the Christ) precedes Christology proper (the statement about the Jesus of faith).

However, the term "soteriology" in this context is ambiguous. It can refer either to the way people *have in fact* apprehended Jesus as significant, or to the way that one thinks they *should* apprehend Jesus as significant for their lives. Thus far it has been used only in the former, purely descriptive, sense. But when statements about Jesus as the Christ state (or at least imply) how men should apprehend Jesus, then Christology proper must precede soteriology. Normative statements about how Jesus should be received, unless they are to be completely arbitrary, can only be based on assertions about what Jesus really was. Only if Jesus is really thought to have had a unique relationship to God is there any reason to say that men should begin or continue to relate themselves to him in a positive way in order to find their salvation, their right relationship to the ultimate reality.

Furthermore, in terms of this analysis, the "question of the historical Jesus," i.e., the question of the theological relevance of Jesus as known through historical research, can be answered. Insofar as we do have historical knowledge of Jesus, no summary statement about his person can be responsibly made which does not include, in a consistent way, this knowledge. Therefore the historical Jesus is central to the total Christological task, since any normative or prescriptive statements about Jesus as the Christ must presuppose a doctrine of Jesus' person.

2. Jesus' Vision of Reality

The remainder of this chapter will attempt to point to the vision of reality expressed through that complex of deeds and sayings that the majority of critical New Testament scholars agree can be attributed to Jesus of Nazareth with a high degree of probability.[2] Jesus' message will be looked at in terms of the idea of the Kingdom of God: its temporal locus, its nature, and Jesus' role in relation to it.

a. *The Kingdom of God as Present and Future.* There is a consensus among New Testament scholars that Jesus preached the Kingdom (or Reign) of God as both present and future.[3] The presentness is suggested by many passages: Satan's power has come to an end (Luke 10:18); John the Baptist was the turning point of the ages (Matt. 11:12);[4] the messianic times have arrived (Matt. 11:5); and the present is a time for celebration (Mark 2:19; Luke 14:16–24). Futhermore, the eating and drinking with sinners was a sign that the *eschaton* was present—the messianic banquet was already being celebrated.[5]

However, there are also many passages pointing to the

futurity of the Kingdom: the Beatitudes contrast the present and the future (Luke 6:20 ff.); the Lord's Prayer contains "Thy Kingdom come" (Luke 11:2); the messianic banquet is still something in the future (Matt. 8:11); a vow of abstinence is made until the Kingdom arrives (Mark 14:25); a resurrection of the dead is expected (Luke 11:31 f.); and reference is made to a Son of Man who is to come (Luke 12:8; 17:23 f.; Matt. 24:37).[6] Further, there are many factors which suggest that Jesus expected the final breakthrough to occur suddenly in the near future, factors such as the urgent tenor of his message, the imminent expectation of both John the Baptist and the early church, and several sayings (e.g., Mark 13:28 f.; Luke 12:54–56). However, even those scholars who doubt the imminent expectation agree that Jesus did expect something greater in the future beyond what was already present.[7]

On the basis of what we have said thus far, this preliminary summary of Jesus' underlying vision of reality can be made: God is active and effective already in the present; but that activity is directed toward a future in which God's rule will be more complete.

The fact that Jesus saw God's Reign as present, as effective here and now, is basic to the Christian vision of reality. This fact decisively separates it from all views which see the "sacred" as totally unrelated to the present world, such as the traditional apocalyptic view, which implied that God's Kingdom was wholly in the future, so that this world would have to come to an end before God's Reign could begin. Although Jesus was influenced by apocalypticism and probably did expect an end to this world, he differed fundamentally by seeing God's Kingdom as already present in it. Thus the total abyss between this world and the holy is overcome, and the present is thereby rendered not totally devoid of inherent significance.

The Christian vision of reality, as based on Jesus' vision of reality, is also different from those views which see God as having acted in the past but as being absent in the present, or at least as not doing anything new. Such a view was prevalent

in the orthodox Judaism of Jesus' time. Jesus of course accepted
the view that God had acted in the past; but he also saw God
as doing something new in the present which superseded what
had occurred in the past.

The fact that Jesus nevertheless also pointed to the future is
equally important. This separates the Christian vision of reality
from any which would absolutize the present, thereby equating
what *is* with what *ought* to be. For, although Jesus saw God's
rule as effective in the present, it was present only in a fragmentary way, and was only anticipatory of what is intended in the
future. Hence, in the Christian vision of reality there is an
essential reference to the future.

b. *The Nature of the Kingdom of God*. There are several
factors relevant to this theme in Jesus' teaching: First, God's
Reign is related primarily to human experience. That is, God's
ruling activity is seen as effective primarily in relation to individuals, rather than to such things as nations and cosmic
events. Second, this activity involves the overcoming of the
various types of ills that afflict individuals, as exemplified by
Jesus' healings (Matt. 11:5), exorcisms (Luke 11:20), and
pronouncements of forgiveness in God's name (Mark 2:7).[8]
Third, the Kingdom of God is a life of joy—the present is
compared with a wedding party, at which fasting is inappropriate (Mark 2:19), and the parables of finding what was
lost conclude with a note of joy (Luke 15:6, 9, 11–32). Fourth,
it is a life of fellowship: in the parables just mentioned the
rejoicing is carried out with neighbors; the symbol for the Kingdom is a banquet; and Jesus' own celebration of it involves
eating and drinking with others. Fifth, the fact that this fellowship was with "sinners" shows that the experience of the Kingdom is based on God's grace. That is, the new life is based on
God's grace; his grace is not based on man's new life.

These factors are relevant to a consideration of the character
and purpose of deity in Jesus' vision of reality. The Christian
community has declared, on the basis of its response to Jesus
as God's decisive revelation, that God's character can best be

indicated by the word "love." The foregoing discussion bears out this response as being appropriate to the message of Jesus himself. God is portrayed as one who rejoices when man finds life, who graciously seeks man, forgives his sin, and thereby offers participation in true life.

Furthermore, God's purpose, the perfect Reign of God, is that which would be experienced by man as the greatest good. The life of joyous fellowship is that which would give man his ultimate fulfillment. And God is active in the present, overcoming all types of obstacles to this life of joy, whether mental or physical afflictions, or past sins against God and one's fellowman.

c. *Jesus' Understanding of His Own Role in Relation to the Kingdom.* Thus far the discussion has focused on Jesus' message about the Kingdom itself. The Kingdom was clearly at the center of his message. Contemporary scholars agree on this. They agree that Jesus probably did not apply any traditional messianic titles to himself. Yet they also agree that his message contains an implicit or indirect Christology. He claimed an extraordinary authority to act and speak in God's place. It was through his words and deeds that God's Reign was being effected as he cast out demons, demonstrated God's love, forgave sinners and accepted them into God's Kingdom.[9] And he said that a decision for or against him was a decision for or against God (Luke 12:8).

These facts are relevant to a consideration of the mode of God's activity in the vision of reality underlying Jesus' explicit imagery. The significant point is that God is understood to be acting through a man. Now the notion of man's having anything to do with the coming of God's Kingdom according to Jesus' message has been rejected in some circles. This was a reaction to the error of some of the older presentations of Jesus' explicit message, according to which the Kingdom of God was to be built gradually by the ethical efforts of man. Insofar as the social gospel theologians assumed that this idea was based on Jesus' explicit teaching about the Kingdom of God, they were in error. A more accurate analysis has shown that Jesus probably conceived of the final arrival of the Kingdom of God in completely supernaturalistic terms. That is, although he differed with the apocalypticists proper in some important ways, he shared their notion of a final, miraculous, catastrophic event that would come suddenly and by God's power alone. Hence those theologies which depended on an agreement between Jesus' *concepts* and their own notion of a Kingdom that would gradually be ushered in by men of good will were left without a foundation. Some theologians emphasized, in reaction, the eschatological, "wholly other" conception of the Kingdom of God in Jesus' preaching. For example, Bultmann says, "The coming of God's Reign is a miraculous event, which will be brought about by God alone without the help of men." [10]

However, there are two factors relevant to a reevaluation of this issue. First, we have now come to see that in Jesus' view, God's Reign was not only a future eschatological expectation, but also a present reality. Second, we have seen that the question of Jesus' perspective can be discussed not only on the level of his explicit images or conceptions, but also on the level of his underlying vision of reality.

In the light of these considerations, Jesus' implicit Christology suggests that God works in the present through man to effect his purposes. And if Jesus drew other men into the proclamation of the Kingdom of God, which is most likely, this further strengthens the case. Furthermore, Jesus' central activity was the proclamation of God's Kingdom. Men were confronted by this message, the offer of forgiveness and life under God's rule, and were thereby challenged to decision. Presupposed in this message is the idea that men are free to accept or reject God's call to them. Hence Jesus' own activity must be regarded as a free response to God's call, as the traditions about Jesus' temptations suggest.

On the basis of the implications of Jesus' implicit Christological claim to be God's agent, then, the following can be added to the previous statements about Jesus' view of God in his underlying vision of reality: God works on man in the present, calling him to participate in his purpose for the world, life under God's rule. And through those who respond to his call, God works to offer participation in this life to others.

Finally, on the basis of this interpretation of the nature of God's activity, the notion of God's "purpose" can be clarified. Within a conceptuality in which God is thought of as omnipotent, in the sense that nothing can resist his will, a cleavage or even a distinction between *God's purpose*, on the one hand, and *what will actually occur*, on the other, is impossible—the two must be identical. And Jesus undoubtedly shared this conception. It was unthinkable that man could hinder God's will. If the complete subjection of all things to God's rule, and that in the near future, was God's will, then that was what was to happen.

But within a conceptuality in which God's power and activity are understood differently, it is possible to distinguish meaningfully between God's will and that which will actually occur. For if God acts by seeking to influence free beings to respond to his purposes for them, then that which God ideally desires may not actually come to pass.

Now, I have implied above that Jesus' *vision of reality* corresponds more closely to this latter *conception* of God than to the conception of a God who brings about the realization of his purposes without the free response of his creatures. Jesus had responded to God's call, becoming the agent of God's purpose, and he calls others to respond; and the present is not a time of simple victory, but a time of conflict. In other words, there is a certain tension between the view of God implied in Jesus' underlying vision of reality and of his own role, and the conception of God which was presupposed in his notion that the present form of existence, with all the obstacles that qualify its goodness, would come to a sudden end.

Accordingly, the essential aspect in Jesus' underlying vision of reality, in regard to the future, is that God's activity in the present is based on his aim that all his creatures respond fully to his call and thereby experience existence as unqualifiedly good. Hence God's present activity always includes a reference to the future, in which his Reign might be more complete. But the idea that the present form of existence, with the ambiguities and risks involved in its temporality and freedom, will be replaced by a final state was based on the particular conceptuality in which Jesus' vision of reality was expressed, and hence is not essential to an explication of that vision as such. Hence the claim of Wolfhart Pannenberg, for example, that Christian theology must affirm such a final consummation if it is to be based on Jesus as God's revelation, does not necessarily follow.

CHAPTER 9

God's Supreme Act
of Self-Expression

THIS IS THE CENTRAL CHAPTER of the book. For, as the critiques
in the first part were intended to make clear, speaking intelligibly of God's special action or presence in Jesus has been
one of the most difficult conceptual problems for Christian
theologians in modern times. And the sketch of process thought
in Chapter 7 was carried out first of all for the purpose of providing a context in which to deal with this most difficult task.

The importance of being able to conceptualize intelligibly
the possibility that a special relationship obtained between God
and Jesus has already been argued. The conceptualization provided here can perhaps best be introduced in terms of a statement by Langdon Gilkey:

> What we desperately need is a theological ontology that will
> put intelligible and credible meanings into our analogical
> categories of divine deeds and of divine self-manifestation
> through events. . . . Only an ontology of events specifying
> what God's relation to ordinary events is like, and thus what
> his relation to special events might be, could fill the now
> empty analogy of mighty acts, void since the denial of the
> miraculous.[1]

Gilkey sees that unless we have a way of thinking of God's
action as analogous to our own (the only type of action of

which we have any real knowledge), we have no way of speaking intelligibly of God's action at all. An ontology adequate to the needs of Christology, and finally therefore to theology as a whole, would have to provide a conceptuality for such an analogy. A second requirement for this ontology is indicated by Gilkey's statement: an adequate ontology would have to allow for the possibility of speaking of "special" acts of God. A third requirement has also been indicated by his phrase, "since the denial of the miraculous": such an ontology would have to meet the previous requirements without implying the interruption of the normal course of natural causation.

Whitehead's philosophy, in which the actual entities are events (actual occasions), has provided us with such an "ontology of events." That it meets the first of the requirements stated above has already been shown, i.e., since all actual entities are of the same ontological type, and since a moment of human experience and a moment of divine experience are both actual entities, God's action can be thought in analogy with human activity. The adequacy of Whitehead's ontology to the third requirement has been partially shown: God is one of the many efficient causes of each finite occasion, being the source of its initial aim. Hence, speaking of his activity, in regard to ordinary events at least, does not imply an interruption of the normal course of natural causation which exists between all events. That Whitehead's ontology also provides a basis for speaking of special acts of God (the second requirement), and finally of a supreme act, and this without violating natural causation, is to be argued in this chapter.

Theologians have always been aware of the fact that, to speak intelligibly of God, it was necessary to think of him in analogy with man. But the analogue that was used for God was problematic. The analogue, at least by implication, was the total human organism, mind and body. This does not mean that theologians used the analogy explicitly in any crude way, suggesting that God had eyes, hands, and a beard. To the contrary—God was incorporeal and absolutely simple. But the type of causality attributed to God was the type appropriate only to a corporeal body, i.e., coercive, deterministic causality. Just as one human body can coerce another "corpuscular society," e.g., a piece of clay, God could (and did) exactly determine the course of events.

In other words, although God was said to be incorporeal and also simple (which first of all meant "not an aggregate"), he was given the type of causality attributable only to corpuscular societies. This attribution implicitly denied his unity, i.e., denied that he is an individual actuality and not an aggregate of such actualities. It was this type of analogy which led to the dilemma regarding God's activity described above: either one had to make the affirmation that some events were totally caused by God and hence had no natural causes, or one had to reject God's causation altogether as a real factor in the world. As we saw, Bultmann assumed that speaking objectively of God's influence necessarily meant asserting an interruption of the natural order.

But this type of analogy is not the only one possible. Furthermore, in view of the fact that God always has been, and must be, thought of as an individual, it is not the most appropriate analogy. Of course, the question of the types of things that are really individuals is an ontological issue. According to Whitehead's ontology, a moment of our own experience is an example of an actual entity, and the only one we know immediately. What is called the mind (soul, or psyche) is constituted by a series of these occasions of experience, and is called a "living person." Hence, for process thought it is the human mind which is technically called the "person," and which is the one enduring individual that we know directly with any adequacy. The human body as a whole is not simply an individual, but is a corpuscular society, with the mind as its dominant member. The body, which is composed of billions of individuals, is the immediate environment of the mind. In each moment of its experience the mind receives countless impulses or influences from the whole body through the brain. The mind constitutes itself in each moment on the basis of these influences, and in so doing it makes decisions that become impulses affecting the brain cells and therefore the rest of the body. To use the term that is generally used for God's influence on the world, we could say that the mind gives "initial aims" to the cells of the brain which express the mind's purposes for its body. As long as the body is functioning normally, the mind exerts a dominating influence over the body.

Hence, the total human organism is a monarchical society. The mind is the monarch; the body is organized so that most of the data or experiences of the members are channeled to it, and the rest of the members are dependent upon its decisions. However, the mind is no tyrant, acting without regard to the feelings of its subjects, but an extremely sympathetic, benevolent monarch. The experiences of the other members are internal to it. It does not observe their experiences impassibly from without, but shares them from within. The injury done to the cells in the foot is felt as pain by the mind; and the healthy exercise of the body is felt as exhilaration by the mind. This is love of one being for others in the deepest sense. The mind literally shares the experiences of the cells in its body; it sympathizes with their sufferings and rejoices with their positive experiences.

Thinking of God's relation to the world as analogous to the mind's relation to its body will not have the intolerable consequences connected with the other type of analogy. Not only is the fact of evil in the world not an insurmountable obstacle to belief in God's goodness.[2] Also God's "special" action in the world can be conceived without implying a suspension of the ordinary process of causation. This will now be explained on the basis of the mind-body analogy.[3] First of all, the sense in which one can speak of acts of the "person" must be distinguished. The person's acts in the *primary* sense are the *psyche*'s acts of *self-constitution* in each moment. These acts of self-constitution include its response to all the impulses from the body and its own past, and also include its decisions for the future. These decisions for the future include aims for the various parts of the body in the next moment of its existence.

The acts of the body are the acts of the person in a *secondary* sense. Insofar as the action of the hand, for example, results from the mind's decision for it, the hand's action can be called the person's action (remembering that "person" in the technical sense refers to the mind or psyche). It is generally in this secondary sense that people speak of a person's acts; and they *are* his acts insofar as they result from the aims for his body which are elements of his acts of self-constitution.

This is how the mind acts in relation to the body. It constitutes itself, and thereby becomes an actual entity in the immediately past world of the cellular occasions of the brain which are in the process of becoming; the mind thereby becomes an efficient cause for them. The brain cells prehend the mind, objectifying it in terms of the mind's aims for them. In a well-functioning body, these impulses are then sent on down the chains of nerve cells to a particular portion of the body. Exactly how all this takes place will probably always remain somewhat of a mystery, but *that* it takes place we know, and *some* idea of how it occurs can be attained in analogy with the influence of one moment of our experience on the next.

Hence, every act in the primary sense is structurally the same. The mind responds to the impulses from the actual entities in its immediate past (most of which are cellular events), making a total decision which includes a cluster of decisions for the various parts of the body. *The mind's action in relation to the body is formally always the same.* The mind always influences the body by formulating aims for it; there is no other way it could influence it. All the actual entities in the body are partially self-creating subjects, which respond to the various efficient causes in their immediate past. They are not mere objects which are simply "there" to be pushed or shoved or otherwise coerced; they can only be influenced by persuasion. (Also the mind itself is not a corpuscular society which, by the

massiveness created by the adhesion between myriads of actualities, can simply coerce other such aggregates.)

But when one is speaking of a person's acts in the secondary
sense, his bodily actions, then there is obviously great *diversity*
in his actions. It is in regard to action in this sense, with its
diversity, that the distinguishing feature of those acts which
can be called the "special acts" of a person can be indicated.

A "person" is not a single actual entity, but a strand of occasions. What makes this strand into a unity is largely the fact
that a certain abstract essence is carried over from each occasion to the next. This abstract essence is the defining characteristic of the person; this is what makes him the same person
over a period of time. Included in this abstract essence are
features which define him as a member of humanity. But also
included are features which are peculiar to him, which can be
called his "personal attributes." Sometimes we sum up these
features by speaking of his "personality." In this essay I am
using the terms "character" and "purpose." One's "purpose" is
his basic subjective aim, that underlying purpose which, although it might not be consciously formulated, ultimately is the
source of all (or at least most) that he does. I use the term "character" to refer to a person's fundamental attitude toward others,
his characteristic subjective form of response to them. In the
broadest sense, the question is whether the person generally
is open to the needs and contributions of others, and allows
these to play a positive role in his own acts of self-constitution,
in which his decisions are made. If not, we say he is inconsid-
erate, unloving, selfish. If so, we describe his character as considerate, loving, unselfish. (The opposite of self*fish*ness is not
complete self*less*ness, but a selfhood which includes other individuals' needs and contributions, sufferings and joys, in its
own quest for fulfillment.)

As mentioned earlier, character and purpose are closely related. For the way a person responds to others is largely a
function of his own deepest aim in life; and the person's aim

will be formed in line with the way he feels about others. Because of this interdependence of the two notions either of them can be used to sum up a person's "personal attributes," i.e., to designate a person's deepest selfhood. But it is best to use both terms often, to emphasize both the passive and the active sides of this selfhood.

Now, some external actions of a person reflect his character and purpose to a greater degree than others. Those external acts which express a person's character and purpose to an especially high degree can be called his *special acts*. For they are really "his" acts in a way that most of his bodily acts are not, for they especially express that character and purpose which constitutes his deepest selfhood, that part of his defining characteristics the description of which indicates what kind of person he is.

There are three considerations involved in an analysis of what constitutes a special act of a person. The first concerns the different *types of actions*. Some external acts are much more suited to express one's basic character and purpose than others. For example, say that Mr. Jones is a considerate person, generally considering the wishes of others. His acts of tying his shoelaces or sharpening a pencil are, at least in most contexts, not especially well suited for expressing this character. This is not to deny that these actions would reflect certain features of his character to some degree. But they are generally not as expressive as some other types of actions. A selfish bigot ties his shoelaces in about the same way a considerate humanitarian does. More suited to being special acts of Mr. Jones are, for example, those acts in which he has his face flash a forgiving smile, his hand give an encouraging pat on the back, or his foot step on the brake of his automobile so that another motorist can have the last empty space in a parking lot.

A second requirement for an external act to be a special act is that the *intention* behind it must be such that the act really does *ex-press* (literally, "press out") the person's character and purpose. If in the last example given above, Mr. Jones had not even seen the other motorist, but only stopped his automobile because he saw a pile of tacks in front of it, then this would not be an act expressing his considerate character, but only his prudence. If the other motorist saw Jones stop, and said to himself, "Jones is a considerate person; that act reveals it," he would be right about Jones's character, but he would be mistaken in thinking that the observed act was an expression of it. For an external act to be a special act of a person it must follow causally from an intention (an aim for his body) which reflects the person's basic character and purpose.

A third consideration is the *degree to which the body conforms* to the mind's aims for it. This factor is often overlooked, since a normal body conforms to the mind's wishes to such a high degree. But even in normal people there are differences; e.g., the ballet dancer and the gymnast are more coordinated than most of us. And when the mind has competition from other influences, such as when the body is weary, drugged, or injured, the fact that the mind's causal control over the body is only persuasive, and hence only a matter of degree, is more clearly seen. For a person's act to be truly his, in the special sense, the body must conform to his aims to a high degree. For example, Jones's considerate nature would not be expressed very well if his intended smile came out a sneer, his intended pat on the back became a karate chop, or if his foot actually pushed on the accelerator instead of the brake, causing his automobile to crash into that of the other motorist.

In summary, for a bodily act to be a "special act" of a person, it must be of a type especially suited to express his deepest selfhood; it must be based on an intention which especially reflects this selfhood; and his body must actualize that intention to a high degree.

This discussion can be applied analogically to God's action. God is thought of here as a living person, a series of occasions of experience. A description of that abstract essence which is his defining essence includes attributes which define his categorical uniqueness, such as his omniscience, omnipresence, everlastingness. It also includes attributes analogous to what

I have called a man's character and purpose, which were designated as God's "personal attributes" in Chapter 7. They differ from man's in being eternal and unchanging. Whereas man's character and purpose develop and can even change significantly in adult life, that cluster of attributes which can be summed up as God's character and purpose "changeth not," to use the language of the Old Testament. To use the language of the Nicene Creed, it is strictly *"homoousion* with the Father" (where "Father" is taken to mean that cluster of attributes defining God's metaphysical uniqueness), i.e., it is part of the eternal essence of God.

God's acts in the primary sense are those in which he responds to the world, receiving its experiences and making decisions for the next stage of the creative advance on the basis of his characteristic response to these experiences and his eternal subjective aim. These decisions are the initial aims which are then objectified by the actual entities which are to come into being next. Hence, *God's acts in the primary sense are formally all the same.* He acts by constituting himself in each moment. He acts on the world in each moment by being what he is, i.e., by creating his concrete state of actuality. For it is this concrete actuality, with all its decisions as to what the world should become in the next moment, that the entities all prehend as they are coming into being.

Accordingly, to speak of God's special acts will not involve saying that he has acted in a different way structurally and therefore interrupted the normal causal relationships. And God's action is always persuasive, never coercive. He seeks to influence the entities in the world by persuading them to actualize those possibilities which would bring them maximum fulfillment, given their concrete situations, and which will provide the basis for even higher values in the future. God never acts in the coercive way which occurs between two corpuscular societies; for he is an individual, not an aggregate. He acts indirectly on the actualities of the world, and they are partially self-creative subjects which can decide for or against the highest possibility he offers them.

God's special acts can be understood in terms of the threefold analysis given above. Here we are speaking of events in the world as being *God's acts in the secondary sense.* Every event in the world is an act of God in the sense that it originates with an initial aim derived from God. But some will be his acts in a special sense, just as some of a man's external acts are the man's in a special sense. First, the event will have to be of a kind which is especially suited for expressing God's eternal character and purpose. Now, every event is to *some* extent an expression of God's nature. But specially suited for this are those words and deeds of a human being through which he expresses a vision of reality, for in such events intelligible expression could be given to God's character and purpose.

Second, the event will have to be based on particular initial aims from God that especially reflected God's general aim. If the specialness of the event were thought to be based only in the finite actuality's decision, then it would be a misnomer to speak of a special act of *God.* Here it is necessary to recall that God's initial aim for a finite actual entity is always for the *best possibility for it given its own actual situation.* That means that, although God acts formally in the same way for every actual occasion, i.e., by providing it with an initial aim, the *content* of his aim for different entities will differ radically. The possibilities open to a molecule in a rock are slightly different from those open to a molecule in an animal body. The possibilities open to an ant are less complex than those open to a monkey. God's aim for a child will generally be less complex than his aim for a man. And his aims for men in different situations will differ; the man's tradition, genetic makeup, training, education, and concrete situation will all affect the determination of the ideal possibility for him at a given moment. For there is an order among possibilities; some are *real* possibilities for a person only when certain other ones have already been actualized. The human race could not produce poetry until it had formed a language; a particular man cannot write a poem until he knows the language. What possibilities God, by means of his initial aims, can lure us to actualize depends upon our past. Hence, God's aims will be different for different human events, and his aims for some of them will more directly reflect his eternal character and purpose.

In the third place, the action of a person, to be a special act of God, must actualize the initial aim presented by God to a high degree. The initial aim given to a man by God contains a hierarchy of possibilities. The human psyche, consisting of a series of very complex actual entities, has a tremendous degree of freedom. Man can reject that highest aim toward which God is luring him in favor of a slightly lower one; he can even choose a much lower one, going radically against God's will and that which would be experienced as best for himself and those around him. Hence a human act cannot be called God's in a very significant sense if the man's own subjective aim does not correspond closely with God's initial aim for him. This means that sinful acts are by definition not acts of God to the same degree as obedient acts: The crucifixion of a proclaimer of God's will is not God's act to the degree that the proclamation itself was.

In summary, a *special act of God* would be a human act (1) in which a new vision of reality is expressed, (2) for which God's aim was a direct reflection of his eternal character and purpose, and (3) in which God's aim was actualized to a high degree. If the second and third points were actualized to an unsurpassable degree in an event in which a new vision of reality was expressed through a man's words and deeds, this would be *God's supreme act*.

The doctrine of Jesus' person that is being proposed here is that he was God's supreme act. First, in his message of word and deed a vision of reality is expressed which contains a view of God's character and purpose. This was presented in Chapter

8. It was not, of course, a totally new vision of reality; all new actualizations are based on a history of actualizations in the past. Jesus' message presupposed the general vision of reality that had emerged in Israel. Its newness consisted in the way the various elements were weighted. God's love was given priority over his justice, so that God's "demand" on men was for that which they themselves would experience as most fulfilling; God was seen as rejoicing over the success of men in finding true life; God's ultimate purpose for men was seen as partially actualized already in the present, so that men could already participate in it. These shifts altered the whole tenor of the extant versions of the Hebrew vision of reality. God's radical love was expressed in the radical forgiveness offered—one could participate in God's Kingdom now simply by accepting the offer to begin living in terms of his kingly activity.

Second, Jesus' active ministry, his proclamation of this God by word and deed, can be understood as being rooted in God's aims for him. Jesus' actual world was such that he was in an optimal position to receive aims that directly reflected God's eternal aim and his correlative character. For Jesus came out of a tradition in which the basic elements in a true vision of reality were already contained. For example, the world was seen as created by a personal God who was interested in the affairs of his creatures, who had purposes for them, and who placed demands upon them based on these purposes. On this basis, the possibility existed for God to give aims to Jesus which, if actualized, would directly express God's character and purpose, whereas this possibility did not exist in relation to men in other traditions.

Hence, the notion that Jesus' revelatory character was based on God's prevenient initiative can be expressed in terms of process concepts. Jesus was not only one who had special insight into the nature of things; his special activity was based on the impulses given him by God. He was not merely a teacher about God, he was a special act of God. And he was a special act of God not merely in the sense of having actualized possibilities which were open to all men, so that Jesus' specialness would have been rooted only in his own decisions. Rather, Jesus' specialness can be understood as rooted first of all in God's aims for him, the content of which was different for Jesus than for all other men. Of course, the divine aims for each man are unique, since the real possibilities open to each person are different from the real possibilities open to all other men. But the content of the ideal aims given to Jesus was unique in a special sense. The content of these aims had an especially close relationship to the content of God's eternal subjective aim for the world. This can be formulated in the following way: *The aims given to Jesus and actualized by him during his active ministry were such that the basic vision of reality contained in his message of word and deed was the supreme expression of God's eternal character and purpose.*

Third, Jesus' active ministry is not to be understood as rooted *only* in God's aims for him. The traditional notion of Jesus' "obedience" makes sense only upon the presupposition that he was free to reject God's aim for him. God does not coerce, but only calls. For Jesus to have been God's supreme act depended not only upon God's aim, but also upon Jesus' free decision to proclaim God's will to men and to continue this in the face of opposition. This third point is already referred to in the summary statement of Jesus' person in the preceding paragraph by the inclusion of the words "and actualized by him."

It is in regard to the second of these three points that most process Christologies have been weakest. They have not made use of the notion that the content of God's ideal aims for men varies. God's aim for a man at a certain time and place is always for that possibility which is best in that concrete situation. If this notion of Whitehead's is not used, the resulting Christology has a somewhat Pelagian quality, suggesting that Jesus' specialness is due solely to human initiative—if Jesus was God's decisive revelation, this did not result even partially from any special activity on God's part in any sense.

An example is provided by Schubert Ogden's Christological

reflections. On the one hand, Ogden believes that the "one-sidedly existentialist character" of Bultmann's theology must be corrected,[4] and that this includes being able "to express in an adequate way the 'objective' reality of the revelatory event Jesus the Christ."[5] This means giving some intelligible meaning to the idea that Jesus is God's decisive act. On the other hand, Ogden believes this should be done without saying that God's action in Jesus differed in any way from his action in all other events. How can the notion of a special act of God be combined with that of the uniformity of God's activity? Ogden attempts this by equating the notion of a special act and a revelatory event. One of my external acts can be called a "special act" of mine if it reveals to someone else my true character. This occurs if someone apprehends one of my acts in such a way that his resulting interpretation of my character is correct. This analysis is then applied analogically to the meaning of a special act of God. Since all finite events are rooted in God's ideal aims for them, they are all acts of God in a general sense. However, those uniquely human events in which man expresses his understanding of existence are especially adapted to becoming special acts of God. These do become God's special acts if they are received by someone in such a way that the resulting understanding of God corresponds to his true nature.

Missing in Ogden's analysis of the meaning of a "special act" is any mention of the intention of the agent whose special act it is supposed to be. No mention is made of the fact that, if one of my acts is really to be one of my special acts, it must really *express* my true character and purpose. It is not enough that someone happens correctly to infer my selfhood from some act of mine. As was made clear by some examples earlier, my external act must follow causally from an intention that especially reflects my basic character. Otherwise it cannot meaningfully be called one of my special acts.

Likewise, in speaking of a special act of God, the specialness of this act must be attributed at least partly to God. Ogden has said that there is no reason to affirm "that God has acted in Christ in any way different from the way in which he primordially acts in every other event." [6] It is really impossible to affirm this totally and also to do full justice to the notion of a special act of God. Unless there is something about God's action in Jesus that differs from his action elsewhere, it is misleading to speak of Jesus as God's special or decisive act. It is the formal-material distinction that can be made in regard to Whitehead's understanding of God's action that makes it possible to overcome this inadequacy. As stated before, formally speaking, God acts in the same way in all events, i.e., by providing them with initial aims. But, materially speaking, God acts differently in different events, i.e., the content of his aims for them differs greatly. Because of this it is possible to conceive of the specialness of Jesus as following partly from the specialness of God's action in him. The content of God's aims for him directly reflected God's eternal subjective aim. In actualizing God's *particular* aims *for him,* Jesus expressed God's *general* aim for his entire creation. Hence, the fact that Jesus was God's supreme act was rooted not only in Jesus' decision to actualize God's aims for him, but also in the content of these divine aims.[7]

The doctrine of Jesus' person that was developed above is intended as an explication of the *objective* side of the statement, "Jesus is God's decisive revelation." Since this is a soteriological statement, it does have a subjective side. For it refers to certain effects that Jesus has had on those men who accept this statement either explicitly or implicitly. It says that Jesus is the decisive factor in their cognitve approach to reality. In the terms used here, this means that their basic model or vision of reality is ultimately derived from Jesus.

But as indicated before, the intention of this statement is not merely to state how men *have in fact* received Jesus as significant for them. It also implies that this reception of Jesus is the *appropriate* one, that other men *should* accept Jesus as God's revelation if they want to be cognitively related to reality as it is. And this implies that there is an *objective* side to the confession of Jesus as the Christ. Something is said not only about men's reception of him; something is also implied about Jesus himself. Only if there was something special about his relation to God is it appropriate to apprehend him as God's decisive revelation. More specifically, it is implied that he was *God's supreme act of self-expression.* Only if this were the case is it appropriate to receive him as God's decisive revelation.

How an objective side is included in a statement about a revelation, and that this objective side can be referred to by the term "expression," can be made clearer by the following example. You have gone with a friend to hear a political candidate. During his prepared speech he seems to everyone to be an idealistic person, truly concerned about the plight of the underprivileged. But one of his responses during the question-and-answer period leads you to change your mind. His facial expression, his gestures, the tone of his voice, and what he says convince you that he is really only a self-centered and power-hungry person, merely feigning concern about the welfare of others. This particular response of his, then, you take to be the revelation of his *true* character and purpose. You take it as the key to understanding everything else you have heard him say and do, including some things about which you had previously been puzzled for they had seemed "out of character," i.e., inconsistent with what you had previously understood his character to be. Now everything seems to fit together.

When you mention this particular response to your companion afterward, you find that he had not perceived it as you had; he did not see it as having special revelatory significance. But you seek to persuade him that it did. This means that you do not think that both interpretations were equally valid, and therefore equally arbitrary. You believe that in that one response the candidate had especially expressed his true character and that he would have expressed it therein even if you had not been there, so that perhaps nobody would have perceived it as revelatory. Of course no "revelation" then would have taken place, and nobody would have been aware that that particular response was a "special act" of the candidate, an especially direct expression of his selfhood. But, having apprehended the statement as a revelation to you, you believe that it was an expression of his character and purpose before and apart from any reaction to it on your part. Hence, to call an event a revelation says something about the subjective form of your own response to the event. But it also intends to say something true about the past event itself. To say that the event was especially "expressive" of the person's selfhood is a way of designating this objective side of a revelation.

It should be clear that revelation as an event is always something that takes place in the present. For a revelation has taken place only if someone receives some past event as a revelation to him, and this reception is a present event. Since this subjective response is an essential aspect, the candidate's utterance of the statement *cannot in itself be called a revelation*. The significance of the statement for his character could have dawned upon you a split-second later, or several hours later. Whatever the case, only then would the revelation have occurred.

But the candidate's act of self-expression was something that occurred in the past. And since this objective side is also essential if the term "relevation" is to be appropriate, to speak of revelation is not only to speak of the present. It is to speak of perceiving in the present what a past event was in itself. This example illustrates the objective intention included when Christians speak of Jesus as God's revelation. On the subjective side, they are referring to Jesus' significance for them, and hence are speaking about the present. But they also mean that Jesus *was* God's supreme act of self-expression, and that he was this before anyone had apprehended him as such.

Implied in this discussion is a further criticism of Ogden's position; for, as mentioned above, he equates a special act of God and a revelation of God. According to Ogden, an event in itself cannot be called a special act of God; Ogden only says that certain events are especially suited to becoming special acts of God. That is, since a special act is defined as a revelation, an act can become a special act only if and when it is received by someone as revelatory of God. Hence, an event in itself cannot "objectively" be a special act of God; the subjective reception of it as revelatory is what constitutes it as a special act.

But this does not do justice to the objective side of Christian faith in Jesus as God's decisive revelation. As the above example indicates, an event does become a revelation only when it is received as such. But when you speak of a person's action as a revelation of his character, you imply that the action was an especially good expression of the person's character before it was received as a revelation, and thus would have been a "special act" even if nobody had apprehended it as revelatory. A distinction must be made between a special act, which is potentially revelatory, and a revelation, which involves the apprehension by someone of the revelatory significance of a special act. Hence, to speak of Jesus as God's supreme act is to speak of his person, of what he was in himself, of the way his activity was related to God's character and purpose. Although, in the order of knowing, these notions are based on an apprehension of Jesus as revelatory, in the order of being God's activity in Jesus must be described as preceding the interpretative reception of Jesus as God's revelation, if that interpretation is to continue to be thought appropriate.

Thus far our discussion of the content of revelation has focused only on the character and purpose of God. However, if Christians claim that Jesus' life provides the decisive revelation of God, then it should be here that they also find the supreme exemplification of the mode of God's *activity* in relation to the world.

The question of the relation between God and the world can with justification be considered the central philosophico-religious question, whether it be called the problem of the one and the many, the infinite and the finite, or the sacred and the profane. The various styles of life are as dependent upon implicit or explicit answers to this question as they are to the closely related question of the character of the divine reality. Yet Christians have for the most part allowed this question to be answered for them by non-Christian systems of thought, in the guise of so-called "natural" theology.

This essay has already registered its protest against one side of this practice by insisting that God's character be defined literally as love. That is to say, one side of the question of the God-world relation is: In what way does the world affect God? The answer that the early Christian theologians took over from Greek thought was: In no way. This was stated in the doctrine of the divine impassibility. In the present essay, however, God's character has been defined in terms of the subjective form of his responses to his creatures. That is, the generic characteristic that God's particular responses to each of his creatures has in common is sympathy, or love. And this clearly corresponds to Jesus' vision of reality much more than did the doctrine that God is not at all responsive to our sufferings and joys.

But the other side of the question is, How does God affect the world? Is there anything about Jesus that could provide a clue to this issue? It is interesting that Whitehead has said, "The essence of Christianity is the appeal to the life of Christ as a revelation of the nature of God and of his agency in the world." (*AI* 213.) But this must be taken more as a prescriptive than a historical judgment on Whitehead's part. He himself sees in Jesus the "revelation in act" of the idea that "the divine element in the world is to be conceived as a persuasive agency and not a coercive agency." (*AI* 213 f.) But historically this was not what the orthodox theologians saw. As Whitehead complains, they saw God as having "no relations to anything beyond himself," and as having an "unqualified omnipotence." (*AI* 217.) Using Whitehead's terms, one could say that they saw Jesus only to an extent as a revelation of the "nature" of God, and not at all as a revelation of his "agency in the world." Rather, they tried simply to add certain Christian ideas about his nature to non-Christian ideas about his nature and his agency. Among the results were Anselm's puzzlement as to how God could be both compassionate and yet without passion, and the notorious problem of evil.

In Chapter 8, Jesus' understanding of his own role in relation to the Reign of God was seen to imply a position as to God's mode of activity. And this corresponds to Whitehead's view of Jesus as revealing God's agency in the world as persuasive. For the "Reign of God" clearly served as the "final cause" motivating Jesus' activities. And Jesus, who saw himself as God's decisive agent in effecting this Reign, tried to persuade others to live in terms of this future reality that was already breaking into the present; and he enlisted disciples to share in this venture. Finally, the Reign of God was preached as the supremely attractive good, that for which man should relinquish every competing good, and that which would bring supreme joy. Accordingly, although Jesus' explicit imagery evidently pictured God's causality in other terms, the vision of reality presupposed in his actual ministry suggested that God effects his purposes by presenting his creatures with a call to the good, a good which goes beyond all those goods achieved in the past.

If Jesus' ministry is the decisive revelation of God's nature (i.e., his character and purpose), it follows that it should be taken also as the decisive revelation of God's agency. For one should look at the place that God has most effectively expressed himself to derive clues as to how he expresses himself always and everywhere.[8] And there is nothing about Jesus' life and fate that suggests that God's activity involves a complete control over the activities of men. The crucifixion of God's agent suggests just the contrary. Of course the early Christians ingeniously reconciled this event with their unreformed conception of God's power by using certain passages from the Hebrew scriptures as proof texts to show that the entire event had been planned by God himself. Whitehead described the Leibnitzian view of "the best of all possible worlds" as "an audacious fudge produced in order to save the face of a

Creator constructed by contemporary, and antecedent, theologians." (*PR* 74.) A similar judgment must be passed on this traditional view of the crucifixion. In terms of our knowledge of the Scriptures, and of the world process, the theological interpretation of the cross offered by Reinhold Niebuhr is more realistic, i.e., the cross is the supreme example of the fact that God's will is continually defeated in the world, even though this defeat is not the whole story.[9]

Contemporary Christians should evaluate proffered views of the God-world relation in terms of four criteria: (1) their rootage in the key events of the Biblical tradition, especially the ministry of Jesus; (2) their consistency with other essential presuppositions and doctrines of Christian faith; (3) their adequacy to the facts of experience, and (4) their illuminating power. In terms of each criterion taken separately, the view that God's power is persuasion fares better than the view that it is all-determining coercion. This is admittedly more ambiguous in regard to the first criterion. However, I believe at least that I have shown that the doctrine of persuasion comes off as well as the competing doctrine even when evaluated in terms of this criterion alone. When this criterion is evaluated in conjunction with the others, as it must be, the balance is clearly tipped in favor of the view that the divine power is persuasive. Of the two doctrines, only it is compatible with the doctrines of freedom and sin, the fact that actuality as such has power, and the fact of evil.

In summation, Whitehead's analysis of the initial aim given each occasion by God can serve as a basis for understanding the objective intention of Christian faith's appraisal of Jesus as God's decisive revelation. For on the basis of this notion, and the analogy it allows between a person's bodily action and acts of God in the world, an idea of God's relation to ordinary events can be formed. Then on that basis an idea of how some events are special acts of God can be formulated. Finally, how an event would have to be related to God to be his supreme act can be formally stated. In this way, the Christian can understand that which he has believed (at least implicitly) to be an *ontic fact* about Jesus to have been an *ontological possibility*. If the above analysis of one of the beliefs about Jesus inherent in Christian faith is correct, the Christian believes that *Jesus was God's supreme act of self-expression, and is therefore appropriately apprehended as God's decisive revelation*. On the basis of the ontology employed in this essay, one can regard as an ontological possibility the idea that God supremely expressed his character and purpose, and concomitantly his mode of activity, in the event of Jesus' ministry. Hence a picture of the "Jesus of faith" which is implied by the cognitive dimension of the confession of "Jesus as the Christ" can be held responsibly.

One further idea needs to be added to complete this discussion of the special presence of God in Jesus. This is an idea that will serve to give a more intelligible basis for the radical difference presupposed in Christian faith between the revelatory significance of Jesus and that of other men. Tillich has spoken of Jesus' being supremely "transparent" to God, so that Jesus as the medium of revelation does not conceal the revealer. Somewhat more precisely, John Baillie has indicated the necessity for the medium of the supreme revelation not to conceal or distort the nature of God beyond that which is inherent in finitude as such. The problem for the theologian is, of course, not merely to assert this, but to conceptualize how this relation of Jesus to God could have obtained. The following suggestion will be an attempt to do this.

The basic notion of this Christological idea was intimated by Schleiermacher insofar as he suggested that the person's psyche can be structured differently, according to how the various elements or dimensions of one's experience are interrelated. The main thing is which one of them forms the organizing center. Schleiermacher suggested further that the experience of God, which is an essential element of every man's life, could be this center, and that in Jesus this was the case. In Jesus the consciousness of God was dominant over the other elements.

Hence the presence of God in Jesus constituted his selfhood in a way that was not the case in other men.

John Cobb has recently developed a Christological sketch along these lines within a Whiteheadian context.[10] He points out that although the human psyche is not ontologically different from other actualities, it is unique in being open to diverse determinations. That is, there are many ways to be human, many ways for the psyche to be structured. In order to indicate the particular structure of Jesus' experience Cobb uses the category of the "I" or the "self." A first step in indicating what is meant by the "self" is to recall that for Whitehead the "person" is not the total human organism, but the psyche. But Cobb does not identify the self even with the psyche, but only with one factor or element within it. The self is that "relatively continuous center within human experience around which the experience attempts more or less successfully to organize itself."[11]

For example, in some men the rational aspect of the psychic activity might constitute the self, whereas in others the affective dimension might have this centrality. Furthermore, Cobb defines the notion of the self in an even stricter sense. In the strict sense selfhood first appeared effectively in history in the Hebrew tradition, for here man came to understand himself as an "I" that transcends the affective and rational dimensions and is therefore responsible for the outcome of the struggle between them.

It is within this context that the special presence of God in Jesus can be articulated in such a way as to make intelligible the distinction between his sense of authority and that of the Hebrew prophets. The prophet experienced himself as called to speak the word of God. But he experienced this call as a demand that encountered him. In fact, in Jeremiah's case it is most clear that it was the conflict between his own natural inclinations and the obligation to communicate the divine word that occasioned the discovery of himself as an "I."

But in the case of Jesus this opposition, at least in some decisive moments of his life, did not obtain. The prehension of the divine aim for him was not experienced as one prehension among others, to be decided about from the point of view of his organizing center. Rather, precisely "this prehension of God constituted in Jesus the center from which everything else in his psychic life was integrated." There was no tension—again, at least in some decisive moments—between his *beliefs* about the relative importance of matters in light of the reality of God, and his own *perception* of things. This perception "was from the perspective given in his prehension of God." Hence one can say that the prehension of God constituted Jesus' self.[12]

Cobb uses this idea primarily to show a way of conceiving Jesus' relation to God that would justify his extraordinary claim to authority. However, the idea can be used equally well to explain further how Jesus' relation to God enabled him to be God's supreme act of self-expression, and hence appropriately received as God's decisive revelation. For the two claims, the one made by Jesus himself and the one made about him by Christians, are very closely related. Each of them is justified only if Jesus' relationship to God was such that his activity, at least in decisive moments of his active ministry, expressed the divine character and will to a high degree. Cobb's way of conceptualizing how Jesus' selfhood can be thought to have differed from that of all other men provides a way of understanding how Jesus could have indeed been "transparent" to God's reality.

And within process thought, where God is thought of as an agent, this transparency need not be attributed solely to Jesus' free response to a possibility that has been open to every man, as it must be in Tillich's thought. Also, within process thought one can formulate more consistently one of the ideas Schleiermacher wished to express. As Cobb emphasizes, one of the ways in which men can differ in regard to the divine presence in them is whether or not they are consciously aware of the fact that the ideal aim they experience has its source in God.[13]

Schleiermacher also saw the relatedness to God as a universal element; and he also saw that the consciousness of this related-ness can vary greatly. The problem in Schleiermacher's thought in this respect is that this variation had to be attributed solely to God's decision, since God's power was defined in such a way that no resistance to his will is possible. In process thought, variations in this consciousness can be attributed partly to the person himself and partly to the history of decisions constitut-ing the particular context in which he finds himself. Accord-ingly, the age-old contradiction within Christian theology of imputing a man's lack of faith to God's decision and then counting this unfaith as sin, is overcome.

The reader will note that Cobb has introduced a third vari-able for differentiating the divine presence in men. That is, besides the difference in the content of the divine aims, and the different degrees to which the aims might be actualized, Cobb also says that the "prehensive objectification of God need not be restricted to the initial aim." [14] That is, the occasion may prehend other aspects of God beyond the particular propo-sitional feeling that constitutes the ideal aim for the occasion in question. Included in this third variable is the possibility of being conscious of God as the source of the initial aim, rather than simply being aware of the urge to actualize some possi-bility.

The fact that this third variable has played no role in the present essay is due solely to the fact that it is not necessary in order to develop the particular thesis of this essay, and implies no difference of opinion as to the legitimacy of this variable. However, the way this idea is employed by Cobb to differentiate Jesus from the prophets does involve a contrast with the leading idea of the present essay. Cobb suggests that for the prophets the *content* of the divine aim, and the fact that its *source* was God, were of equal importance. But in Jesus' case the specific content of the ideal aim is said to have been secondary in importance to the fact that it was divine in origin. This was what was decisive for the peculiar subjective form of Jesus' experience, i.e., his unique sense of authority.[15]

I have stressed, on the other hand, precisely the particularity of the divine aims given to Jesus, suggesting that their content was such that, although radically particularized to Jesus' concrete situation, they nevertheless directly reflected the general aim of God for his creation. It was because Jesus actualized these particular aims that the divine Logos, the character and purpose of that reality in which the whole creation is grounded, was supremely expressed through him.

This difference is partly due to different concerns. Cobb is primarily interested, in making these distinctions, to account for the extraordinary sense of authority Jesus evidently had. I am primarily interested in showing how it is conceivable that the vision of reality that we derive from Jesus can be understood as divine revelation. Accordingly, the focus in the present essay has been primarily on the objective datum of Jesus' prehension of God, whereas Cobb is interested primarily in the subjective form of Jesus' response to God. I believe these both to be valid interests. But I do not see that the importance of the content of the divine aims for Jesus has to be depreciated in order to account for his sense of authority. For one thing the sense of authority to speak in God's stead should not be separated from the sense of *what* should be expressed. Also, no depreciation of the importance of the content of the initial aim is needed to distinguish Jesus from the prophets. Rather, this difference can be adequately accounted for in terms of Cobb's distinction summarized above, i.e., that in the prophets the divine will was experienced as being in some opposition to their own wills, whereas in Jesus the prehension of the divine aims constituted his self (at least in certain decisive moments), so that the antithesis of desire and duty was transcended.

In summary, then, the Christian belief that Jesus is God's decisive revelation can be understood to be a real possibility in terms of the following conceptualization. Partly because of the content of the divine aims given to Jesus during his active ministry, and partly because of Jesus' conformance to these aims, the vision of reality expressed through his sayings and actions is the supreme expression of God's character, purpose, and mode of agency, and is therefore appropriately apprehended as the decisive revelation of the same. The finality of this expression is due to the fact that at least at decisive moments Jesus identified himself with the divine aims for him, so that he provided no hindrance to the expression of the divine Logos other than that which is inherent in human nature as such.

CHAPTER 10

Revelation
and Christian Existence

To RECEIVE JESUS as the Christ means to receive saving benefits from him. Thus far in this essay the focus has been upon Jesus' direct significance for the cognitive dimension of our existence. In Gordon Kaufman's words, we receive him as the decisive revelation insofar as we derive from him "the meaning that illuminates all our existence, giving us means to understand even the most elusive corner of ourselves and our world." [1] Inasmuch as Jesus' vision of reality is appropriated, the cognitive side of our being is brought into right relationship with God and the rest of reality. And this is good in itself. Nevertheless, a meaningful salvation must involve the other dimensions of human existence as well. It has been suggested in the Introduction that Jesus does mediate wholeness to these other dimensions indirectly, by means of his revelatory significance.

One traditional position has stressed the notion that salvation is achieved by God alone, apart from man's cooperation. There is one sense in which process theology affirms this. H. Richard Niebuhr stresses that in revelation God is known as the one who knows and values us. The implication of this is of utmost importance for Charles Hartshorne. He regards the question of the ultimate significance of our experiences as the supreme question that arises for the mature religious consciousness. Human posterity certainly provides no answer, since only the most minute portions of our lives are effectively retained by future generations. Also, even that retention will be only temporary, since our world will one day perish (Hartshorne rejects personal or subjective immortality). Only an omniscient, everlasting, loving God can rescue us from the fate of total oblivion. Without belief in such a God we would have to accept the fact that in the long run it will be as if we had never been, that all our hopes, fears, struggles, tragedies, and triumphs will count for naught. But belief in God can bring the ultimate gift of peace, of knowing that the value one has experienced and contributed will be valued everlastingly.

Another traditional view is the "Abelardian," i.e., that God saves us by revealing his love for us through Jesus Christ. Process thought emphasizes along with Bultmann the importance for Christian existence of the belief that God makes demands upon us. We are confronted with normative possibilities. They come from beyond ourselves, from God, and yet they are our "ownmost," or authentic, possibilities, calling us beyond the past to that which is right and best for us, given our concrete situation. Also, John Cobb has stressed the importance of the belief that God "looks upon the heart," for this is important to the concern for motives, as opposed to merely external obedience to the law.[2]

But the demand for radical obedience, for inward purity of motive, can by itself lead to a self-defeating works-righteousness, a self-preoccupation and rigidity that hinders that freedom, spontaneity, and genuine concern for others which is of the essence of Christian existence. It is recognized that these virtues are only possible if we know ourselves first loved, prior to any righteousness on our part.[3] Hence, the revelation of the love of God is essential. Since the one who ultimately matters, God himself, loves us, we need not strive inordinately to secure our own place in the scheme of things.[4] And since this God loves us, in spite of the sin and errors in our past, we can become free from any unnecessary dominion of that past over our present and future. Since God forgives us, continuing to urge us to actualize that which is best for us in our present situation, there is no reason to continue to fret about the past, which cannot be changed. What counts is the present and the future. Of course, the best possibility for the present and the future may well include making whatever amends can be made for past mistakes. But this can be done in an attitude of genuine concern for others and not primarily in an effort to rectify one's own position in the world's eyes, in order to secure some future advantage.

Also, knowledge of God's purpose always to bring about the greatest possible value for his creatures in the present, and in a way that will make possible even greater value in the future, frees us from our past achievements as well as our past failures. Despite the inadequacies in his own doctrine of God, Henry Nelson Wieman has rightly urged that we are to worship the source of good, the creative good, not the created good.[5] The purpose of God as intimated in Jesus' message of the Kingdom as both present and future should prevent any Christian from being a pure conservative. As Whitehead says, "the pure conservative is fighting against the essence of the universe." (*AI* 354.)

Knowledge of God's purpose and his activity in the world pursuant of this purpose also saves us from ourselves in another way. John Cobb and James Gustafson have both stressed the importance of belief in a power beyond ourselves working for good.[6] Apart from this belief we easily fall into despair, or into fanaticism. Since God works through his creatures, we will know the importance of our activity for good against evil. But we will know that all is not lost if our particular projects fail. For God can bring good out of evil. And he is working through others and in other ways. Hence, we can avoid the fanaticism of assuming that the good depends upon the success of our scheme, and that all who oppose us are necessarily enemies of the divine good. Moreover, we can avoid the despair that will follow upon this fanatical attitude when our projects fail, as they often will. This has been one of the major themes of Reinhold Niebuhr.[7]

Another related aspect of the saving effects of the revelation of God has also been stressed by Reinhold Niebuhr. The Christian view is that God is the God of creation, and that he loves all his creatures. It is therefore God who is the center of things, the source of norms, and that alone which is worthy of worship. All things have their meaning therefore in relation to God. Through the revelation of the true God, man can learn to accept his own place as one among others, and, thereby, to return somewhat to the intended harmony of creation.[8] This emphasis of Niebuhr's is especially needed in our time, as we are becoming more aware that the wholeness of man's spirit cannot be separated from his relation to his body and the rest of nature.

All the saving effects of the self-revelation of God in Jesus Christ mentioned in the preceding five paragraphs fall within the Abelardian doctrine. The only change in the God-man relation is in man's attitude. Through revelation he comes to know things about God that were already true, and this knowledge affects the subjective form of his experience.

The tradition also contains two views which hold that Jesus' saving effects are more "objective." One of these, the "classic" view, stressed that something happened to man through his faith in the Christ event, that he no longer had to fight the powers of evil completely on his own, but that Christ or the Word comes to dwell in him. The "Anselmian" view stressed that something objective happened in the God-man relation, so that the divine causality is different for those in Christ and those outside. A process doctrine of Jesus' significance cannot say that it is first through Christian faith that God works savingly in man, aiding him to find wholeness of life. For God as Holy Spirit is always influencing man toward that end which will bring him the greatest fulfillment consonant with the good of the rest of creation. Neither could a process view say that

God's attitude is different toward Christians and non-Christians. God loves all men equally, feeling their joys and sorrows alike, and willing each man his maximal fulfillment.

And yet an element of truth can be allowed these two views. This element of truth can be conceptualized in terms of the difference in the content of God's aims for different occasions. This content is always the highest ideal that is possible for the occasion, given its total situation. In man, one of the most important factors constituting this total situation is the beliefs that are held. A man's beliefs will largely determine which of the things that are *ontological* possibilities for man in general are *real* possibilities for him in his concrete situation. Of particular importance are the man's beliefs about matters of ultimate concern: his beliefs about deity, ethics, and values will largely determine the types of values he can be lured by God to actualize. This is partly the case because man's character, his habitual way of responding, and his life purpose are formed according to his real convictions about these matters.

This is also the case because his fundamental convictions about the nature of deity precondition him to pay special heed to those impulses upon him which are consonant with these convictions. For example, the man who closely identifies "God" with reason will give special attention to the impulse to be rational, to seek intellectual truth. As for other impulses, especially those to eschew reason in favor of other passions, the man will ignore them as far as possible and regard them as demonic. He will attempt to form a harmonious existence centered around his rationality, with all other impulses subordinated to it.

The man who understands God primarily in terms of moral will is apt to give more attention to acting rightly than to thinking correctly. He will seek to achieve a unified existence around his will, with all else subordinate to it. The search for truth as a good in itself may even be seen as a ploy to avoid real engagement in life. And a distinction will likely be made between theoretical and practical truth. Of course these first two views of deity could be somewhat merged, so that seeking truth would be seen as a moral duty, and thinking would be regarded as one form of acting.

One who has a more Dionysian, Romantic understanding of deity will tend to focus more upon his immediate bodily and emotional feelings. The impulse to rational thought and moral behavior will not be totally absent, but their role in experience will be greatly diminished. They will likely be seen as dangerous tendencies, threatening to lead man away from that harmony that is attainable at the level of the basic vitalities. It belongs to man's freedom or transcendence to be able to select which aspects of his experience will be allowed to play an important role. The Dionysian will tend to emphasize the lust for life, to give a dominant role to the impulse to seek immediacy and intensity in feeling and expression, and to play down the impulse to rationality of thought and action.

It is man's radical self-transcendence, his ability to organize his existence around any of the dimensions of his being, that makes the revelation of God so central. Because the "sacred," or the "holy," or the "divine" is that which is intrinsically good and self-authenticating, the relation to it is what gives all finite things their meaning. Accordingly, man's idea of what is holy will be the dominant factor in his ordering of his own existence, since the search for meaning finally underlies all his fundamental decisions. Since there are a variety of competing impulses on man that can be claimed to be the spirit of God, man needs some standard by which to "test the spirits," to decide which one is the *Holy* Spirit. For the Christian, that standard is Jesus as the Christ. The Christian takes that which was revealed in him as the Logos of reality, as the clue to what the truly divine reality is, and what it is leading us toward.

It is basic to the Christian vision of reality that the divine is creator of our world. The world is thereby regarded as finite, and yet good. There is no being, and no dimension of being, that is inherently evil. Since God is the creator of life, the vitalities of existence and the values possible at the level of bodily and emotional existence will not be despised and refused recognition.

However, since God is the loving creator of *all* beings, the question of the relation between competing values must be recognized. Because God wills the good of every part of creation, insofar as it is consonant with the harmony of the whole, harmony with God entails moral attitudes and behavior. The good of the whole must be considered. Hence, although the vitalities of life should not be *repressed* as inherently evil, they often must be greatly *suppressed* out of respect for the intrinsic value and rights of other beings. These ethical values are thereby recognized as higher values than those of private gratification. Accordingly, those impulses to actualize justice and in general to seek the greater good will be recognized by the Christian as divine impulses. Although these impulses will not be totally absent in any man, they will play a larger role in the sensibilities and the decision-making of one who sees things in terms of the Judeo-Christian vision of reality.

It should be noted in passing that, although the process conceptualization of the Christian vision of reality suggested in this essay does not support a *primarily* "social gospel" interpretation of the Christian message (at least not in the conventional sense of that term), it does strongly support a social emphasis. That is, the Christian message is not understood *first of all* as a call to achieve a just society, but as an answer to man's ultimate questions of meaning and destiny, his quest for wholeness, his desire to be in harmony with the ultimate reality. And yet, because of the content of the Christian vision of reality, these ultimate issues cannot be clearly distinguished from the so-called penultimate issue of the structure of society. For God is envisaged as a loving, purposive, continually creative Process that is constantly seeking the highest possible good for all his creatures. Also, although the primary emphasis is on the quality of experience of individuals, this implies no reduction in the importance of the structure of society. Due to the social nature of reality, and the great extent to which the individual is conditioned by his society, the structures of society are of decisive importance. Accordingly, one cannot really be in harmony with the *Christian* God without genuinely willing the good of all of God's creatures and working for structures that enhance the possibilities for fullness of life. Further, the process conceptualization of the Christian vision of reality implies an extension of the scope of the Christian's concern beyond what is generally suggested by the term "social gospel." Although man is objectively of much greater value than the other creatures, there is nevertheless no absolute distinction between him and the lower forms of life. Accordingly, the "social gospel" emphasis of Christianity must become an "ecological gospel" emphasis, since the "society" for which God is concerned includes the totality of beings, especially the totality of living beings.

Since God is the perfect knower, the life of reason is important. Striving to know things as they truly are is important and rewarding in itself. It is also necessary in order to make responsible moral judgments. And as has been repeatedly stated, the exercise of reason is the only way to test the veracity of that which one has received as the decisive revelation of reality. The Christian is not only called upon to test the spirits in terms of Jesus as the Christ. He is also called to test this standard itself, to see if it can prove itself as authentic. The call to truth will be recognized by the Christian, along with the call to a full and a just life, as the call of God.

Recognition of the vital, moral, and rational impulses as all being essentially good means a development of one's individuality, not a suppression of it because of the finitude involved in its distinction from others. This development of self, the fulfillment of its potentialities rather than the negation of one's individuality, is rooted in the personhood of God. If the deity of *God* is not negated by his being distinct from other beings, then the task of human life is not to try to overcome our finitude by the annihilation of our own distinctness from others.

However, although God is distinct from others, he is not separate from them. There is a divine individual, but no divine individualism. The experiences of others enter fully into his unity of experience, and are allowed to affect its state. This implies that our individuality should not be that kind of independent, self-sufficient individualism that was promoted by the traditional idea of deity as impassible and independent in every respect. Rather, the highest form of individuality, of true personhood, would include the highest appropriation of the experiences of others that is possible for man. As Tillich has said, participation and individuation are not antithetical. They do not rise in inverse proportion to each other, but in direct proportion. Accordingly, in harmony with this reformed idea of God, which is more consistent with the vision of Jesus than was traditional Christian theism, the modern Christian will give special heed to the impulse to develop his individuality by sharing the feelings of others, allowing them a constitutive role in his selfhood. Again the "others" should not be understood as limited to other human beings, but as including God and nature as well.

The implications of the above line of thought can now be brought out fully. Although, according to the process conceptuality God's grace is a positive influence on all men, regardless of what they believe, it is not to be concluded that their beliefs are thereby irrelevant to the saving work of God. The true revelation of God does not merely inform man as to what God has done in the past, and/or what God is always doing, so that the only change is in man's attitude toward God. Rather, the revelation of God's character, purpose, and mode of activity also actually *changes the way in which God can act* in relation to man, and therefore what he can effect in him.[9]

As intimated above, revelation changes the content of the aims that God can provide for man. This allows for an element of truth in the Anselmian view. Before revelation, God could only present those aims which were the best real possibilities for the man who had an inadequate, even idolatrous, view of the sacred. But after the Christian revelation, after the man begins to see God, the world, and himself in terms of the Christian vision of reality, he is open to receiving different aims. *After the revelation in Christ man is capable of receiving aims which more directly express God's character and purpose, the divine Logos.*

Accordingly, whereas before revelation God was present in man as Holy Spirit, afterward God can begin to be in him also as Logos. This gives one way of conceptualizing that experience which earlier Christians expressed in terms of the presence of Christ in them. Of course, insofar as Jesus is vividly appropriated as the Christ, Jesus himself is objectively present in believers. But Christians have expressed their experience in stronger terms than this. They spoke not only of a memory, even a memory in which there was a "real presence" of that which was remembered. Rather, they spoke also of a presently acting, empowering reality. In terms of the process conceptuality employed here, this should be taken as referring to the ever-present ideal impulses from God, based upon his Logos, which has been supremely revealed in Jesus as the Christ. The imagery of Christ's presence in the believer, battling against evil, can thus be interpreted as referring to the active impulses of God, the content of which is based directly upon that same Logos whose supreme presence in Jesus was fundamental to his Christhood.

More can be said along the lines of these two "objective" doctrines. The revelation through Jesus not only changes the content of God's aims for man, it also increases the possibility that the aims that are proffered will be actualized to a high degree. Insofar as man's reception of Jesus is truly a revelation, it involves a change in man's basic intention, or life purpose, as well as in his intellectual beliefs. For if he truly finds *this* God to be *God*, he will want to make his own character conform to God's character, and his own purpose conform to the divine purpose. Insofar as this change is effected, the divine aims will be received with a different subjective form. Even though the divine aims were "ideal" only in a very qualified way prior to revelation, since they were ideal only in relation to quite hampering conditions, they nevertheless were those real possibilities which would be best in those conditions. But the man's life purpose was oriented in a different direction; he was serving a different god. Accordingly the divine aims would likely, more often than not, be experienced as somewhat restrictive, repressive, and counter to the type of fulfillment that was sought by the man. For if man is not seeking a fulfillment consistent with the loving creator who seeks the fulfillment of all beings, the divine aims will continually run counter to the human aims. Insofar as they are noticed at all, they will be experienced as heteronomous, alien demands.

But after a genuine revelation, in which man's will has been converted, the divine aims will be experienced as empowering rather than restrictive, as stimulating self-fulfillment rather than seeking to repress it. They will be experienced as gifts as well as demands. In these terms we can formulate the experience that was expressed in the Anselmian doctrine as a change in God's attitude from wrath to mercy.[10]

Furthermore the notion of Christ's presence in the believer can be given a stronger interpretation than that presented above. In Schleiermacher's view of salvation, the presence of God in the Christian is different only in degree from the presence of God in Jesus. Just as the divine impulses in Jesus constituted his selfhood, so that there was no struggle between the divine impulse and that which Jesus himself *really* wanted, so the believer could approximate to this state. Of course, in the Christology set forth in the present essay, the presence of God in Jesus is considered to have been different in content as well as in degree from God's presence in other men. However, once the situation of true revelation and thereby conversion is presupposed, this difference is somewhat reduced in importance. As we said above, the particular aims for the believer come to be rather directly expressive of God's general aim, as was the case supremely in Jesus. Accordingly, it is possible for the Christian to approximate a state in which the divine impulses, directly expressive of the divine Logos, constitute the center of one's selfhood. (Luther said that we are to become "little Christs.") Insofar as this occurs, the Christian life is not one of constant struggle against other impulses, but can take on that kind of spontaneity that is essential to real wholeness and harmony of being. The Christian can approximate to that transcendence of the tension between desire and duty that is ascribed to Jesus. For this kind of person, situation ethics would be appropriate. In Luther's terms, this person could "love and then do as he pleases."

In summary, Christian existence is rooted in the Christian vision of reality, which is the content of the Christian revelation. According to this vision of things, the world is created by a personal God who loves all his creatures for what they are, yet urges them on to become what they can be. God's self-authenticating Reign is always present, yet also always refers to a greater future in which the intrinsic goodness of life, lived in harmony with God and therefore with all creatures, will be less fragmentary.

The impulse to fullness of life is understood as rooted in God's purpose for us. Yet the full character and purpose of God requires that the vital values be balanced by a concern for the values of truth and justice, respect and concern for others. Because God constantly calls us to do and become more, the impulse to rest content with the achievements of yesterday cannot be identified with God's will. Nor can it be God's will that we flee from the precarious, divided state of an only partially realized Christian existence by trying to return to a simpler harmony oriented around the natural impulses. God calls us to rise to a new level of existence, at which a higher harmony can be achieved, not to sink back to a lower level. These demands to become what we can are placed on us by a God who knows, values, and loves us. Hence we are freed from paralysis caused by past failures and from inordinate striving caused by the anxious attempt to deny our finitude and to make ourselves the center of meaning.

Also the knowledge that the divine power is a persuasive power, not absolutely omnipotent in the sense of being the only power, makes us take seriously the reality of sin and evil and the importance of our fighting against it. Yet we are freed from presumption on the one hand, and from despair on the other, by the knowledge that this God, whose goals are constantly distorted by finite agents, is the God who brought order out of relative chaos, life out of nonlife, centered life out of mere multiplicity, and symbolizing consciousness out of mere awareness. Furthermore this God has brought men, who are naturally self-centered and tribalistic, to have a concern for universal values, and sometimes a genuine concern for those who are far beyond their immediate circle. Sometimes men even seek truth and justice to their own pain and disadvantage. Also this God has led men from very primitive, tribalistic, self-serving notions of deity to the idea that their God is the creator of all men, who loves all his children equally. This has entailed the recognition that special knowledge of God does not increase God's love for man, but increases man's responsibility before God. The knowledge that God has achieved all this, in spite of the unviolated freedom and the natural egoism of the creatures, is an adequate ground for hope.

Finally, the knowledge of God's character, purpose, and mode of activity enables and sensitizes us to distinguish the promptings of the *Holy* Spirit from the welter of the other impulses operating upon us at any moment. A change can take place in our lives, whether suddenly or gradually, so that the divine Spirit is felt as empowering us to do what we want to do, whereas in the past that Spirit was felt only as a call of conscience, reminding us of what we ought to do. And besides his other effects, Jesus stands as a ground of hope that the precariousness of responsible, historical existence can be overcome in a higher synthesis, in a life in which the natural vitalities, unconscious symbolizations, moral will, and reason are reconciled by being subordinated to the divine aims. And this new level can return the sense of spontaneity and community that the emphasis on will and reason so often destroys, and it can do this in a more fulfilling sense than was possible at the level of bodily and tribal emotions. Because God is love, life under the Reign of God will be a life of fulfillment and harmony with ourselves and all of creation.

NOTES

Preface

1. Cf. Wolfhart Pannenberg, *Jesus—God and Man*, tr. by Lewis L. Wilkins and Duane A. Priebe (The Westminster Press, 1968), pp. 135 f.

Introduction: Revelation and Christology

1. F. Gerald Downing, *Has Christianity a Revelation?* (The Westminster Press, 1964). There are many problems with this book. First, sometimes Downing gives a negative answer to the question in the title (pp. 143, 204, 222, 289), but in other places he suggests only that revelation is subordinate to salvation (pp. 86, 141, 166, 264). Second, Downing spends half of the book arguing that the term "revelation" is not adequately supported by the Bible and the history of theology; but then he admits that this historical argument, even if sound (and only the Biblical part of it appears to be), would not be conclusive (p. 161). The third and major problem involves his insistence that the term "revelation" means "to provide clear information" (p. 237). Since Christians cannot agree on such things as how to unify the church, whether to accept Biblical criticism, and how to stem the de-Christianization of the West, the so-called "revelation" is too partial to merit the term (pp. 204, 227 f.).

Yet Downing himself seems to assume there are many things held in common by Christians, e.g., that God has purposes, is Creator of the world, graciously acts preveniently (pp. 264, 275), is love omnipotent (p. 277), and that all events are his (p. 245). Hence, while Downing presents a cogent, but by no means novel, argument against a revelation that provides "clear information" regarding strategic details, he presupposes unanimity among believers on certain basic ideas about deity. A fourth problem in the book involves the nature of religious language. At times Downing takes a purely conative view. For example, he says that "'I believe in God . . .' should, as Braithwaite suggests, be taken as declaration of an intention to live in a particular way" (p. 185). He uses this theory to argue that Christians do not really have a revelation of the Christian God; for to "know God" would be to be completely Godlike, to live "agapeistically" (pp. 193, 206). And yet he later says that it is only to the non-Christian that Christian language appears to be a "poetic, pictorial way of expressing moral decisions" (p. 290). For Christians "God must be said to 'act' now, and really to have 'acted in Christ'" (p. 185). There is no Christian commitment to agape "with the understanding 'as though "God" were real (but he is not)'" (p. 186). In sum, Downing presents no cogent argument against the propriety of speaking of revelation in contemporary theology. He does make one valid point, that of the difficulty of speaking of Jesus in himself as the final revelation, since all revelation is in the present (p. 210). But this difficulty can be handled in terms of a distinction between God's activity and self-expression, on the one hand, and his revelation, on the other, a distinction which Downing himself suggests (pp. 287 f.), and which will be developed below in Chapter 9.

2. Carl L. Becker, *The Heavenly City of the Eighteenth-Century Philosophers* (Yale University Press, 1932), p. 63.

3. Lewis Mumford lends support to this understanding of human nature in *The Transformations of Man* (Harper & Row, Publishers, Inc., 1956), p. 144: "The integration of the person begins at the top, with an idea, and works downward till it reaches the sympathetic nervous system, where organic integra-

tion in turn probably begins and works upward, till it emerges
as an impulse of love or a vital image. In this replenishment of
the whole self under a formative idea lies the promise of
reducing the distortions, conflicts, isolationisms, infantilisms,
and obsessions that have limited human growth."

4. Although Albrecht Ritschl did not hold consistently to his
doctrine that religious assertions are judgments of value, not of
being, he did employ it in regard to Jesus' relation to God. He
says we are not in a position to understand "the special conditions of Christ's dependence on God," the problem of the relation between divine activity and human freedom (*The Christian Doctrine of Justification and Reconciliation,* tr. by H. R.
Mackintosh and A. B. Macaulay [Edinburgh: T. & T. Clark,
1900], pp. 438, 439). This question "is not a subject for theological inquiry, because the problem transcends all inquiry"
(p. 451). Furthermore, "the fruitless clutching after such explanations only serves to obscure the recognition of Christ as
the perfect revelation of God" (p. 452). Melanchthon was right
to find the deity of Christ in his saving benefits (p. 396). That
is, we affirm Christ's deity because he has the value of God for
us, since he saves us (pp. 391, 398).

Although Emil Brunner criticized Ritschl's use of Melanchthon's dictum to support a "religious pragmatism," and said
the doctrine of the person of Christ should not be subordinated
to that of his work, he agreed that we should not "try to probe
into the mystery" of the incarnation (H. Emil Brunner, *The
Mediator: A Study of the Central Doctrine of the Christian
Faith,* tr. by Olive Wyon [The Westminster Press, 1947], pp.
407–409, 411). In this early book Brunner did nevertheless
construct a Christology proper, which, unfortunately, was quite
docetic (cf. pp. 317–320, 360). However, in his later work he
held consistently to an agnostic position. How the statements
that Jesus is "true God" and "true Man" can be combined,
especially without destroying the unity of his person, is "utterly
beyond the power of human understanding, and it is also
beyond all that really concerns faith." Every attempt to go
beyond the affirmation that "the Eternal Son became man" is
useless speculation (H. Emil Brunner, *The Christian Doctrine*

of Creation and Redemption [*Dogmatics,* Vol. II], tr. by Olive Wyon [The Westminster Press, 1952], pp. 360 f.)

5. Cf. Brunner, *The Mediator,* pp. 322 n., 333, 345. But in *The Christian Doctrine of Creation and Redemption,* p. 331, Brunner mocks the Schleiermachians by saying that if you ask them, " 'How then can a man like ourselves be sinless and thus perfectly, ideally, good?' they can only say 'It is so!' " It is surely unfair to demand of one's opponents that they explain the conceivability of their doctrines and then excuse oneself from this task on the grounds that, since the events described actually happened, they had to be possible!

6. Cf. Maynard Kaufman, "Post-Christian Aspects of the Radical Theology," in Thomas J. J. Altizer (ed.), *Toward a New Christianity: Readings in the Death of God Theology* (Harcourt, Brace & World, Inc., 1967), esp. p. 346.

Chapter 1. BEING-ITSELF AND SYMBOLIC LANGUAGE

1. John B. Cobb, Jr., *Living Options in Protestant Theology: A Survey of Methods* (The Westminster Press, 1962), pp. 276–283.

2. Cf. John B. Cobb, Jr., "Speaking About God," *Religion in Life,* Vol. XXVI (1967), pp. 28–39; and Paul Edwards, "Being-Itself and Irreducible Metaphors," in Ronald E. Santoni (ed.), *Religious Language and the Problem of Religious Knowledge* (Indiana University Press, 1968), pp. 46–55.

3. Thomas Aquinas, *Summa Theologica,* Vol. I, q. 13, art. 2.

4. Cf. Whitehead, *PR* 28, 36 f., 68, 73.

5. Tillich, *ST* I, p. 134; Tillich tries to soften our liberation from Jesus' ethics by saying "any legalistic understanding of his ethics." But we would seem to be free from his ethics in *every* sense, since a person's ethics is equally as "finite" as his tradition and his world view.

6. Van A. Harvey, *The Historian and the Believer: The Morality of Historical Knowledge and Christian Belief* (The Macmillan Company, 1966), p. 152.

Chapter 2. THE RELATIVISTIC MEANING
OF REVELATION

1. It is possibly true that, subsequent to *The Meaning of Revelation*, Niebuhr's writings were less relativistic in intention, and that they enunciated ideas more compatible with an adequate understanding of revelation. However, a perusal of commentators suggests that there were no changes that would require serious qualification of the conclusions reached in this chapter; cf. Cobb, *Living Options*, p. 285, n. 3; Lonnie Kliever, "The Christology of H. Richard Niebuhr," *Journal of Religion*, Vol. L (1970), pp. 33–57. Hans Frei does see a substantive shift in Niebuhr's thought. See Hans Frei, "Toward a Definition of Christ," in Paul Ramsey (ed.), *Faith and Ethics: The Theology of H. Richard Niebuhr* (Harper & Row, Publishers, Inc., 1957), pp. 65–116, esp. pp. 107–116. Kliever disagrees (*loc. cit.*, p. 46, n. 57). In any case, the shift that Frei sees is in the direction of the reformulation that I suggest would be necessary to make Niebuhr's position consistent.

2. Kliever, *loc. cit.*, p. 34.

3. Van Harvey, to whose analysis I am somewhat indebted, refers to this second meaning of external history as "alien internal" history (*op. cit.*, p. 238). This expression has the virtue of stressing that the history is internal in the sense of "committed." But I have preferred "alien external" history. The term "alien" is sufficient to indicate that the historian has a perspective of his own; and this usage corresponds to Niebuhr's own use of "faithful external history" (p. 88) to refer to the Christian's use of his own principles to construct a history of other communities.

4. The five real possibilities would be: (1) internal in both senses; (2) internal epistemically and external ontologically; (3) alien external epistemically and external ontologically; (4) alien external epistemically and internal ontologically; (5) objective external epistemically and external ontologically. The sixth logical possibility (objective external epistemically but internal ontologically) does not seem a real possibility, since an account that remained "objective" in the sense of giving an

in principle universally acceptable reconstruction would have to remain at a high level of abstraction from the concrete decisions and feelings of selves.

5. Harvey, *op. cit.*, p. 239.

6. This claim brings us back to the problem discussed previously, i.e., that some affirmations about God cannot intelligibly be understood relativistically. Here Niebuhr is using the Christian idea of God as universal creator and provider to support his relativism. He says our own Christian belief requires us to think of God as active in other traditions, perhaps as revealing himself there in other ways. While this may sound relativistic, it is in fact not. For, as Niebuhr says, the idea of God as revealing himself in worldly events requires that God be active in the world. This requires that God be the type of being who can act in the world, and that the world be open to this activity. Hence, quite a lot is implied about God and the world that rules out as equally true all conflicting doctrines of deity and the world.

7. For my criticism of a recent attempt to make sense of this notion, see my "Divine Causality, Evil, and Philosophical Theology: A Critique of James Ross," *International Journal for Philosophy of Religion*, Vol. IV, No. 3 (1973).

8. The quotation is from Whitehead, *RM* 31.

9. The text has "adequate images," but this is surely an error.

Chapter 3. PARADOXICAL IDENTITY OF DIVINE AND WORLDLY ACTION

1. Cf. Schubert M. Ogden, *Christ Without Myth: A Study Based on the Theology of Rudolf Bultmann* (Harper & Brothers, 1961), pp. 49–54.

2. The essence of Ogden's argument demonstrating Bultmann's inconsistency is the incompatibility between affirming that (1) authentic existence is possible only as Christian faith, which involves an essential reference to a particular event, Jesus of Nazareth, and that (2) all men are responsible for their failure to actualize authentic existence. Ogden takes "responsible" to mean *equally* responsible. This is perhaps done with some justice, insofar as an interpretation of Bultmann is

concerned. But whether this is the best option systematically
is another question. The other way to have a self-consistent
position would be to deny that all men are equally responsible
for actualizing what Christians consider authentic existence.
Each would be responsible in accord with the truth and op-
portunities available to him, and this would differ according to
the environment. The argument in Romans used to support the
idea that all men have the possibility of authenticity, and hence
are "without excuse," also suggests, as Bultmann points out,
that this possibility was *especially* given to the Jew. (Bultmann,
EF 83; quoted by Ogden, *Christ Without Myth*, p. 154.) This
position would be in line with the prophet Amos' recognition
that being the "chosen people" increased the Hebrew's responsibility. It would be in harmony with the historical character of
man, i.e., the fact that we are largely formed by our particular
culture, and largely limited to the possibilities it presents to us.
This would also be in harmony with Whitehead's way of understanding the relation between general and real possibilities.

3. In view of this double emphasis, Bultmann's position
formally is not as far from Barth's as is often pictured. While
Barth stresses that we should concentrate on the *fides quae
creditur* and let the *fides qua creditur* take care of itself, he
also admits that this latter, the subjective form of faith, "cannot possibly be quite excluded from proclamation" (Karl Barth,
Dogmatics in Outline, tr. by G. T. Thompson [Harper & Brothers, 1959], pp. 15 f.). James M. Robinson has pointed out an
interesting contrast between Barth and Tillich, saying that in
Barth the act of faith is a mere shadow of the content, while
in Tillich the opposite is true. He then suggests, as a way of
overcoming this antithesis, that "the content of faith is itself
the act of faith." That is, the *fides qua creditur* of Jesus and the
apostles confronts me as a possible act for me, "so that 'believing' that content means carrying through in my case the act of
faith" (James M. Robinson, "New Testament Faith Today,"
Journal of Bible and Religion, Vol. XXVII [1959], pp. 233–242).
However, if my interpretation is correct, then Bultmann should,
at least in terms of his intention, be placed halfway between
Barth and Tillich, giving equal weight to the content and the
act of faith. Robinson, to be sure, does not claim that he is set-

ting forth Bultmann's position, but rather seems to be trying to resolve a felt inconsistency in the Bultmannian position.

4. Cf. Ogden, *Christ Without Myth*, pp. 146–153; cf. also Schubert M. Ogden, "Theology and Objectivity," in his *The Reality of God, and Other Essays* (Harper & Row, Publishers, Inc., 1966), pp. 71–98; and his "Bultmann's Demythologizing and Hartshorne's Dipolar Theism," in *Process and Divinity: The Hartshorne Festschrift: Philosophical Essays Presented to Charles Hartshorne*, ed. by William L. Reese and Eugene Freeman (Open Court Publishing Co., 1964), pp. 494–513.

5. In speaking of Paul's (normative) theological approach, Bultmann implies a parallel between speaking of man and of God: Just as Paul's theology "deals with God not as He is in Himself but only with God as He is significant for man," it also "does not deal with the world and man as they are in themselves, but constantly sees the world and man in their relation to God." (*TNT* I, 191.) But Bultmann equivocates on the idea "in itself." Whereas he does not treat God or the world "in themselves" in *either* sense, he does deal with man in himself in the sense of developing general concepts to provide a meaningful context for ontic assertions.

6. Cf. Chapter 2, note 7, above.

7. Explicitly in regard to Christology, Bultmann makes it clear that the figure of Jesus cannot be understood simply from his inner-worldly context. The figure and work of Jesus Christ "must be understood in a manner which is beyond the categories by which the objective historian understands world-history." For "such detached historical inquiry cannot become aware of what God has wrought in Christ." (*JCM* 80.)

Chapter 4. GOD'S OBJECTIVE PRESENCE IN JESUS

1. Cf. Schleiermacher's *Brief Outline on the Study of Theology*, tr. and with introductions and notes by Terrence N. Tice (John Knox Press, 1966). Dogmatics is listed as one division of "historical theology" and apologetics as one division of "philosophical theology." Also in his *The Christian Faith* the very important propositions 11–14, which define the essence of

Christianity, its relation to other religions, and the relatively
supernatural nature of Jesus, are said to be "borrowed from
apologetics" (*CF* 52).

2. He does qualify this somewhat, saying that the God-consciousness apart from connection with Jesus cannot *fittingly* be
called an existence of God in man, and that in fact Jesus himself is the only one in whom there is an existence of God "in
the proper sense" (*CF* 387, 388).

Chapter 5. POINTING A WAY FORWARD

1. This is the major point on which I agree with the constructive position developed by Donald Baillie in *God Was in
Christ: An Essay on Incarnation and Atonement* (Charles
Scribner's Sons, 1948). He argues that we should affirm an
analogy between Jesus' experience of God and that of Christians (pp. 127–129). Though we affirm that "that which was
incarnate in Him was of the essence of God," this does not
mean "anything like a conscious continuity of life and memory
between Jesus of Nazareth and the pre-existent Son," or that
Jesus' personality was preexistent (pp. 150, 151).

2. John Baillie, *The Idea of Revelation in Recent Thought*
(Columbia University Press, 1956), pp. 68–70.

3. This is the major substantive point on which I disagree
with Donald Baillie (*op. cit.*). He says that God's grace is not
only prior to our acts, but that it "even covers the whole," so
that one cannot speak of "divine initiative and human cooperation" (p. 116). This follows from Baillie's rejection of the
idea that God could be limited in any way, and his consequent
affirmation that everything is wrought directly by God (pp.
111 f.). He admits this is paradoxical, since God's all-determina-
tion is said not to abrogate human freedom, and since there
are many things "which are directly contrary to the will of
God" (pp. 111 f., 114). Certain passages show that Baillie
accepts the traditional schema of primary and secondary causation (pp. 111 f., 118), a view which I consider self-contradictory. There is no dispute on this point, since he defines a
paradox as "a self-contradictory statement" (p. 110). Hence

the substantive disagreement as to the relation of divine and human causation is closely related to the formal disagreement as to the importance of the demand for self-consistency.

4. John Baillie, *op. cit.*, p. 123.

5. Albrecht Ritschl, *The Christian Doctrine of Justification and Reconciliation: The Positive Development of the Doctrine*, tr. from the 3d German edition by H. R. Macintosh and A. B. Macaulay (Edinburgh: T. & T. Clark, 1902), p. 467.

Chapter 6. VISION OF REALITY AND PHILOSOPHICAL CONCEPTUALIZATION

1. This is quoted from Anselm's *Proslogion* in Charles Hartshorne and William L. Reese, *Philosophers Speak of God* (The University of Chicago Press, 1953), p. 99.

2. This term has been used by John B. Cobb, Jr., *A Christian Natural Theology: Based on the Thought of Alfred North Whitehead* (The Westminster Press, 1965), pp. 263–270; *God and the World* (The Westminster Press, 1969), pp. 117–119.

3. Cobb, *A Christian Natural Theology*, pp. 252–257; Gordon D. Kaufman, *Systematic Theology: A Historicist Perspective* (Charles Scribner's Sons, 1968), p. ix.

4. For discussions that reflect this understanding of the nature of philosophy, and thereby its similarity to theology, cf. Cobb, *Living Options*, pp. 312–318; Cobb, *A Christian Natural Theology*, pp. 262–270; Kaufman, *Systematic Theology*, pp. 16–32; Langdon Gilkey, *Maker of Heaven and Earth: A Study of the Christian Doctrine of Creation* (Doubleday & Company, Inc., 1959), pp. 155–162; Thomas Ogletree, "A Christological Assessment of Dipolar Theism," *Journal of Religion*, Vol. XLVII (1967), pp. 87–99, esp. pp. 92 f.; Frederick Ferré, *Basic Modern Philosophy of Religion* (Charles Scribner's Sons, 1967), pp. 367–370; Harvey, *op. cit.*, pp. 253–258.

5. William Warren Bartley III, *The Retreat to Commitment* (Alfred A. Knopf, Inc., 1962), pp. 88–175, esp. p. 151.

6. Adolf von Harnack, *What Is Christianity?* with an introd. by Rudolf Bultmann, tr. by T. B. Saunders (Harper & Brothers, 1957), pp. 14, 15.

7. *Ibid.*, pp. 52–57.

8. On the difference between a "meaning" (which Whitehead calls a "proposition") and a verbal statement, see Whitehead, *MT* 48 f., and Ferré, *Basic Modern Philosophy of Religion*, pp. 382 f.

9. Cf. Ferré, *Basic Modern Philosophy of Religion*, pp. 156–166, 379, 380.

10. Cf. Cobb, *Living Options*, p. 311; Frederick Ferré, *Language, Logic, and God* (Harper & Row, Publishers, Inc., 1969), pp. 161 f.

11. Paul van Buren, *The Secular Meaning of the Gospel: Based on an Analysis of Its Language* (The Macmillan Company, 1963), p. 155.

12. Cobb, *A Christian Natural Theology*, p. 268.

13. Ferré, *Basic Modern Philosophy of Religion*, pp. 89–93, 372 f.

14. *Ibid.*, pp. 381 f.

15. James M. Robinson, "The Biblical View of the World," *Encounter*, Vol. XX (1959), pp. 470–483, esp. p. 482.

Chapter 7. A Process Conceptualization of Reality

1. For the development of Whitehead's idea of God, see Cobb, *A Christian Natural Theology*, pp. 134–168. For a summary of the character of Whitehead's argument for God's reality, cf. *ibid.*, 168–175, and Charles Hartshorne, "Whitehead's Idea of God," in P. A. Schilpp (ed.), *The Philosophy of Alfred North Whitehead*, 2d ed. (Tudor Publishing Company, 1951), pp. 515–559.

2. Peter C. Hodgson, *Jesus—Word and Presence: An Essay in Christology* (Fortress Press, 1971), p. 87, n. 58, claims that Heidegger offers a more adequate philosophical basis than Whitehead for the idea of God as one who calls us forward by presenting us with novel possibilities (cf. also pp. 289 f.). My general reason for disagreement has been stated in the critique of Tillich, i.e., if God is not conceived as *a* being, it is impossible meaningfully to ascribe causal activity to him. This is the central problem in Hodgson's position, with his identification of God with being, qua primordial language or word. On the

one hand, Hodgson accepts the idea that God must exert benef-
icent activity *and* power to be God (p. 15). And he uses
phrases suggesting divine agency: being is said to be an event
"which 'grants' or 'gives forth' more than any cause or ground"
(pp. 84 f.); it "calls" men forward (p. 87); it "wills" to be with
us (p. 88); it uses human speaking as an "instrument" (pp. 89,
97); the word of God is the "initiator" of the relation with man,
who is at its "disposal" (pp. 112, 129), and whose word is
"brought to" authenticity by it (p. 102). To be meaningful, this
talk not only requires a distinction (Heidegger's "ontological
difference") between being as language-event-itself (God) and
human speaking, which Hodgson can affirm (p. 97, cf. p. 92, n.
73); but it also requires that God have the transcendent unity
required for activity (Whitehead's "ontological principle").
Hodgson does sometimes refer to God as "the one who . . ."
and even once refers to him as *a* being as well as being itself
(pp. 116, 118). However, more in line with his position as a
whole, he denies that God is *a* being (pp. 114, 116), and he
wants to be more clear than Heidegger that "word" is not an
"active, speaking subject" with "independent subsistence as a
metahistorical entity" (pp. 103, 112, 147, 149). Rather, word
(the word of God) is the same as authentic human words;
being is always the being of some (finite) being (pp. 102, 118,
146). Hodgson's concept of "finite transcendence" (p. 103)
seems merely to affirm God (as being itself or primordial language event) as the material cause of man, and thus of the
world, since man constitutes it by his linguistic activity (p.
136). Hence Hodgson no more than Tillich gives God the
transcendent unity necessary to legitimatize language implying
divine efficient and final causation.

John B. Cobb, Jr., in *God and the World* (The Westminster
Press, 1969), first spoke of God as the "One who calls us forward." Hodgson claims that Cobb never explains the "means"
by which God calls the world forward, even though Cobb does
explain this (pp. 80–83), referring the advanced reader (p. 66)
to his discussion of the divine initial aims in his *A Christian
Natural Theology.* Hodgson's failure to see this explanation is
evidently due to his notion that God is present to the world
only through language (*op. cit.*, pp. 22 f., 102), so that any

divine "call" would have to involve language. From a White-headian viewpoint, this limitation is due to a failure to recognize the pre-linguistic relation between a person and his bodily activity, and to use this relation analogically. Hodgson does speak of the world as God's "body" (p. 128); but the relation has to be a type of identity, since he holds that "a man *is* what he says and does in the world; he *is* his words and deeds. . . . There is no person 'behind' the word" (p. 136). Besides the fact that this doctrine seems inconsistent with Hodgson's own recognition that language can be deceitful (p. 134, n. 143), it provides no analogical basis for meaningful talk of God's causal relation to the world.

3. This follows Cobb's interpretation. See *A Christian Natural Theology*, p. 201.

4. Martin Heidegger, *Being and Time*, tr. by John Macquarrie and Edward Robinson (Harper & Row, Publishers, Inc., 1962), pp. 212 f., 303, 307, 310 f.

5. Bultmann, *ET*, pp. 102–110.

6. Bultmann, *JW*, p. 51; translation of first sentence slightly corrected.

7. Cf. Cobb, *A Christian Natural Theology*, pp. 176–192. He follows Hartshorne in this regard, as does Schubert Ogden.

8. Charles Hartshorne, *The Divine Relativity: A Social Conception of God* (Yale University Press, 1948), pp. 121 f., 146.

9. *Ibid.*, pp. 127 f., 139, 142; Hartshorne and Reese, *op. cit.*, p. 83.

10. Cf. Hartshorne and Reese, *op. cit.*, pp. 11, 21, and especially the passage from Socinus, pp. 225 f.

11. Hartshorne, *op. cit.*, p. 138.

12. Hartshorne and Reese, *op. cit.*, p. 277.

13. It is primarily the assumption that the reality designated by "God" must be infinite in the strict sense that supports the idea that God cannot be thought of as *a* being. If he is a being, the argument runs, then he is merely one being alongside others, and hence is not infinite. For example, Tillich says, "To be something is to be finite" (*ST* I, 190); "To be a being would be to be finite" (*ST* I, 273). He clearly indicates that whatever is infinite would be God (*ST* I, 206, 237, 252). On this basis, he says that God is "being itself," which is infinite (*ST* I, 237).

Also cf. Paul Tillich, *The Courage to Be* (Yale University Press, 1952), p. 184: "But theism . . . must be transcended because it is wrong. It is bad theology. . . . The God of theological theism is a being beside others and as such a part of the whole of reality." Wolfhart Pannenberg also apparently assumes that Fichte's criticisms to this effect are valid against the notion of God as a being; cf. his "The God of Hope," *Cross Currents,* Vol. XVII (1968), pp. 284–295, esp. p. 284. There are several objections to raise about this type of argument. For example, what right does this notion of infinity, with its connotations, have to this favored status, especially among Christian theologians? In the Biblical vision of reality it seems quite clear that God is one being interacting with others. Also, this type of argument presupposes that one cannot make a distinction between God's essence and his actuality, which would make it possible to say that God is a being and that there are other beings, without using the persuasive language, "a being *beside* others," which suggests that the others are equal to and "outside" of God. To be sure, classical theism did not allow a distinction between God's essence and actuality; but there is no justifiable reason, especially in our day, to speak as if this were the only possible notion of God as *a* being.

14. Cf. Aquinas, *Summa Theologica,* Vol. I, q. 20, art. 1, ans. 1 and 3; also Hartshorne, *op. cit.,* pp. 16, 26, 54 f.

15. Cf. Cyril Richardson, *The Doctrine of the Trinity* (Abingdon Press, 1958).

16. Cf. Claude Welch, *In This Name: The Doctrine of the Trinity in Contemporary Theology* (Charles Scribner's Sons, 1952); Kaufman, *Systematic Theology,* Chs. 6, 17.

Chapter 8. CHRISTOLOGY AND THE HISTORICAL JESUS

1. Brunner, *The Mediator,* pp. 184 f.

2. The original draft of this chapter included, besides methodological discussion, extensive documentation indicating the support among contemporary scholars for the authenticity of the passages cited, and discussion of disputed passages and interpretations. Because of limitations of space, this part of the book had to be drastically shortened.

3. James M. Robinson, *Kerygma und historischer Jesus*, 2d ed. (Zurich: Zwingli Verlag, 1967), p. 227.

4. James M. Robinson, *A New Quest of the Historical Jesus*, Studies in Biblical Theology, No. 25 (London: SCM Press, Ltd., 1959), p. 117.

5. Norman Perrin, *Rediscovering the Teaching of Jesus* (Harper & Row, Publishers, Inc., 1967), p. 77; Günther Bornkamm, *Jesus of Nazareth*, tr. by Irene and Fraser McLuskey with James M. Robinson (Harper & Brothers, 1960), p. 81.

6. Regarding the authenticity of these Son of Man sayings, see Heinz Tödt, *The Son of Man in the Synoptic Tradition*, tr. by Dorothea M. Barton (The Westminster Press, 1965), pp. 329–347; Pannenberg, *op. cit.*, pp. 58–63.

7. Cf. Perrin, *op. cit.*, pp. 161–164, 191, 198, 203; Eta Linnemann, *Jesus of the Parables*, tr. from the 3d German ed. by John Sturdy (Harper & Row, Publishers, Inc., 1966), pp. 102, 132.

8. Cf. Bornkamm, *op. cit.*, p. 81; Perrin, *op. cit.*, pp. 102–108.

9. Cf. Joachim Jeremias, *The Parables of Jesus*, rev. ed., tr. by S. H. Hooke (Charles Scribner's Sons, 1963), pp. 128–132; Perrin, *op. cit.*, pp. 103, 107, 139; Bornkamm, *op. cit.*, pp. 80 f.

10. Bultmann, *TNT* I, 4.

Chapter 9. GOD'S SUPREME ACT
OF SELF-EXPRESSION

1. Langdon Gilkey, "Cosmology, Ontology, and the Travail of Biblical Language," *Journal of Religion*, Vol. XLI (1961), pp. 203, 200. These two sentences were quoted in this order by Gordon Kaufman at the head of his article, "On the Meaning of 'Act of God,'" *Harvard Theological Review*, Vol. LXI (1968), pp. 175–201 (reprinted in Gordon D. Kaufman, *God the Problem* [Harvard University Press, 1972], pp. 119–147).

2. Cf. Cobb, "Evil and the Power of God," in his *God and the World*, Ch. 4; Lewis Ford, "Divine Persuasion and the Triumph of the Good," *The Christian Scholar*, Vol. L (1967), pp. 235–250 (reprinted in Delwin Brown *et al.*, eds., *Process Philosophy and Christian Thought* [The Bobbs-Merrill Company, Inc., 1971], pp. 287–304).

3. The following discussion is partly dependent upon Schubert Ogden's analysis in his article "What Sense Does It Make to Say, 'God Acts in History'?" *Journal of Religion*, Vol. XLIII (1963), pp. 1–19 (reprinted in Ogden, *The Reality of God*, pp. 164–187). I developed my criticism of it in "Schubert Ogden's Christology and the Possibilities of Process Philosophy," *The Christian Scholar*, Vol. L (1967), pp. 290–303 (reprinted in Brown *et al., op. cit.*, pp. 347–361). This criticism revolves around a distinction between the *degree* to which creatures actualize the divine aims for them, and the *content* of these ideal aims. This distinction had already been made, and in connection with Jesus' person, by John Cobb in "The Finality of Christ in a Whiteheadian Perspective," in Dow Kirkpatrick (ed.), *The Finality of Christ* (Abingdon Press, 1966), pp. 122–154. These notions were further developed in my article "Is Revelation Coherent?" *Theology Today*, Vol. XXVIII (1971), pp. 278–294.

4. Ogden, *The Reality of God*, p. 170.

5. Ogden, *Christ Without Myth*, p. 158.

6. Schubert Ogden, "Bultmann's Project of Demythologizing and the Problem of Theology and Philosophy," *Journal of Religion*, Vol. XXXVII (1957), p. 169. There is nothing in Ogden's subsequent writings to suggest that he has modified this judgment. In fact, his criterion for nonmythological language about God's action still implies it, i.e., nothing must be affirmed about God's action at one place in time and space that does not apply to God's action at all places. Cf. Ogden, *The Reality of God*, p. 173.

7. Another example of the same inadequacy is found in Norman Pittenger's process Christology. Because he does not employ the distinction between the content of God's aims and the degree to which they are actualized, his description of Jesus' specialness involves merely a difference in degree from other men, i.e., Jesus was special solely because he actualized that which is the divine purpose for all men; cf. W. Norman Pittenger, *The Word Incarnate: A Study of the Doctrine of the Person of Christ* (Harper & Brothers, 1959), pp. 176 f., 179, 181, 182, 188; also cf. his *Christology Reconsidered* (London: SCM Press, Ltd., 1970), pp. 112, 114, 120, 124, 142 f. For my criticism

in this regard, cf. my article "The Process Theology of Norman Pittenger: A Review Article," *Process Studies*, Vol. I (1971), pp. 136–149, esp. pp. 140–142. Peter N. Hamilton has also alluded to the notion that God's aims for different events vary in his *The Living God and the Modern World: Christian Theology Based on the Thought of A. N. Whitehead* (United Church Press, 1968), p. 209. However, he does not make it central to his Christological reflections, but mentions it only in passing. Like Pittenger, Hamilton limits the specialness of the divine presence in Jesus to the degree of intensity of this presence, and seems to see Jesus as having actualized a potentiality open to all men; cf. Hamilton's "Some Proposals for a Modern Christology," in W. Norman Pittenger (ed.), *Christ for Us Today* (London: SCM Press, Ltd., 1968) (reprinted in Brown *et al., op. cit.*, pp. 362–381; cf. esp. pp. 373, 377).

8. To express the fact that the claim of an incarnation is a revelatory claim about the "basic character of the whole process of reality and the principles underlying each particular event," David A. Pailin has entitled his process article "The Incarnation as a Continuing Reality," *Religious Studies*, Vol. VI (1970), pp. 303–327. I am in fundamental agreement with most of his points, e.g., that propositions expressing what is revealed are of the order of metaphysical propositions and should be tested accordingly (pp. 320–324); that an incarnation is not an interruption of the general processes but an event making known the basic character and purpose of these processes (pp. 314 f.); that although God is changing he has a constant character, and it is this to which the ideas arising from revelatory events refer (p. 317); and that God's metaphysical attributes, such as his infinity and necessity, cannot be expressed incarnationally, whereas his personal qualities, such as his love and mercy, can be expressed in a human life (pp. 308, 318). However, Pailin's way of distinguishing between God's abstract qualities and his actuality, and his correlative way of relating reason and revelation, seem confusing; cf. esp. pp. 308–310, 317.

9. Reinhold Niebuhr, *Leaves from the Notebook of a Tamed Cynic* (Meridian Books, Inc., 1957), pp. 106, 123; *Does Civilization Need Christianity?* (The Macmillan Company, 1927),

p. 237; *Reflections on the End of an Era* (Charles Scribner's Sons, 1934), p. 202; *Beyond Tragedy: Essays on the Christian Interpretation of History* (Charles Scribner's Sons, 1938), pp. x, 155 f. I have argued Niebuhr's compatibility with process theology in general, and I have referred to his interpretation of God's relation to evil in particular, in my article "Whitehead and Niebuhr on God, Man, and the World," *Journal of Religion*, Vol. LIII (April, 1973), pp. 149–175.

10. Cobb, "A Whiteheadian Christology," in Brown *et al.*, *op. cit.*, pp. 382–398.

11. *Ibid.*, p. 391.

12. *Ibid.*, p. 393; cf. pp. 395 f.

13. *Ibid.*, pp. 388, 392.

14. *Ibid.*, pp. 387 f.

15. *Ibid.*, pp. 392 f.

Chapter 10. REVELATION AND
CHRISTIAN EXISTENCE

1. Kaufman, *Systematic Theology*, p. 73. This definition, while similar to that of H. Richard Niebuhr, overcomes the limitation of the relevance of revelation to the concerns of the "practical reason."

2. John B. Cobb, Jr., "The Intrapyschic Structure of Christian Existence," *Journal of the American Academy of Religion*, Vol. XXXVI (1968), pp. 327–339, esp. p. 339; and *The Structure of Christian Existence* (The Westminster Press, 1967), pp. 103 f., 114.

3. Cobb, *The Structure of Christian Existence*, pp. 135 f.

4. Reinhold Niebuhr, *The Nature and Destiny of Man: A Christian Interpretation*, Vol. I (Charles Scribner's Sons, 1941), pp. 15, 252, 271 f.

5. Cf. H. N. Wieman, *The Source of Human Good* (The University of Chicago Press, 1946).

6. Cobb, *God and the World*, pp. 99 f.; James M. Gustafson, *Christ and the Moral Life* (Harper & Row, Publishers, Inc., 1968), p. 244.

7. See Reinhold Niebuhr, *op. cit.*, pp. 69 f., 86, 91, 273 n. 4.

8. *Ibid.*, pp. 16, 57 f., 179, 251 f.

9. This conceptuality provides a way of resolving one of the obstacles standing in the way of a wholehearted acceptance of Jesus as the Christ, the so-called "problem of particularity." It is thought by many, especially by many standing somewhere on the borderline between Christian faith and skepticism thereof, that it is not only irrational but also unchristian to claim that Jesus mediates a higher revelation of the divine reality than can be found in other traditions. What is seen as problematic is the idea that a loving and just God would have made himself more known to one group of people than to another. And this certainly is problematic as long as one is thinking of God within the context of the unqualified omnipotence of traditional theism. But if God's power is seen as persuasive, as in the process view, so that he can effect his purposes only gradually, step by step, then the problem disappears (just as does the theoretical side of the problem of evil in general, of which the problem of particularity is only one dimension). Since God's ideal aim is always for the highest possibility in the concrete situation, it is largely dependent upon the past history of decisions constituting the traditions leading up to the present moment. Accordingly, God could present the ideal aims that he did to Jesus only because of a long history of decisions, beginning back in prehistoric times, that allowed ideal aims directly expressive of the divine character and purpose to be *real* possibilities for a historically conditioned person to actualize.

10. Incidentally, it should be remembered that, in line with his doctrine of the divine impassibility, Anselm himself had to interpret the change in terms of man's *experience* of God's causality, rather than in terms of an actual change in the divine attitude behind the different experiences.

INDEX